Mosaic of Tongues
Multilingual Learning for the Arabic-Speaking World

Edited by

Carine Allaf, Fabrice Jaumont, Selma Talha-Jebril

CALEC – TBR Books
New York – Paris

Copyright © 2024 by Carine Allaf, Fabrice Jaumont, Selma Talha-Jebril

All rights reserved. No part of this publication may be reproduced, distributed, or transmitted in any form or by any means without prior written permission.

TBR Books is a program of the Center for the Advancement of Languages, Education, and Communities. We publish researchers and practitioners seeking to engage diverse communities on education, languages, cultural history, and social initiatives.

CALEC – TBR Books
750 Lexington Avenue, 9th floor
New York, NY 10022
USA
www.calec.org | contact@calec.org
www.tbr-books.org | contact@tbr-books.org

Cover illustration © bgstock72 via Canva (One-design use license)
Cover design © Nathalie Charles

ISBN 978-1-63607-395-8 (Hardback)
ISBN 978-1-63607-360-6 (Paperback)
ISBN 978-1-63607-396-5 (eBook)

Library of Congress Control Number: 2023950691

TABLE OF CONTENTS

Foreword
Stavros Yiannouka, CEO, World Innovation Summit for Education .. i

Unraveling the mosaic: A journey into multilingual learning in the Arabic-speaking world
Carine Allaf, Fabrice Jaumont, Selma Talha-Jebril 1

1. The pathway to bilingualism in the Middle East: Stories from the borderland
   Majd Sarah 9

2. Negotiating language and identity: A reflection on the self-identification of European Arabs in the diaspora
   Janaan Farhat 21

3. The social motivations for code-switching among Jordanian speakers
   Issam Albdairat 31

4. Pedagogical translanguaging in kindergarten classrooms in the UAE: Reflections on co-teaching to facilitate Arabic and English medium education in the early years
   Anna Marie Dillon 41

5. Language status and usage in multilingual Algeria
   Mehdi Lazar 55

6. Bilingualism in Arabic language training sets
   Zeynep Ertürk 73

7. Multilingualism in Northern Ireland: The challenges and opportunities of introducing Arabic in schools
   Rym Akhonzada 93

8. The role of parents and the community in preserving the Arabic language: The case of Qatar Reads
   Hanieh Khataee, Fatema M. Al-Malki, Logan Cochrane 109

9. Arabic dual language immersion programs in U.S. public schools
   Robert Slater, Gregg Roberts, Carine Allaf 123

10. "Mama, are you speaking Spanish?" Experience of parents developing their children's standard and colloquial Arabic
    Aishah Alfadhalah 141

11. Unveiling the shared heritage of Arabic and Amazigh
    Mohamed Foula 159

12. Learning Arabic outside the Arab world: A language of identity that opens doors of opportunity
    Sarab Al Ani 167

13. Arabic in the digital era: Reaching a new concept of language
    Hossameddine Abouzahr 179

14. Voices of home: A multilingual journey
    Marina Chamma 193

15. The language I knew without knowing
    Hakim Benbadra 201

16. Arabic for all, why my language is taboo in France?— An interview with Nabil Wakim
    Fabrice Jaumont 209

17. The history and development of the teaching of the Arabic language to students of Arab origin in Florence and Tuscany
    Haifa Alsakkaf 225

18. Linguistic consciousness-raising: A reflection on critical thinking and mainstreaming gender vocabulary in the Arabic language
    Munirah Eskander 237

Mosaic of languages: Shaping the future of education in the Arabic-speaking world
    Carine Allaf, Fabrice Jaumont, Selma Talha-Jebril 249

About the authors 253

References 259

About CALEC 284

Praises

Mosaic of Tongues presents a skillfully crafted mosaic of chapters that chart a new frontier for Arabic as it asserts its presence as a global language. Bilingualism and multilingualism are increasingly shaping the linguistic situation in Arabic-speaking countries and communities worldwide and the educational systems in which Arabic is embedded. Utilizing Arabic as a model, the volume provides a wealth of insightful perspectives on language learning and education within a global context, making it a must-read for educators, parents, and policymakers.

— Dr. Mahmoud Al-Batal, Professor Emeritus of Arabic, The University of Texas, Austin, USA

A fascinating mosaic of personal and research-based accounts that explore what it means to come to terms with our mother tongue(s) in the face of socio-political realities that challenge our very identities. Arabic language educators will be inspired to reflect on how to train multilingual and multicultural citizens who can positively impact the world with kindness and compassion.

— Dr. Laila Familiar, Senior Lecturer of Arabic Language, NYU Abu Dhabi, UAE

A captivating fusion of insightful anecdotes and rigorous academic inquiry, this exploration delves deeply into the nuanced interplay between cultural heritage and educational philosophies. It prompts educators across disciplines to foster critical thinking and compassionate global citizenship by weaving diverse cultural narratives and interdisciplinary methodologies into their pedagogy.

— Dr. Laëtitia Atlani-Duault, Professor of Social Anthropology and Global Health, IRD-University of Paris, France

An engaging blend of personal narratives and scholarly analysis that delves into the intricate relationship between our native languages and the socio-political forces that shape our identities. This work invites Arabic language educators to contemplate the cultivation of globally-minded, empathetic individuals through multilingual and multicultural education.

> — Darcey H. Hale, Former Head of School, International School of Boston, USA

Through the collective efforts of its contributors, *Mosaic of Tongues* presents a richly woven narrative of essays highlighting the critical role of multilingual education. This collection marks a significant milestone in the discourse surrounding the evolution of Arabic language teaching.

> — Layla Tabbal, Language Consultant, Lebanon

A masterful collection of insights and perspectives on multilingual education within the Arabic-speaking world. This book brilliantly shines a light on the complexities and opportunities of language learning.

> — Dr. Jane Ross, Author and International Educator, USA

A compelling and enlightening read! *Mosaic of Tongues* provides an insightful exploration into multilingualism, making it an essential resource for educators, students, and policy makers alike.

> — Dr. Teboho Moja, Professor of Higher Education, New York University, USA and University of the Western Cape - South Africa

The 24 authors of *Mosaic of Tongues* weave together an exquisite tapestry of thought-provoking essays on the importance of multilingual education. This book is an invaluable contribution to the ongoing dialogue on the future of Arabic language education.

> — Viviane Motard, Teacher Trainer, France/Tunisia

Acknowledgment

The editors would like to express their appreciation to everyone who has encouraged and participated in this book project and to all supporters of multilingualism and bilingual education in the Arabic-speaking world. This project has brought together many voices, each with a unique story and perspective, and inspired by exciting and enlightening conversations with many chapter authors.

Special thanks to Stavros N. Yiannouka, CEO of the World Innovation Summit for Education (WISE), a global think tank of the Qatar Foundation, for his willingness to author the Foreword, gracious interest and encouragement, and all he does to promote Arabic as a global language. Heartfelt thanks to the chapter authors for sharing their stories, perspectives, and experiences—Issam Albdairat, Hossam Abouzahr, Sarab Al Ani, Fatema M. Al-Malki, Haifa Alsakkaf, Aishah Alfadhalah, Rym Akhonzada, Hakim Benbadra, Marina Chamma, Logan Cochrane, Anna Dillon, Zeynep Ertürk, Munirah Eskander, Janaan Farhat, Mohamed Foula, Hanieh Khataee, Mehdi Lazar, Gregg Roberts, Majd Sarah, and Robert Slater.

We would also like to thank The Center for the Advancement of Languages, Education, and Communities, its board of directors, advisory council, and global supporters for their belief in the value of multilingualism, cross-cultural understanding, and linguistic empowerment. Hearty appreciation is extended to Toscane Landrea, Milène Elisabeth Klein, Xiao Peng, and the CALEC team for their invaluable assistance in reviewing and preparing this manuscript.

— Carine Allaf, Fabrice Jaumont, and Selma Talha-Jebril

Foreword

Stavros N. Yiannouka, CEO of the World Innovation Summit for Education (WISE), a global think tank of the Qatar Foundation

The region encompassing the Middle East and North Africa has been a fulcrum of multi-cultural civilization for over five millennia. From the edubas of Sumer and Babylon, where young scribes learned to read and write by studying the Epic of Gilgamesh, to the Library of Nineveh, where in the seventh century BC, the Assyrian King Ashurbanipal collected tens of thousands of texts written on clay tablets that still survive to this date —how's that for battery life— the region also pioneered many of the institutions and practices that today make up the education enterprise. While this expansive and diverse region stretching from the Atlantic coast to the Hindu Kush has often been bound together by a lingua Franca —whether that be Akkadian, Aramaic, or Arabic—it has always been a region of polyglots. It is perhaps no accident that the *Book of Genesis* (11:9) identifies Babel as the place where the Lord first confused the language of and dispersed its people across the face of the Earth.

It is against this rich historical backdrop that *Mosaic of Tongues: Multilingual Learning for the Arabic-Speaking World* tackles the challenges and opportunities of multilingual education in the modern Middle East and North Africa. Through a series of essays that are in equal measure academically rigorous and deeply personal, the book's editors and authors make the case anew in favor of multilingual education by persuasively arguing that:

> 1. Multilingual education is a vital tool for preserving the rich cultural heritage of the MENA region. Nurturing indigenous languages alongside global languages like Arabic helps maintain the unique identities of various communities.

2. Multilingualism fosters enhanced cognitive abilities, problem-solving skills, and adaptability among students. Multilingual individuals often exhibit a deeper understanding of language nuances and a heightened capacity for critical thinking.

3. In an increasingly interconnected world, multilingual education equips students with the skills needed for effective communication and collaboration on the global stage. It positions them to engage in diplomacy, trade, and cultural exchange with ease.

4. Achieving effective multilingual education requires collaborative efforts among governments, educators, families, and communities. It calls for collective action to promote linguistic diversity as an asset rather than a challenge.

5. Ultimately, multilingual education is a means of empowerment and unity. It encourages embracing linguistic diversity as a celebration of unique identities and a commitment to a more interconnected future.

The chapters within this book offer insights, strategies, and inspiring stories that illuminate the path to realizing these key ideas and fostering a brighter educational future in the MENA region.

Unraveling the mosaic:
A journey into multilingual learning
in the Arabic-speaking world

Carine Allaf, Fabrice Jaumont, Selma Talha-Jebril

In an increasingly interconnected world, the art of multilingualism and language learning has emerged as an essential skill, especially among Arabic-speaking communities scattered across the globe. With numerous individuals fluent in multiple languages, the exploration and understanding of multilingual education have never been more vital. Our new book, a mosaic of insights and reflections, aims to navigate the diverse landscapes of multilingual learning within and beyond the Arabic-speaking world, revealing its realities, unearthing its opportunities, and confronting its challenges.

Our collective volume uniquely investigates how colonial legacies have significantly shaped bilingual education in the Arab region, emphasizing the lasting impact on linguistic policies and practices. With a timeline rich in complexities and nuances, the Arab world's saga has been significantly marked by the legacy of colonial rule. The colonial powers, imposing their languages, have indelibly shaped language education and bilingualism within the region. Acknowledging this legacy is paramount to understanding the multifaceted challenges and opportunities concerning multilingual education in the Arab world. It sets the stage for a nuanced exploration, adding depth to our understanding and grounding our perspectives in historical realities.

Moreover, we delve into scenarios where bilingualism extends beyond two distinct languages, exploring instances where two varieties of the same language coexist within a community. Often, the same speakers utilize these language variants under different conditions, thereby magnifying the complexities surrounding language learning and multilingual education in the Arab world.

We firmly believe that multilingual education is more than a learning strategy—it fosters diversity, inclusiveness, equity, and quality. It is a pathway to economic growth and human capital development within the global community of Arabic speakers and their multilingual habitats. Consequently, we spotlight the dedication to various forms of bilingual and language education across the Arabic-speaking world, drawing reflections from different angles. Our book's primary objective is to illuminate the multilingual education landscape from diverse perspectives, offering practical solutions and recommendations to foster the growth and scalability of these programs. To achieve this, we have curated contributions from a broad spectrum of stakeholders—educators, researchers, students, practitioners, and parents. These unique voices narrate their experiences, presenting essays on local applications of bilingual education or language immersion models, such as Arabic in conjunction with other languages like French or English. These case studies paint a comprehensive picture of the challenges and opportunities in the Arab world concerning multilingual education and language learning. As such, our book serves as a platform to foster discussions and inspire a broader vision for multilingualism. It is structured into three detailed sections that draw on various insights to illuminate the complexities of Arabic language education in a global context.

Our journey begins with **Part 1: Bilingualism and multilingual dynamics**. The voices of Majd Sarah, Janaan Farhat, and Issam Albdairat resonate with tales of bilingual pathways, personal linguistic identities, and societal motivations, respectively. Anna Dillon and Mehdi Lazar delve deeper into the topic, emphasizing pedagogical translanguaging in the U.A.E. and multilingual practices in Algeria. To conclude this section, Zeynep Ertürk discusses the benefits of bilingualism in Arabic language training sets.

Part 2: International approaches to Arabic education steers our focus towards the methodologies and challenges of Arabic teaching worldwide. Rym Akhonzada reveals the emerging multilingual landscape in Northern Ireland, and the team of Hanieh Khataee, Fatema M. Al-Malki, and Logan Cochrane highlights community-driven efforts in Qatar. The narratives of Carine Allaf, Gregg Roberts, Robert Slater, Aishah Alfadhalah, Mohamed Foula, and Sarab Al Ani further magnify the nuances of Arabic education, from dual immersion programs in the U.S. to heritage learning and native teaching strategies.

Our voyage culminates with **Part 3: Arabic in the global context.** Hossam Abouzahr delineates the transformative potential of digital tools in Arabic instruction, while Marina Chamma and Hakim Benbadra recount personal linguistic journeys amidst global influences. Fabrice Jaumont offers an enlightening conversation on the state of Arabic in France, Haifa Alsakkaf reminisces about Arabic teaching initiatives for Arab-Italians, and Munirah Eskander sheds light on the urgent need for linguistic consciousness in Arab universities.

Our book sets out to illuminate the transformative impact of multilingual education within the Arabic-speaking community, encouraging proactive engagement and dialogue to enhance its value and reach. We aim to offer a thorough resource for those captivated by language learning, the dynamics of multilingual education, and the evolving linguistic landscape of Arabic speakers, both within the Arab region and globally.

We navigate through the realms shaped by globalization and technological advancements, highlighting how these forces have revolutionized language learning. This era of digital progress and global interconnectivity has rendered language learning more attainable and compelling, especially for Arabic speakers navigating an increasingly globalized environment.

Our exploration delves into the crucial elements of language policies and strategic planning in the Arab world, recognizing their fundamental role in shaping the success and breadth of language learning initiatives. Our analysis is designed to spotlight effective practices and identify opportunities for growth, thereby fostering an environment where multilingual education can thrive.

Central to our discussion is the commitment to inclusivity, ensuring that the discourse on multilingual education includes the voices of marginalized groups and learners facing distinct challenges. This approach aims to cultivate a more comprehensive and equitable understanding of the multilingual education landscape and its varied implications. Moreover, our narrative extends beyond the acquisition of language skills to explore the cultural richness that multilingualism unlocks. We emphasize languages as pathways to cultural insights, fostering empathy, understanding, and dialogue among diverse communities. Our book aspires to spark meaningful conversations and encourage a broader vision for multilingualism's role in society.

Each contribution to this anthology acts as a unique mosaic piece, collectively assembling a vibrant and holistic view of the Arabic language's significance and possibilities in today's world. Every chapter, story, and insight draw us nearer to grasping the intricate mosaic of multilingual education in the Arab realm. This work seeks to motivate educators, students, parents, and policymakers to cherish the splendor of multilingualism and to pursue a future where language learning is embraced not merely as a task, but as a gateway to understanding, connecting, growing, and thriving in our global community. In this expansive journey of multilingual learning, every voice is essential. We eagerly anticipate engaging with your perspectives and gaining from your insights. *Mosaic of Tongues: Multilingual Learning for the Arabic-speaking World* is not just a compendium of views—it represents a worldwide dialogue, an open exchange, and a collective aspiration.

PART 1:

BILINGUALISM AND MULTILINGUAL DYNAMICS

1. The pathway to bilingualism in the Middle East stories from the borderland

Majd Sarah
The University of Texas at El Paso

This chapter reflects my experiences as both an English-language learner and an educator and how they have been shaped and reshaped by my move from Syria to the U.S.-Mexico border. It is divided into three sections. In the first one, I reflect on my language-learning experiences and how I became an Arabic-English speaker with limited resources, saving for a mind filled with strong will and a great desire to achieve bilingualism. In the second, I discuss conflicting ideas I encountered when I moved to the U.S. and began living and teaching on the U.S.-Mexico border, the different language ideologies I came across, and the obstacles to learning a second language on the border. Then, I compare these obstacles to the ideologies of bilingualism in the Middle East. In the final section of this chapter, I conclude with an analysis of the educational, financial, social, and cultural benefits bilingualism offers to those who pursue it, in the hopes that my dual insight as learner and educator will serve as a guiding star to readers seeking bilingual or even multilingual education.

Air conditioner or hair conditioner?

AC units were in high demand in Syria, especially during the hot summer days of August when temperatures often exceeded 40° C. The word "conditioner" has migrated from English to Arabic (just like the universal word "taxi" before it). So many Arabic speakers in the heart of Homs, my hometown, would frequently use كونديشن (condition) instead of its Arabic equivalent, مكيف (mukayf), to refer to this magnificent, cold-air-blowing machine—but with a pinch of

Arabic's unique vowel and consonant pronunciation. When I was about ten years old, my uncle, who lived abroad, visited us and brought a bag filled with little bottles of sample hair products he had collected from hotel stays abroad. I had never traveled outside the country, and my hotel experience was limited to apartments on the beaches of Latakia and Tartus, two Syrian cities on the Mediterranean coast. I vividly remember removing one bottle at a time from the small bag, opening their top caps, and—Ah! A sweet, minty scent filled my nose. Many samples did not have the word "shampoo" printed on them. I carefully spelled out the familiar word printed on what looked like a shampoo bottle—to my surprise, it read "conditioner." "CONDITIONER?" I thought, confused. After a few minutes of analysis, I thought: "Aha! This lotion must be used to cool off one's skin. YES, NO DOUBT!" Eager to validate this conclusion and careless about the potential risks that testing my hypothesis might present, I quickly set aside four bottles to hide in my drawer so I could later take them on my next hike.

At that time, hiking had only recently been introduced to the millennials of Homs. This new activity was exported, organized, and ultimately led by Frans van der Lugt, a priest from the Netherlands who moved to the Middle East to join a Jesuit order in the 1960s. Father Frans loved Homs so much that he decided to spend his whole life there. He learned colloquial Arabic and was dedicated to enriching the lives of new and upcoming generations. I was lucky to have had the opportunity to partake in most of his hiking adventures as a teen. One day, before we were to set off on a ten-hour-long hike in the nearby mountains of Wadi Al-Nasara, I said to myself, "Majd, you better not forget that conditioner—it is going to be so hot out there in the mountains, especially while walking under the sun for hours and hours." And so, when we departed, they were in my pack: all four bottles, arranged nicely next to my water and snacks. Two hours into the hike, I proudly produced my first bottle and bragged about this magical lotion from ANOTHER country and how it would instantly begin cooling my body temperature once I put it on my arms and neck. I still did not fully understand the conditioner's use during that hike. However, my application's unwanted results taught me the practical consequences of my assumption; my skin felt stickier than ever. WHAT AN EMBARRASSMENT! I shied away from taking any more bottles out for the remainder of the hike, and I did not say a word further about this "skin-cooling" lotion. I waited until we reached the nearest village and quickly searched for a home where I could access water to rinse the conditioner off my arms and neck.

Yes, I am a bilingualism seeker!

Associating new words or phrases with prior linguistic knowledge is expected in language learning and second-language acquisition. It is indeed one of the strategies learners use to increase their lexical knowledge—essentially, the number of words they know and can use to express their thoughts and ideas. In this section, I will continue to reflect on my own language learning experiences, but with particular focus on the strategies I used to reach my goal: learning the English language.

However, before I start narrating my English-language learning story, I would like to introduce the term "Bilingualism Seeker," which best describes my identity in the language-learning journey. We often hear the term "job seeker," meaning a person looking for employment, or "talent seeker," meaning someone hired to recruit talented individuals to their association. But what about all those who seek bilingualism? To many individuals worldwide, myself included, bilingualism may be the only tool to open new doors to employment, education, or travel. I have coined the term "Bilingualism Seeker" to identify individuals committed to acquiring a new language. These learners proactively pursue various methods to enhance their proficiency in critical areas such as speaking, listening, reading, writing, and grammar, aiming for effective communication with native speakers of the language they are learning.

My journey toward bilingualism started at a very young age—my earliest clear memory of pursuing bilingualism dates back to my fifth-grade year. Being the fourth child in my family came with some privileges, including attending a private school with an English-language program—a magnetic attraction for many of Homs' families. During English class at this private elementary school, we learned from four unique, colorful books imported from outside Syria. I remember how I loved turning their pages and staring at the bright images and the stunning letters and words inscribed on them. One recurring thought these classes evoked was that I wanted to speak English as fluently as I speak Arabic. My heart was filled with love for how English sounded, especially in music. All my free time was spent hours listening to songs by the Backstreet Boys and Britney Spears!

At school, my English-language classes mainly focused on grammar, as opposed to speaking or reading. I had to find another way to improve my pronunciation and speaking—but how? Exposure to the target language is critical to learning, but I lived in a third-world country, and foreigners were not frequent visitors to Homs. My family's finances and young age did not allow me to pursue study abroad either. So, how could I expose myself to native English-language sources while I lived in Syria and lacked the means to do so in person?

A self-taught bilingual speaker

We had just gotten a new desktop—that old, bulky computer with a single big monitor and its cream-colored frame—and a dial-up Internet line. My siblings and I were fascinated by the capabilities of this new, expensive device, and we each took turns using it throughout the day. When it was my turn, I looked up songs and lyrics and spent hours listening to my favorite band, Backstreet Boys. What started as an activity I enjoyed in my free time soon became an organized learning session. Whenever I had the opportunity to use the computer, I came prepared with a notebook titled '*My Personal Dictionary.*' I created alphabetical tabs, sectioned the notebook like any other dictionary, and filled each page with two columns and as many rows as I could fit (Table 1). In the following section, I will describe how I used music, the computer, and my notebook to create a language-learning tool.

Table 1

English	Arabic
Anywhere	في كل مكان
as long as	طالما

First, I picked a song and looked up its lyrics. I let the song play on one tab, taking up half of the computer screen, and pulled up a tab with the corresponding lyrics to occupy the other. Listening to the song, I paused frequently to write down vocabulary I had never heard or seen before. After I wrote them down in the English column of *"My Personal Dictionary,"* I pulled out my English-Arabic dictionary and started translating each word. As I filled the two columns with words, I repeatedly listened to the same song and sang aloud—just like karaoke!—until my time was up and I could no longer use the computer. I would lie in bed every night and review what I had learned. The next day, I would do a dictation drill repeatedly, covering one column—for example, the English words—and reading and translating each word in Arabic on paper. I would then uncover that column and check my answers. The next step would be to cover the opposite column, practice translating from memory, and write down my answers repeatedly. I had no one to dictate to me or to conduct any learning checks, but creating these columns helped me dictate to myself. Repetition was the key to making these new words and phrases a part of my lexicon. Music offered me two essential resources: a way to learn and check my pronunciation and a way to learn how to spell and improve my writing. Improving my speaking fluency and automaticity was a bonus that came with listening to music and singing along.

Music significantly influenced my learning of a second language, but the key to success was my determination and consistent effort to maintain a challenging routine. Remembering that learning a second language is a lengthy and demanding process is vital to prevent discouragement. This reminder holds particular importance for young people in countries where the target language is less common and for adults juggling language study with other responsibilities. Because these groups must dedicate time and effort to daily language-learning activities and everything else they have on their planners, I want to highlight the difference between learning and acquiring a language. The former is a conscious process that entails engaging in activities to learn a specific language; the latter, on the other hand, is natural and unconscious and comes about mainly by unintentional exposure to the target language. For this reason, youth living in a non-target language country—those like me, living in Syria and learning English—and professional adults must go the extra mile to learn a new language.

Other language sources

Though music was the most significant source of language exposure for me and had the greatest impact on developing my writing and speaking skills, other sources played a role, too. For example, going to the public library was another source I used. In my hometown, Homs, we had دار للنشر — Dar lil-Nasher, which translates to a house for printing books—that carried a vast selection of 'bilingual' texts. The pages of these books had English on the left and Arabic on the right (Table 2), making grasping their meaning and translating easier. I highlighted each new word; I remember that the first ten books I read were filled with highlighted sections, but the number of highlights declined throughout my middle and high school years.

Achieving proficiency in a second language is a gradual process that requires persistent effort over time, not an instant change that can be achieved with a simple action. Don't give up if you don't see immediate results! And, most importantly, celebrate even the smallest of victories. For example, if you are watching the news in your target language and find yourself able to recognize two or three new words you have just learned, celebrate that! Every new word or phrase you know brings you closer to achieving bilingualism.

Table 2

English Words	Arabic Words

Another source that helped me improve my English language skills was my work as a volunteer tour guide. Even though Homs is not a big tourist attraction, it houses Al-Baath University, Syria's fourth-largest university, which hosts many exchange programs. Because of the popularity of these programs, the Office of Foreign Student Exchange was always short on staff capable of translating between English and Arabic and, accordingly, taking students on tours. Below is a picture of one of the tours my dear friend Hania and I led as both translators and guides for tourists. Now, think of your hometown. Do you have volunteer opportunities to help you practice your target language?

"No hables como Pocho!"

In October 2012, I moved permanently to the United States and claimed El Paso—a city on the US-Mexico border—as my new hometown. Before my move, I knew very little about Hispanic culture in general and even less about the borderland in particular. Before my arrival, I had worked as an Arabic and ESL instructor for five years in Syria and the U.A.E. Still, my goal in moving was to continue my education, so I applied to a graduate program at the University of Texas at El Paso and earned my master's degree in Applied Linguistics. A year after graduation, I was hired as program coordinator for El Paso Community College's Language Institute. I want to highlight my academic and professional gains on the borderland to give my reader a background on the kind of engagement with and exposure to the language I encountered in the borderland—a complex place teeming with different language ideologies and cultures. El Paso, specifically, being the second most heavily trafficked borderland in the nation (see Table 3), offered me a unique opportunity for language exploration.

Table 3

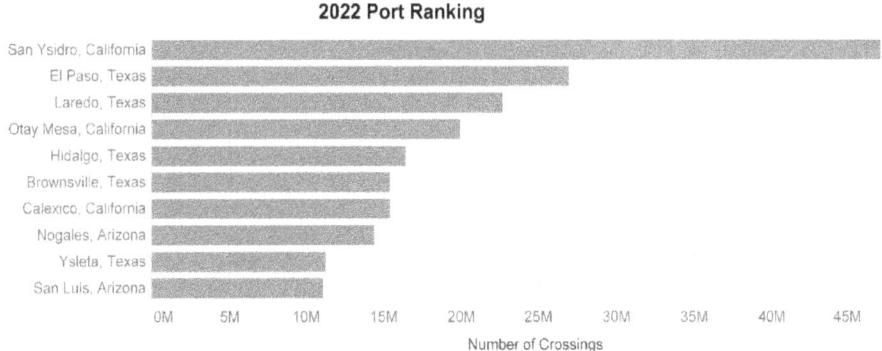

Data retrieved from explore.dot.gov

The significant difference between the language-learning ideologies I encountered on the border and those I lived through in Syria is how bilingualism is perceived and practiced. In the Middle East, mixing languages in speech is a lauded practice; using, for example, Arabic, English, and French all in one conversation signifies that the speaker is highly educated and occupies a high socio-economic status. In Syria, it was often the case that a friend would approach and greet me with "Hello! Kifek, Ça va?", mixing English, Arabic, and French to convey a simple "Hello, how are you (fem.), how are things going?" A typical response might be "Bonjour, all's well, w enti?" meaning "Good morning, all's well, and you (f)?". When I moved to El Paso, I expected the same fluidity between English and Spanish, especially given the bicultural nature of the border. To my surprise, a frequent response to mixing English and Spanish was "No hables como pocho!" meaning "Do not speak like a *pocho*!". The word *pocho*, as well as its feminine counterpart *pocha*, is Spanish slang describing a person of Mexican ancestry who cannot speak proper Spanish and has poor knowledge of Mexican culture. Though younger generations often use Spanglish, the kind of Spanish a so-called *pocho* might speak, it remains widely frowned upon in El Paso. Teachers at school usually call out students mixing languages and correct them, "Either English or Spanish, ¡Habla bien!"

This phrase, which translates to "talk right," made me question who and what determines how languages can be used—and what it means to use them right. What makes mixing languages in the Middle East admirable, while the same practice is discouraged and often perceived as a marker of poor language abilities and thus corrected on the U.S.-Mexico border? I cannot help but wonder: how do these differing language ideologies affect language learners and influence their language-learning journeys?

Reflecting on my experience as a self-taught bilingual, I recall being hungry for every opportunity to slip English words into conversation to practice what I learned with others. Mixing languages gave me a scaffolded means of putting my knowledge of English into practice even when I had not yet mastered the language fully. It also helped to empower me in my identity as a bilingualism seeker. I could use the Arabic equivalents of words I did not know in English while communicating with an Arabic/English bilingual speaker. From my standpoint as a language educator, I often notice that my students worry about what their peers and those around them think of their linguistic ability—that they fear being judged for their mistakes. Some students have even told me that they will not speak English until they are at the level of a native speaker. This is a fundamental misunderstanding of the language-learning process, which is all about practice and engagement in conversations in the target language at every acquisition stage. When constructing a building, do you demolish the first floor to build the second or use it as a base for future expansion? Analogously, your first language will always be the base that you consistently lean on until your 'second floor'—in this case, your second language—is built. The pillars and walls of these two floors are connected, and the weight of the whole building rests on them both. When you acquire a second language, you no longer switch between one and the other as you speak; instead, you draw on both languages simultaneously as resources for conveying your intended meaning when communicating.

But why?

The rise of new technologies and the instant access to information that the Internet offers us in today's world connected people across the globe more than ever before, and with that vastly increased contact comes the heightened importance of learning a second, third, or even fourth language. In this concluding section of the chapter, I will not list the benefits of bilingualism; instead, I want to share with you how learning a second language turned my life around and opened doors to opportunities I never dreamt would be possible for me. Looking back at living in Syria, I always planned to move abroad to study and work. Being bilingual, I had a much easier time navigating immigration paperwork and requirements than my monolingual peers—I was at ease during my interview with the embassy, which continued when I moved to and ultimately settled in the U.S. Small things—grocery shopping, applying for a driver's license or ID,—and big things—starting school or looking for a job— are much less troubling for immigrants who speak the language of their new home country. And even if your plans are not to migrate, being bilingual provides you with skills that make finding a job even in your home country much more accessible. In our globalized world, those who speak different languages are needed in virtually all fields: politics, medicine, trade, teaching, and many more.

Being bilingual set me up for educational success. As I enrolled in graduate school to pursue a master's degree and later a Ph.D. at the University of Texas at El Paso, I could navigate an ocean of new knowledge through the university's library and academic resources. Being bilingual made reading and writing in the target language a much easier task. If, in your plans, you have certain degrees or certifications from a country where anything other than your native language is spoken, seeking bilingualism is your gateway to a successful academic journey. In my own experience, even during networking events and conferences, being bilingual helped me to connect with other attendees and build a personal and professional network that, to this day, I often find myself putting to use.

To conclude, being bilingual has provided me with the educational, financial, social, and cultural benefits to which I credit my success. At the beginning of my journey, I was a little girl from a small city in Syria, the youngest of four children in a hard-working family whose residence in a third-world country alone limited available opportunities. Today, I am a successful educator, a doctoral candidate, and—above all—a bilingual speaker!

2. Negotiating language and identity: A reflection on the self-identification of European-Arabs in the diaspora

Janaan Farhat

Sheikh Saud bin Saqr Al Qasimi Foundation
for Policy Research

"An Arab is whoever speaks Arabic, wishes to be an Arab, and calls himself an Arab."—Sati al-Husri

Language influences the development of most national and ethnic identities throughout the world.[1] This is particularly applicable to the relationship between the Arabic language and Arab identity, where the ability to speak a dialect of Arabic has often been casually defined as the sole criterion required for Arab identification, regardless of ethnic background.[2] Interestingly, this definition extends to all Arabs, irrespective of whether they live in a diaspora or their country of origin.[3] Within Arab communities living abroad, language

---

[1] Edwards, 2009.
[2] Despite acknowledging high genetic heterogeneity among present-day Arabs (Hajjej et al., 2018), this study does not delve into the intricacies of what makes a person genetically Arab and instead understands "ethnically Arab" to mean someone whose parent comes from a Middle Eastern or North African country with a sizable population of self-proclaimed Arabs e.g. Syria, Egypt, Morocco, Tunisia, Iraq, etc.
[3] Suleiman, 2003.

typically plays an essential role in "constructing and negotiating diaspora identities and relationships."[4]

Similarly to Arabs in Arabic-speaking countries, those living in the diaspora who speak Arabic often learn to speak using a colloquial dialect. One of the more unique features of Arabic is that it is a diglossic language, where two different varieties exist. The standardized variant of Arabic is Modern Standard Arabic (MSA) or *fusha*, a modified version of Classical Arabic. The other variant of Arabic is colloquial, encompassing a wide variety of vernacular languages or dialects regularly spoken by most native Arabic speakers. MSA is typically taught in schools, and most native speakers do not use this variety of Arabic except in formal settings, such as religious texts, news reports, and letter writing, among other instances.

Language is often deemed integral to forming one's identity,[5] which applies to Arabic. However, since the ability to speak the Arabic language is often closely tied to Arab identity, this may exclude ethnic Arabs who cannot speak Arabic well and discredit the self-identification of people from Arab backgrounds. Hence, this research aims to ask: How has learning Arabic influenced the self-identification of second-generation Dutch- and German-Arab students living in the Netherlands? This research is particularly relevant because it attempts to formulate a new understanding of whether and how language learning can affect the self-identification of people living in the diaspora. It also seeks to problematize the prevailing notion that knowing Arabic or being fluent in the language is the cornerstone of Arab identity. In this way, this essay attempts to inform the scope of research conducted within the field of Arabic sociolinguistics to assess how and why second-generation Arabs

---

[4] Canagarajah and Silberstein, 2012, 81.
[5] Bucholtz and Hall, 2004.

living in the diaspora, regardless of their fluency in Arabic, identify in the way they do.

My interest in this topic stems from personal experience. Born in the United States to Syrian parents, I could understand and speak Arabic to a minimal extent as a young child. Following our relocation to the United Arab Emirates (U.A.E.) when I was nine, I struggled to develop my Arabic language skills despite being enrolled in "Regular" as opposed to "Special" Arabic classes. As someone who continued to study predominantly in the English language in American private schools, my use of Arabic was restricted to some interactions with friends, relatives, and family members. However, English remained my preferred language of communication. I longed for my language only after I left the U.A.E. to relocate to the Netherlands, which led me to immerse myself in Arabic music and Arab TV shows. My relocation to the Netherlands also made me feel much more Arab—perhaps due to apparent differences in traditions and culture. Nonetheless, it also made me more curious about the experiences of other Arabs living in the diaspora. Since my fluency in Arabic has always influenced my perceived "Arabness" in some ways, this research was inspired by my negotiations with language and identity.

Dutch- and German-Arab participants

In this study, seven questionnaires were distributed to five Dutch-Arab and two German-Arab participants who had completed studying Arabic for at least one and a half semesters while majoring in the International Studies program at Leiden University as of September 2018. The questionnaire consisted of six open-ended questions assessing how their increased fluency in Arabic affected their self-identification.

Firstly, all the students were between the ages of 20 and 23 when the study was conducted in 2018 and had at least one self-proclaimed ethnically Arab parent. Secondly, none of the students can speak, read, and write fluently in Arabic. However, at least three students have described themselves as proficient native speakers of their respective dialects. Thirdly, most students have spent most of their lives in Europe, except for one student who spent approximately half of his life there. Interestingly, the selection process, which did not fully or partially evaluate the students' Arab heritage, resulted in five biracial students, typically of half-European and half-Arab descent. This outcome, with many students having a European ethnic background and being raised in European countries, may have influenced the study's results.

The decision to rely on qualitative research for this study was influenced by the approach providing a more comprehensive overview of the association between identity and language. By focusing on qualitative research, this work rejects the hierarchy embedded in Arabic sociolinguistics that favors the quantitative research method as more objective and scientific.[6] Renowned Modern Arabic Studies scholar Yasir Suleiman argues that relying on the qualitative approach "add(s) depth and insight into the study of Arabic in the social world."[7]

Hence, a qualitative approach to studying language can provide greater insight into how using and learning Arabic influences the identity construction of people living in the diaspora. Once the data was gathered, it was analyzed and categorized in different ways using MAXQDA, a software program designed to assist in organizing qualitative data using codes and coded segments.[8] There were also a few limitations experienced when conducting this research, especially the small sample of participants included, which are briefly discussed in the conclusion.

---

[6] Suleiman, 2011.
[7] Suleiman, 2011, 6-7.
[8] VERBI Software, 2017.

Common themes pertaining to learning Arabic

Upon analyzing the numerous questionnaires using MAXQDA, 76 references (coded segments) were identified within the data. These references could be grouped into four categories: political, cultural, relational, and personal. Nine references to Arabic and one's political affiliation were made, whereas 11 were made to ties to Arab culture. However, references to Arabic and its impact on relationships were mentioned a total of 19 times, specifically regarding (1) discrimination influencing willingness to learn Arabic, (2) judgment on linguistic fluency, and (3) connection to other Arabs. Lastly, participants mentioned personal references at least 37 times, nearly twice as often as relational references. These personal references focused in particular on (1) personal reasons to learn Arabic, (2) an "incomplete" identity characterization, (3) identification as both Arab and European, (4) non-identification as Arab, (5) learning Arabic as strengthening Arab identity, and (6) a shift in identification as Arab, Dutch, or German.

Most references are linked to the personal categorization discussed above, with the fewest references relating to political affiliation. In simpler terms, there is a strong correlation between increased fluency in Arabic and personal identity and a weak correlation between increased fluency in Arabic and political identity. The following section addresses categorizing the 76 references in greater detail, specifically regarding their influence on political, cultural, relational, and personal matters and identities.

Reflecting on participants' political, cultural, relational, and personal identification

In the questionnaire, students were asked a single question about whether their increased fluency in Arabic influenced them to become more supportive of typically Arab causes. Interestingly, the students' answers to this question are remarkably similar, with none of the samples indicating that studying Arabic strengthened their affiliation toward Arab causes. Six students stated they were already previously inclined to support Arab causes, thus indicating that other matters about upbringing were far more salient in influencing identification.

Concerning cultural affiliation, only one question explicitly addressed culture in the questionnaire. Firstly, it is significant that most students (about five) concurred that their increased understanding of Arabic strengthened their connection to "Arab culture." Interestingly, however, greater familiarity with "Arab culture" was simultaneously associated with greater rejection of the culture by one of these five students. He emphasized his stronger rejection of certain elements he associates with Arab culture now that he has a deeper understanding of them (Egyptian-Dutch, male, 22).

Of the remaining two students who did not feel that they better understood Arab culture since they started learning Arabic, one stated that he grew up watching and listening to Arab movies and songs and, therefore, already felt connected to his heritage before formally studying the language. The other student indicated that he does not feel more linked to Arab traditions but instead feels more strongly European. Hence, the findings suggest that while improving their fluency in Arabic strengthened most students' identification with Arab culture, increased identification can coincide with increased rejection of perceived cultural attributes (such as sexism). In addition, increased fluency does not necessarily strengthen one's connection to Arab culture.

The fourth and fifth questions in the questionnaire are explicitly relational, as they inquired how experiencing judgment and discrimination from others influenced the students' inclination to learn Arabic. Firstly, it is significant that six out of the seven students indicate that they have been judged based on the level of their Arabic fluency, and others have discriminated against all five Dutch-Arab students. This also fueled their desire to counter negative stereotypes about their backgrounds. Interestingly, one of the students who did feel judged based on her Arabic fluency noted that she was taken more "seriously" by her family once she became more fluent (Egyptian-Dutch, female, 21). Secondly, all three students who described themselves as native speakers of their respective dialects indicated that they were also judged based on their ability to speak Arabic or their identities as Arabs in general. One student suggested that she was discriminated against for not being "Arab enough" and being too Dutch (Moroccan-Dutch, female, 21).

Thirdly, three students have indicated feeling closer to other Arabs due to their increased fluency. These findings demonstrate several things: firstly, being fluent in Arabic and identifying as an Arab does not exclude one from being discriminated against in their European home countries for being "brown and Arab and Muslim" (Egyptian-Dutch, male, 22). However, this does not preclude one from being treated differently by Arabs in the Middle East and Europe, who may perceive identification with a European national identity as detracting from one's Arab identity. Secondly, the influence of external or relational factors is much more significant than either cultural or political factors, as it had a more substantial impact on the students' decisions to learn Arabic and their overall identification as Dutch, German, or Arab.

The first and sixth questions of the questionnaire are explicitly personal and broadly assess the students' identification as Arab, the degree to which they feel Arab, the impact that language has had on their Arab identity, and whether the students can identify a shift in their self-identification. It is also clear that personal categorization is the most relevant of the four identified since it is prominently featured in the data. A few notable themes emerged concerning this particular category. Firstly, the most commonly cited reasons that students give for studying Arabic pertain to communication, and more specifically, (a) the desire to learn to read and write (for the three native speakers exclusively), (b) the intent to reconnect with their Arabic-speaking family members, and (c) to use Arabic in their careers. Secondly, some students address learning Arabic as filling a perceived gap in their identities that previously existed due to an inability to communicate in Arabic. Thirdly, some students indicated their experience of alienation or disinterest in being Arab, although the reasons for this differ for each person. Fourthly, six of the seven students declared they identify as Arab and European.

Much can be extrapolated from the students' personal reasons. Firstly, the students' reasons for learning Arabic are fascinating and diverse, with none indicating that they wanted to learn Arabic to relocate to an Arab country. This would generally concur with the findings of recent works that argue that many second-generation diaspora members have a hybrid and more complex relationship with their "home" country.[9] Secondly, increased fluency in Arabic sometimes served to paradoxically distance some of the students from their Arab identity instead of making them feel more Arab.

Thirdly, despite the students' statements that they identify equally with their Arab and European identities, many of their answers subtly indicated hesitation in identifying more strongly with their Arab identity. For example, one student proclaimed: "I am both Dutch and Egyptian, and I do not have to choose. As said before, however, where before I felt 50% Dutch and 25% Egyptian, I can now safely say that maybe I now feel 50%-50% indeed" (Egyptian-Dutch, male, 22). The words "safely" and "maybe" demonstrate the student's continued attempts to reconcile his Arab heritage with his more dominant Dutch identity, thereby challenging his statement that he feels equally Dutch and Egyptian. However, this is also demonstrative of the shift in identity that many students spoke of, whereby identity can be perceived not as "a stable, predefined entity but an ongoing dynamic process that is constantly negotiated and co-constructed between the interactants."[10]

Reassessing identity through language: The impact of learning Arabic on second-generation European Arabs

In sum, the process of learning Arabic has influenced the self-identification of the participants in diverse ways. While learning Arabic had little influence on the political identification of the

---

[9] Canagarajah and Silberstein, 2012.
[10] Angouri, 2012, 106.

students, it more strongly influenced the ability of students to relate to Arab culture. However, improved fluency in Arabic also led, in some cases, to rejection or greater alienation from one's heritage. Although people's judgment and discrimination against the students influenced the majority by encouraging them to study Arabic and prove their *Arabness*, the personal reasons discussed belie their assertiveness about being simultaneously Arab and European.

This hesitancy to fully claim their Arab heritage indicates that while many students are more comfortable with being Arab than before, their claim to their European identity continues to be stronger. Interestingly, however, all the students indicated some level of re-assessment of their identity after starting to learn Arabic at university, even though it did not necessarily encourage them to associate more strongly with their Arab heritage. Hence, the process of learning Arabic has influenced the self-identification of these second-generation Dutch- and German-Arab students by bringing them closer to the realization that their identities are truly hybridized and the understanding that they will likely continue to negotiate and reform their dual and potentially competing identities for the rest of their lives.

Although my experience differed significantly from that of the students who partook in my research, I also resonated with their perceptions of their identities as hybridized. My experience of living in multiple countries has affected my identity in various ways. However, unlike the sample of students, living in an Arab country in my late childhood and throughout my adolescence has made me feel more *Arab* as opposed to Syrian or American. Nonetheless, this may also be because I have never lived in Syria and instead resided in the U.A.E. Despite having lived in the U.S. briefly during my childhood, my parents were immigrants there, unlike the students sampled, four of whom had at least one ethnically European parent. In addition, as someone who has studied Arabic for ten years in school, my experience also differs due to my greater fluency in speaking, reading, and writing in MSA and Syrian Arabic.

There are a few limitations to this study, one of which is that it does not explore the impact that being biracial has had on five of the seven students who partook in the questionnaire due to time and space constraints. In addition, this study oversimplifies "Arab culture" and subsumes the participants' cultures under a single label. Moreover, the results of this study are primarily non-generalizable because they are based on the experiences of a few individuals from a particular demographic, as all participants were young university students at Leiden University in the Netherlands at the time of writing. As such, the results of this study would need to be replicated in larger samples across different universities and countries to verify the results.

Nonetheless, this small-scale research could encourage other academics to investigate the links between identity and language among student youth in the European Arab diaspora. I also hope this essay helps destigmatize the lack of language fluency and identification with a particular ethnic background, especially concerning the Arabic language. While increased fluency may facilitate greater communication between Arabs, I believe it is not and should not be the sole or main criterion that dictates who may be considered an Arab. In my opinion, destigmatizing the language learning process can encourage non-fluent "Arab" speakers to make the mistakes they need to become more comfortable with the language and within their skin.

3. The social motivations for code-switching among Jordanian speakers

Issam Albdairat
Indiana University, Bloomington

Understanding code-switching for everyone

What is code-switching? Being fluent in more than one language, known as bilingualism, is quite common and has been studied extensively. When we talk about someone being bilingual, we mean someone who uses two or more languages regularly in their daily life. Grosjean put forward this concept in 1982. When bilingual people or those learning a new language switch between these languages in learning settings or everyday conversation, it is called "code-switching." Simply put, code-switching is like jumping back and forth between two languages or even two ways of speaking the same language. You'll often see this happening when people chat rather than in writing.

There are a few ways that people switch between languages. In 1993, Myers-Scotton explained that sometimes the switch happens between two whole sentences and sometimes in the middle of a single sentence.

For instance, look at this example where someone switches from Arabic to English:
- انا حطيت أغراضي على *lab bench*
  I put my stuff on the *lab bench*
- شو في عندك *comments* على *Facebook post*
  What other *comments* do you have on your *Facebook post*?

In the above examples, the switch happens within the sentence, so we call it intra-sentential code-switching.

But what about when the switch happens between whole sentences? Here's an example:

- *We are typical students,* بندرس يوم الامتحان
  We are typical students; we study on the day of the exam

In this case, the switch is between two main ideas or clauses, called inter-sentential switching.

Muysken, in 2000, introduced three ways to understand code-switching:

1. Alternation is when someone completely switches from one language to another, including the rules and words of that language.

2. Insertion – This happens when just one word from a second language is added to a sentence from the first language.

3. Congruent Lexicalization – This is a bit complex. It means that the sentence structure is common to both languages, and you can use words from either language to complete it.

Why do people code-switch? People have different reasons for switching between languages. Some reasons are based on the situation around them, like where they are or the topic they are discussing. For example, two friends might speak one language and switch to another when someone else joins their conversation. This kind of switch, based on external factors, is known as situational code-switching.

On the other hand, sometimes the reason for switching is more personal. It can be about how a person wants to present themselves or relate to others. This personal motivation for changing linguistic styles is known as metaphorical code-switching.

In summary, code-switching is a fascinating way for bilingual people to communicate. Whether they switch between sentences or within them or do it because of the situation or personal reasons, it offers a unique insight into multilingual communication.

The languages of Jordan: A closer look

Jordan's linguistic landscape

Jordan, located in the heart of the Middle East, primarily speaks Modern Standard Arabic (MSA). This version of Arabic is typically reserved for official matters, education, media broadcasts, and other formal events. That said, you'll also hear plenty of English spoken as it is taught to children from their early schooling years. While most public schools instruct in Arabic, some private schools prefer English. Despite MSA's prevalence in formal environments, the day-to-day chatter on Jordan's streets is primarily in Jordanian Arabic, a variant of the Levantine dialect spoken in neighboring countries such as Palestine, Syria, and Lebanon.

Interestingly, the Arabic spoken in Jordan isn't uniform; there are distinct varieties. While standard Arabic remains consistent in written form, spoken dialects show differences. Holes (1995) noted three main dialectal varieties: Madani (Urban), Rural, and Bedouin. These dialects are unique to Jordan and can be identified in specific regions or cities. El Salman (2003) provided an in-depth look at Al Karak's city dialects, categorizing them as Karaki, Fallahi, and Urban.

Neighboring cities have often influenced urban dialects and come with their specific markers. One such marker is the [ʔ] sound, so distinct that some Jordanians refer to this dialect by this sound. Interestingly, this urban variant carries prestige, making it a preferred choice among women. This phenomenon, called "leveling" by Abu-Melhim (2014), is when speakers modify their language to mirror a more respected variant.

As the name suggests, rural dialects are predominant in villages and cities around Amman, including Al-Karak and Al-Tafilah. The Bedouin dialect, on the other hand, is recognized by its distinct use of the [ʧ] variant (similar to the "ch" in "church") and the [g] variant.

Different Bedouin dialects can be traced back to specific tribes, as Sakarna (1999) did, identifying dialects of tribes like Bani Hasan and Bani Saxar.

Why do Jordanians switch between languages?

People might bounce between Arabic and English in conversation for various reasons. Some bilinguals claim they switch because they can't find the right word in one language and opt for the other. This "filling in the gaps" reasoning is debated among researchers. Hughes et al. (2006) recognized this rationale, but Bassiouney (2009) argued there's more to code-switching than simply substituting words. The surroundings, a specific event, or even the situation might influence this linguistic dance, as noted by Gumperz (1976). Myers-Scotton (1993) took a universal view, suggesting that there are established rules guiding when and how people switch languages. Many researchers, including Ritchie and Bhatia (2004) and Azlan et al. (2013), have delved deep to uncover the motivations behind code-switching, and this study aims to explore these in detail.

Diving into Jordan's language dynamics offers valuable insights into how people communicate and why. Specifically, this study probes why someone might switch from a rural to an urban dialect or between Arabic and English in particular settings. The research also shines a light on the influence of education on language choices and how Jordanians perceive various dialects. It is important to note that this study's findings stem from a select group of participants—specifically, from three Jordanian cities- and are limited to ten individuals per city. The age group of the participants is restricted to those between 19 to 25. Given that the research spanned from March 2021 to May 2022, the findings provide a snapshot of Jordan's linguistic landscape during this period. Regardless of these limitations, the study offers an insightful glimpse into the sociolinguistic choices of Jordanian speakers.

Researching Jordan's linguistic patterns: How we did it

Our study journeyed across different corners of Jordan, focusing primarily on three major universities, each representing a unique city. We employed a qualitative methodology to shed light on the intricate dynamics of code-switching in diverse social settings. Arabic, especially the local dialects, dominated the linguistic repertoire of our participants. To provide an in-depth and broad overview, we amassed 10 hours of recorded conversations spanning almost an entire year.

For this exploration, 30 individuals—comprising both men and women—contributed their voices and experiences. Specifically, the participant breakdown was 12 males and 18 females. The choice to have more female participants was backed by numerous studies suggesting that women are more inclined towards code-switching. A shared characteristic among all participants was their bilingual proficiency in Arabic and English, attributed to their English-medium education at school and university levels. Moreover, their linguistic profiles were colored by diverse dialects, reflecting their origins and residential locations.

To ensure a rich and varied data set, participants were carefully selected based on several demographic factors, including their origins, age, educational background, and gender. The term 'origin' here refers to whether the participant hailed from an urban or rural backdrop in one of the three key cities, subsequently influencing their dialectal choices.

Our participants were undergraduate students from three distinct educational institutions: Jordan University in Amman, The Jordan University of Science and Technology in Irbid, and Mutah University in AlKarak. Below is Table I, offering a concise overview of the participants' backgrounds.

Informant code	Gender	Age	Field of Study	Origin
1	Female	20	Nursing	Al-Karak
2	Male	21	Business	Al-Karak
3	Male	19	Engineering	Irbid
4	Female	23	English	Al-Karak
5	Male	20	Pharmacy	Irbid
6	Male	25	Chemistry	Amman
7	Female	19	Chemistry	Amman
8	Female	22	Business	Al-Karak
9	Female	21	Dentistry	Irbid
10	Male	22	Engineering	Amman
11	Female	19	Physics	Al-Karak
12	Male	22	Engineering	Irbid
13	Female	25	Arabic	Amman
14	female	19	Engineering	Al-Karak
15	Female	23	Law	Amman
16	Male	21	Dentistry	Irbid
17	Male	22	Agriculture	Al-Karak

18	Female	23	Engineering	Amman
19	Female	20	Computer Science	Irbid
20	Male	21	Business	Amman
21	Male	23	Arabic	Al-Karak
22	Female	22	Architecture	Irbid
23	Female	20	Law	Amman
24	Female	22	Engineering	Irbid
25	Male	19	Law	Al-Karak
26	Female	21	English	Amman
27	Female	19	Engineering	Amman
28	Female	22	Agriculture	Irbid
29	Male	23	Islamic Study	Al-Karak
30	Female	20	Mathematics	Irbid

Table I. Personal Background of Informants

Unraveling the tapestry of language: Navigating code-switching

The role of relationships in language decisions

Our research reveals that interpersonal relationships play a significant role in determining language choices. As observed, university students use an informal dialect during casual chats at the campus café but switch to a more formal tone during lectures. Additionally, the language used with elderly family members often differs from those reserved for siblings or peers. The nuances in these choices underline the influence of respect and formality in linguistic decisions.

Responding to uncertain language scenarios

Adapting to language preferences is another observed motivation. For instance, during an interview at the U.S. Embassy in Amman, one participant began conversing in English but shifted to Arabic when the officer did. This adaptability isn't just limited to official settings. Immigrants, as Mahsain (2015) mentions, sometimes prefer not to be addressed in their native language, while others might have a preference for formal language over informal.

Balancing dual identities through language

A fascinating facet of our study highlights the complexity of balancing dual identities. A student shared his challenge in addressing his uncle, who also plays the role of his professor. The student felt a tug between using a formal tone, which is expected on campus, and the informal language of family gatherings.

Adjusting language to the situation

Context-specific language switches were commonly observed. At a social gathering, while the majority of women inquired about beverages using the urban dialect: شو بدكم تشربوا؟ نهوة و لا شاي؟, one participant, coming from a village, felt the need to switch from her regular rural dialect. These decisions often reflect underlying influences of age, gender, and social class.

Choosing neutrality to fit in

Sometimes, individuals resort to a neutral language to blend with their surroundings, as seen in a conversation where a participant, wanting to distance herself from her Bedouin tribe's identity, deliberately avoided dialect markers, such as [tʃ] and [g], thereby opting for neutrality over identity.

Emphasizing through dual languages

Bassiouney (2013) emphasizes how code-switching can be employed for message emphasis. An illustrative example from our research is of students discussing math problems. After explaining a concept in Arabic: هاي معادلة تفاضلية من الدرجة الأولى, a student reiterated the point in English: هاي first-order differential equation. This shift, although the idea was initially understood, accentuated the message.

Filling linguistic voids with dual languages

Specific scenarios demand language switching due to the absence of direct translations, especially in technical domains like STEM. For instance, students found themselves weaving English terms like "scientific calculator" and "complex numbers" into their Arabic conversations. Alkhlaifat et al. (2020) and Yaseen et al. (2021) found similar tendencies in medical and aviation settings, underlining code-switching's utility to bridge linguistic gaps.

The subconscious dance of languages

Lastly, some bilinguals, as Bullock and Toribio (2010) point out, switch languages spontaneously without any apparent motivation. An example that stood out was a student's use of the term "calculus" within an Arabic sentence: اشتريت كتاب ال calculus؟. When questioned, he was unaware of the linguistic dance he had performed.

This exploration of code-switching offers a window into the intricate world of bilingual communication. It emphasizes that beyond grammar and vocabulary, language choices are deeply embedded in our social contexts, experiences, and identities.

Linguistic navigation and identity: Exploring code-switching practices among Jordanian speakers

Some patterns distinctly emerge when investigating the code-switching habits of specific Jordanian speakers across varied social settings. Participants displayed a heightened propensity to code-switch when engaged in dialogues with peers and coworkers, as opposed to more routine conversations with family.

Notably, the interchange between Arabic and English among Jordanians varies significantly based on their proficiency in English and the motivations steering this linguistic shift. English and Arabic code-switching appears to be more prevalent among STEM professionals than their counterparts in fields where Arabic dominates the instructional methodology. Analytical insights suggest that the primary catalyst for this bilingual shift is to fill lexical voids when transitioning from Arabic to English, often due to the lack of a parallel word in Jordanian Arabic. Some interviewees acknowledged instances where they struggled to recall the Arabic equivalent, finding it reasonable to employ the English counterpart. This inclination suggests that the shift to English facilitates enhanced clarity and comprehension, especially in academic settings with colleagues and educators. In this context, education emerges as a dominant factor propelling individuals to oscillate between the two languages, while attributes like gender and social standing seem to exert a lesser influence.

Addressing the interchange between distinct Jordanian dialects, a sentiment of pride and emotional connection to the rural dialect was evident among students from Mu'tah University in Al Karak city. They perceive this dialect as symbolic of their identity. Yet, most female participants favored transitioning from the rural to the urban dialect. They believe that adopting the urban dialect presents them in a more favorable light, particularly within the university milieu. Albirini (2014) proposes that Jordanian rural speakers chiefly utilize their multifaceted dialectal range to optimize their self-portrayal in interactions with a diverse audience. They aim to harness different social capitals and extract maximum value from these varied interactions. One of the driving forces behind women's inclination to migrate linguistically from the rural to the urban dialect lies in the perception of the urban dialect as the epitome of prestige in Jordanian society, as articulated by Al-Tamimi (2001).

This comprehensive review underscores the rich tapestry of linguistic choices prevalent in Jordanian society and their intricate ties to aspects of identity, educational background, and social aspirations.

4. Pedagogical translanguaging in kindergarten classrooms in the UAE: Reflections on co-teaching to facilitate Arabic and English medium education in the early years

Anna Marie Dillon
Emirates College for Advanced Education, Abu Dhabi, UAE

This chapter reflects on how two teachers co-teaching in a kindergarten classroom were observed working together to facilitate emergent writing in both Arabic and English. This reflection on a fifteen-minute segment of a recorded lesson observation conducted in one Kindergarten Two (KG2) classroom occurred within a more extensive study. Five and a half hours of recordings were gathered in six Kindergarten classrooms in the emirate of Abu Dhabi in the United Arab Emirates. The researcher was prompted to reflect on this lesson segment because it appeared to be a pedagogical moment of wonder. At the outset, it is essential to acknowledge this paper's limitations as a researcher's reflection on a fifteen-minute segment of an observed lesson. There is no intention on the researcher's behalf to generalize these reflections to the broader field, but rather an acknowledgment that moments of wonder are worth exploring, as they may have something to teach us.[11]

This reflection on an occasion where emergent writing was facilitated in a bilingual classroom is grounded in the literature on co-teaching, emergent writing among bilinguals, and a translanguaging

---

[11] Burgess, 2021.

pedagogy in early childhood education. It is also contextualized by a summary of the curriculum and education system in place at the macro level at that time and how that curriculum was enacted at the micro level by co-teachers facilitating emergent bilingual writing, thereby promoting a translanguaging pedagogy in that particular early childhood setting. The paper takes up wonder as an analytic approach, allowing researchers to hold space in surprise at uncertain moments.[12]

Co-teaching dynamics and literacy development in Abu Dhabi's kindergarten classrooms

This reflection took place while gathering data in the field for a project exploring teachers' experiences of co-teaching during literacy lessons at the kindergarten level. It was based in the emirate of Abu Dhabi, which has seen a significant transformation of the public education system since 2010 under the Abu Dhabi Education Council (ADEC) umbrella. The mid-2010s saw the peak of the reformation of the education system at the K-12 level, leading to a "qualitative transformation."[13] The present study is concerned with the kindergarten level, which saw a push towards having English Medium Teachers (EMTs) and Arabic Medium Teachers (AMTs) co-teaching in the same classroom. AMTs were responsible for teaching Arabic, social studies, Islamic studies, and civics through the medium of Arabic, the native language of the children. At the same time, EMTs were responsible for teaching English, math, and science through English. While not every KG1 and KG2 classroom in the emirate of Abu Dhabi had this model, my research focused on classrooms that did. KG1 includes children aged four to five, while KG2 includes children aged 5-6.

---

[12] Burgess, 2021.
[13] Gallagher, 2019, p. 3.

Curriculum

The ADEC curriculum at that time was based on learning outcomes. It was not (and is not) publicly available and was received through my role as a Head of Faculty in a kindergarten at that time. For English, the same learning outcomes applied to KG1 and KG2. The writing strand, which is the focus of this paper, encompassed the strand units of text type, writing process, and conventions. The curriculum included differentiated versions of the outcomes (at the mastered, accomplished, developing, and beginning levels), along with explanatory notes. The notes have suggestions for teacher/ child activities and information about the potential for negative language transfer. For Arabic, different learning outcomes applied to KG1 and KG2. For KG2, the writing strand included four units: writing process, appropriate use of language according to an audience in the writing process, efficiency in writing, and scientific research.

Literacy centers

Regarding the emergent writing observed in the lesson, the writing occurred in two literacy centers—one facilitated by the AMT and one promoted by the EMT. The lesson was based around the theme of community helpers and having set the scene during the whole group lesson. The writing activities were based on the children being prompted to think about items a doctor or a baker might need (e.g., a bowl or a spoon), then drawing a picture of that item, then sounding it out and writing it down in both English and Arabic depending on which center they were at. While five groups of children spent time at various learning centers, two moved between the English and Arabic writing centers. Therefore, if the child started at the English center, having chosen a bowl as a piece of equipment a baker would use, then she started by drawing the bowl, then sounding out and writing the word in English using approximated spelling, then moving to the Arabic center to sound out and write the word in Arabic.

Moving between the English and Arabic learning centers in this scenario may sound obvious and intuitive in terms of good practice. However, in my two years observing co-teaching in eighteen KG1 and KG2 classes in the school where my role as Head of Faculty involved conducting classroom observations within the school and in other KG schools in the emirate of Abu Dhabi as part of Continuous Professional Development (CPD), and in my role as researcher following on from that, I never observed such seamless weaving together of English and Arabic writing. I had never witnessed such a skillful and supportive co-teaching approach. Drawing on what I already knew about co-teaching and emergent writing among bilingual young children, as well as some of the principles of a translanguaging pedagogy, this short observation led me to appreciate this as a moment of wonder and reflect on what I had observed to learn from it and disseminate to those who may find it helpful for practice.

Exploring co-teaching, emergent bilingual literacy, and translanguaging pedagogy in early education

The literature review focuses on three main areas, which will be discussed in turn—co-teaching as a practice in classrooms, emergent writing among bilingual children, and the potential of a translanguaging pedagogy in the early years.

Co-teaching

As a model for facilitating teaching and learning, educators can implement co-teaching in various ways.[14] Quite a few factors influence what co-teaching might look like in a given situation. Co-teaching is often utilized to manage inclusive classrooms, where a special education teacher and mainstream class teacher work together within the classroom to meet pupils' needs, rather than

---

[14] Pancsofar and Petroff, 2016.

implementing the traditional withdrawal method. It also has a place in classrooms where an experienced mentor teacher hosts a student teacher, and the student teacher gradually takes more and more responsibility for leading teaching and learning over time. The usefulness of co-teaching for teacher/musician partnerships has been highlighted by Kerin & Murphy.[15] Friend and Cook describe six widely cited approaches to co-teaching. These approaches include one teach/one assist, one teach/one observe, station teaching, parallel teaching, alternative teaching, and team teaching—these six approaches range from the least collaborative to the most collaborative.[16] Depending on the approach, each teacher has specific roles and responsibilities to facilitate teaching and learning. Co-teaching pairs or teams may implement several of these approaches at different times depending on what they try to achieve with children. Indeed, co-teaching as an approach should include not only the practice itself but also the planning and evaluation of the practice.[17]

The success of implementing a co-teaching approach may depend on the number of co-teaching teams a teacher is working with within a given period, the amount of choice that teachers have in selecting their co-teacher, the length of time the co-teachers have worked together well, and the quality of CPD availed of by teachers involved in co-teaching, if any.[18] The amount of teaching experience a teacher has can also either negatively or positively influence the experience. Teachers' attitudes towards co-teaching are also a factor in its successful implementation, with teachers having had a previous positive experience being more positively disposed towards co-

---

[15] Rabin, 2020; Soslau, Gallo-Fox, and Scantlebury, 2019; Kerin and Murphy, 2018.
[16] Friend and Cook, 1992; Pancsofar and Petroff, 2016.
[17] Kerin and Murphy, 2018.
[18] Dillon, Salazar and AlOtaibi, 2015; Pancsofar and Petroff, 2016.

teaching.[19] Regarding traditional teacher education programs, co-teaching tends not to receive much attention. So, if co-teaching is required within a district, this presents an opportunity for schools to provide CPD in this area. However, one difficulty is the variety of purposes of co-teaching and the approaches that may be suitable within particular contexts. There is no 'one size fits all' approach to this practice, which depends on so many factors, and therefore, in many ways, it is part of one of those intangible aspects related to the craft of teaching.

The development of co-teaching relationships can be compared loosely with developing a relationship leading to a long-term commitment such as a marriage.[20] The most successful co-teaching partnerships have often been in place for some time. When the co-teachers are initially placed together, they can be seen as in the 'getting to know you' phase of the relationship, perhaps unsure of their place as they negotiate their way within the new relationship. As the relationship grows and matures, and issues are ironed out, leading to more and more harmony within the dynamic, this becomes the more committed phase of the relationship, similar to the engagement period. Over time, as more and more decisions are made as a team and co-teachers are at the point of finishing each other's sentences and speaking with one voice, the relationship can be likened to a long-term relationship such as a marriage. It can lead to great success for teachers and students.

Emergent writing—bilingual children

The cognitive benefits of literacy development in two languages are well-researched in the literature.[21] These include heightened cognitive flexibility, metalinguistic awareness, the development of

---

[19] Pancsofar and Petroff, 2016.
[20] Friend, 2015.
[21] Bauer and Mkhize, 2012; Cummins, 1979, 2008; Bialystock, 2001.

interlanguage, increased working memory, and many more. The foundations of literacy are established in early childhood, with the term *emergent literacy* being used to account for what children know about reading and writing from birth to the early years of nursery and school. It is termed *emergent* since the accepted conventions of writing and reading develop during that developmental stage. Gort and Bauer's work on emergent biliteracy states that this term refers to "the ongoing, dynamic development of concepts and expertise for thinking, listening, speaking, reading, and writing in two languages."[22] The use of the word dynamic is noteworthy in this definition, as the word connotes that emergent biliteracy is ever-changing, that languages may be rubbing off on each other, that one may spark a change in the other, and that we may expect different rates of change and development in each language. Indeed, emergent biliteracy is challenging to assess at progress points that may be utilized with monoliterate children.

Literacy includes more than reading and writing, whether in one, two, or more languages. Text is constructed using more than just letters, words, and sentences, especially in the early years. Pictures and other types of signs are an essential part of the process. As children go through the stages of emergent writing, drawing is critical to that development. Drawing and writing are similar systems of "mark-making capable of carrying meaning."[23] However, drawing is an invented form of mark-making with no clear definitions, whereas writing is a closed system "determined by cultural context and constrained by rules."[24] Therefore, it is essential to include drawing as an encouraged aspect of emergent writing as a type of visual text construction.[25] This is particularly important in emergent

---

[22] Gort and Bauer2012, p. 2.
[23] Mackenzie and Veresov, 2013, p. 23.
[24] Ibid., p. 23.
[25] Mackenzie and Veresov, 2013.

biliteracy, where the drawing aspects are related equally to both languages, but the rules differ. Emergent bilinguals apply what they learn in one language to their other language in a way that helps the other when writing.[26] Kenner has long maintained that even where different writing systems are involved, it adds a linguistic resource to children's repertoires rather than being a challenge.[27] For example, she found that in terms of metalanguage, children tend to make comparisons and connections between their known writing systems, that young children explicitly talked about which direction reading and writing started in Arabic, and that children understood that Chinese characters correspond with words and concepts rather than letters. She also found no barrier to emergent biliteracy depending on a different directionality. Kenner cautions against educators assuming children will be confused by simultaneously engaging with text construction in two languages. Instead, she highlights children's "expanded range of semiotic resources."[28]

Translanguaging pedagogy in the early years

Translanguaging sees the languages of individuals as forming a repertoire of linguistic features that have been socially assigned, from which bilinguals choose to communicate effectively. Velasco and García see translanguaging as a "bilingual theory of learning,"[29] as language forms an integrated system. They stress that emergent bilinguals engage in language practices "in functional interrelationship with other languages."[30] In the past, each language had been viewed as a separate linguistic system, emphasizing a monolingual ideology, but translanguaging firmly focuses on

---

[26] Gort and Bauer, 2013; van den Bosch, Segers, E. and Verhoeven, 2020.
[27] Kenner, 2004.
[28] Kenner, 2004, p. 53.
[29] Velasco and Garcia, 2014, p. 7.
[30] ibid.

affirming multilingual identities.[31] Research on code-switching has tended to look at the alternation of languages in and between sentences as two separate languages. Translanguaging is much broader than understanding the linguistic behavior of bilinguals and multilinguals as drawing from one linguistic system. García and Lin explain this briefly as follows:

> Code-switching [...] is based on the monoglossic view that bilinguals have two separate linguistic systems. Translanguaging, however, posits the linguistic behavior of bilinguals as being always heteroglossic [...] always dynamic, responding not to two monolingualisms in one but to one integrated linguistic system.[32]

Translanguaging is commonly understood to have originated with Williams' research on *trawsieithu* in bilingual Welsh-English schools in Wales.[33] In classrooms where a translanguaging pedagogy is intentionally planned, we may see an alternation of languages between modes of teaching and learning. For example, information might be presented in one language, with students encouraged to produce responses in another.[34] The practice of pedagogical translanguaging primarily focused on switching the input and output language, for example, reading a text in one language and writing about it in another.[35] These original pedagogical practices, which still saw some language separation, have become more flexible in recent years. Learners may be encouraged to mediate their understanding and demonstrate knowledge by translanguaging flexibly.[36] They may be prompted to co-construct meaning with peers by drawing flexibly

---

[31] Goodman and Tastanbek, 2021.
[32] García and Lin, 2016, p. 120.
[33] Williams, 2000.
[34] Goodman and Tastanbek, 2021.
[35] García and Lin, 2016; Lewis, Jones, and Baker, 2012.
[36] Poza, 2017.

on their combined linguistic resources in collaborative work.[37] Intentional pedagogical translanguaging also allows teachers to scaffold learning—not by directly translating but by drawing on their linguistic resources or others to support learners' conceptual understanding.

A translanguaging pedagogy can also go a long way to challenging language dominance and fostering equal relationships between speakers of different languages, as languages are not seen as separate entities but rather a well of linguistic resources from which to draw.

Emergent biliteracy and translanguaging in a KG2 classroom

This discussion explores how the EMT and AMT in the KG2 demonstrated their co-teaching practices, facilitating emergent biliteracy and implementing a translanguaging pedagogy. These will be analyzed in terms of how they stood out as moments of wonder.

Regarding co-teaching, these teachers had reached the 'marriage' stage of the co-teaching relationship (Friend, 2015). Having worked as co-teachers for a couple of years, they often finished each other's sentences and had a very respectful working relationship. Children used one language per teacher, mainly because the EMT had minimal knowledge of Arabic, and the AMT spoke only Arabic with the children, although she did speak English with the EMT. Regarding linguistic leadership in the classroom, the AMT had slightly more power because she could draw on the linguistic resources of English and Arabic. In contrast, the EMT could only draw on English. Therefore, the AMT could communicate freely with everyone in the classroom, while the EMT was more limited in communicating with these young children. How both teachers had their students working on similar learning outcomes in both English and Arabic (considering that many of the learning outcomes are

---

[37] Hamman, 2018.

different between the languages) stood out as a moment of wonder regarding co-teaching. To have the students work in such an aligned manner, moving between drawing and writing in English and Arabic on the same piece of paper and for the same purpose, showed a level of co-planning for the literacy lesson I had not observed before. The fact that it happened so seamlessly indicated that the children were used to the team approach taken by their teachers during learning centers.

The teachers facilitated emergent biliteracy in various ways, particularly in the Arabic and English learning centers. By moving between the literacy centers so freely and equally, sounding out the exact words in English and Arabic, and then forming the letters, the children indicated they were similarly comfortable writing both languages.[38] The writing of the words in both languages based on their drawing of the item showed that their knowledge of the vocabulary was equally scaffolded in both languages. This equal valuing of both languages and drawing on the potential of drawing pictures as part of emergent writing created a fair and equitable environment and resulted in a beautiful language mosaic. In contrast, they drew on their linguistic resources and the language of drawing to contribute to a piece of text.[39]

There is no one way of implementing a translanguaging pedagogy, but this classroom succeeded by encouraging children to use whichever language felt most appropriate. While the children naturally spoke to the EMT in English and the AMT in Arabic, it was not because of a rule-driven language separation policy in that classroom. This is common in many classrooms with co-teachers speaking one language each. It was simply a natural circumstance of the teachers' linguistic resources. Despite not understanding Arabic, the EMT supported children's emergent writing in both languages by

---

[38] Kenner, 2004.
[39] Mor-Sommerfeld, 2002.

not insisting on language separation. Despite not being an official translator, the AMT did everything possible to clarify any linguistic barriers between the children and the EMT. The philosophy of translanguaging was evident, as everyone in that classroom drew on their linguistic resources to communicate and learn.[40]

Insights and implications for translanguaging pedagogy

In a classroom with co-teachers responsible for different languages and subject areas, pairing teachers who can work together effectively is essential. If the co-teaching team does not work smoothly together, achieving success in teaching and learning practices will be very difficult. This can be a challenge in the U.A.E. where there can be a high teacher turnover rate due to the nature of the expatriate lifestyle. Still, in areas with a lower rate of teachers, turnover measures could be taken to emphasize the importance of developing and maintaining the co-teaching relationship through ongoing CPD and sufficient timetabled planning time. In terms of fostering emergent biliteracy, one of the reasons for the success of this lesson is that the expected learning outcomes were the same for English and Arabic. This can be difficult to foster if learning outcomes differ significantly between the native language and the additional languages of learners. It is worth exploring and learning from other contexts where teaching and learning activities are provided in two languages, such as in Ireland, where the Primary Language Curriculum has recently been revised so that it includes the same structure and strands for both English and Irish, thereby seeking connections and supporting transfer between the languages.[41] It appears that to implement a translanguaging pedagogy, one of the essential aspects is for teachers to have a conceptually deep understanding of the importance of all members of the learning environment, drawing on their linguistic funds of

---

[40] García and Lin, 2016.
[41] Department of Education and Skills, 2019.

knowledge.[42] Once that is in place, teachers and learners can work together to create equitable environments for teaching and learning that value all the languages of teachers and learners. Certain pedagogical practices may be more appropriate depending on the context, whether co-taught or not, or whether teachers are bilingual or monolingual. It would be wonderful to see more action research projects[43] in classrooms implementing a translanguaging pedagogy. This would open up more doors for teachers' voices to be heard in their recommendations for best practices in re-conceptualizing how the linguistic repertoires may be valued and encouraged. It was a privilege on this occasion to have the opportunity to observe these beautiful moments that glowed on me as a researcher and learn from the experts in the area—the teachers and the children.

---

[42] Wei, 2014.
[43] similar to those described in Hathorn and Dillon, 2018.

5. Language status and usage in multilingual Algeria

Mehdi Lazar
International School of Boston

The first time I returned to Algeria after a decade of absence due to the civil war was in February 2003. I was eagerly going back, trying to escape the gloomy Parisian weather, and, most importantly, I was impatient to see many family members again and conduct research for my master's degree thesis. As a young geographer, languages were not usually considered central in our geopolitical analysis, so I went to Algiers, Blida, or Médéa without overthinking it. Soon, however, I discovered two things. First, I saw a vast difference in language proficiency, particularly in French, between my parents' generations and mine. I noted it because, like many second-generation immigrants in France, I had limited Arabic proficiency, and French was my *lingua familia*. Secondly, I learned that the civil war during the *décennie noire* (Black Decade) was, to some degree, also a "linguistic war." Of course, languages are never neutral, but in the 1990s, they reflected strong power relationships and intense sociopolitical realities.

During my research that semester in 2003, I realized that since independence in 1962, languages have been a political, social, and ideological issue in Algeria. The colonization of Algeria by France and the length of occupation (132 years) profoundly affected Algeria's society (more so than its neighboring countries, Morocco and Tunisia). France's domination also happened when Algeria's linguistic unification was still underway, which had profound implications for Algeria's linguistic situation.[44] After 1962, Algeria's new leaders chose Arabic as the language representing its identity and religion. As a result, Algeria's language policy changed significantly during the 20th century but fell short of satisfying the various speakers.

Genuine and significant linguistic diversity is nevertheless present in Algeria. First, the Arabic dialect (Algerian Arabic, or colloquial Arabic, also known as *Darja*) is spoken by most Algerians (around 80% of the population). It differs from the Modern Standard Arabic taught at school or used in the media. Second, the Berber (Tamazight) language, with its different regional forms, is widely spoken (by around 20 to 25% of the population). Third, French is a colonial heritage and is still widely present in Algeria in the education system or the Algerian language, although it has no official status. Fourth, the English language is progressing in the country, and despite a low user base, regular calls demand that it replace French as the first foreign language in schools.[45] In addition, *Ethnologue* counts 18 living languages within Algeria, splitting Arabic and Tamazight into several different languages.[46] Finally, Algerian Sign Language is also widely used by the deaf community in the country and is sometimes seen on national TV.

Following the strict Arabization policy post-independence, developments regarding the Berber, French, and English languages have shown a new approach to language status in Algeria. Today, the practice of French and, to a greater extent, English, or the promotion of Tamazight as a national language and medium of instruction, are viewed differently. The recognition of Tamazight has been of particular importance. It transformed Algeria into an official multilingual country, confirming a *de facto* multilingualism.

---

[44] Saad, 1992.
[45] Amara, 2010.
[46] ethnologue.com/country/DZ

Before discussing the current situation in Algeria, it is necessary to provide a brief historical overview of the country's linguistic diversity. The spread of existing languages in Algeria can be traced back to various conquests and can be analyzed in terms of their uses in different domains. Language has also brought to light several contentious issues in contemporary Algerian society, especially concerning the definition of the Algerian Nation. The ongoing dispute over languages is most explicitly manifested in the Arabization policy. Finally, a multilingual education model will be proposed to address some of the persisting linguistic issues, beginning with multilingual practices as a source of tension and an opportunity.

Historical perspectives on language practices

Algeria has been a place of invasion and a crossroad of civilizations, making linguistic plurality reign among its speakers since Antiquity.[47] During the Neolithic period, many Berber cultural elements were already in place. Those elements include the Berber language, Tamazight, a primarily oral language using the Libyco-Berber alphabet. Some experts believe that this alphabet has its roots in the Phoenician alphabet.

Later, Romanization forced the Berber people to learn Latin. The following Christianization process also strengthened the position of Latin. Starting in the 7th century, however, the linguistic fabric of Algeria began to change following the first Arabic conquest, although Arabic remained mainly a religious and academic language. Tamazight remained the language of communication between the people, even if, during the reign of the Almoravids (1050-1147) and the Almohad Caliphate (1147-1269), educated elites were bilingual in Tamazight-Arabic. The Spanish and Ottoman conquests changed the language mix slightly, but those effects remained limited. The Turkish language did not replace the Tamazight and Arabic

---

[47] Chami, 2009.

languages used by the inhabitants. That said, in Algeria, the cohabitation of languages and cultures has always been challenging.[48] Still, social and cultural divisions were not as marked along religious, cultural, or linguistic lines as they were along regional areas. In addition, Arabs and Berbers were less ethnic than linguistic groups, and multilingual practices were already a reality, particularly around contact zones such as markets, cities, or limits between plains and mountains.

Contrary to the Spanish and Ottoman conquests, the French conquest introduced significant changes in Algeria. The colonial system had a tremendous influence on what Algeria was then, including language practices. French became significant over the 132 years of the French presence in the country. Another consequence of French colonization has been dismantling the existing education system (centered around koranic schools *kuttabs*) and the decreasing literacy rate, negatively impacting generations of Algerians. Parallel was the development of French public or church primary schools, some *collèges* and *Lycées*, and faculties that would become l'Université d'Alger. The first bilingual schools, known as the écoles arabes-françaises, were created in 1833 as an experiment. Most schools were monolingual, and more natives were increasingly enrolled.[49] It is within this context of French domination that the Algerian nationalist movement emerged. In 1962, when Algeria became independent, the question of the newly independent state's language(s) became quite central.

The founding myths of Algerian nationalism have been underlying the importance of Arabization and Islamization as a frame of reference.[50] Indeed, the Arabic conquests primarily structured society with the Arabic language, which spread widely

---

[48] McDougall, 2017.
[49] Ruedy, 2005.
[50] Harbi, 1998.

(except in the mountains), while Islam significantly organized society. It was only with the French conquest and then domination that Algeria entered modernity and developed a nationalist feeling. This nationalism developed first within the French-speaking elites, then within minority groups of the Muslim religion or non-French language (Arabic speakers, Tamazight speakers), mainly around two ideologies. Initially, there was the ethnocultural movement of Messali Hadj, which viewed the Algerian nation as Arab-Muslim. This movement was followed by the ideology of Ferhat Abbas, who considered the nation a political construction; the francophone elites mainly supported him. The duality of the conception of the Algerian nation is clearly expressed in the languages spoken by the partisans of this approach: Arabic for the Hadjian concept and French for the Abbassian concept. The status of languages (Arabic, Tamazight, French) was therefore integrated into the very conception of the Algerian nation. This conception of the Algerian nation remained central to many quarrels and controversies over the years. Finally, after independence, the FLN (*Front de Libération Nationale*, the one-party for many years) chose the establishment of an ethnocultural nationalism, one of the most significant traces of which remains the Arabization policy implemented in the 1970s.

The first constitution (1963) and principal constitution (1976) of post-independence Algeria consequently omitted all references to French and Berber languages. The 1976 constitution stated in Article 3 that "Arabic is the national and official language." The Algerian authorities rejected the use of the word "Berber," either on the secular grounds that the term undermines national unity or on the religious grounds that it is hostile to Islam. Therefore, the Arabization that started after independence was a political language policy that was not fully representative of the Algerian linguistic landscape.

Moreover, its implementation conflicted with the extensive practice of the French language and Tamazight.[51]

Algeria, throughout its history, remained a *de facto* multilingual country. The Algerian linguistic environment has native Arabic speakers and Tamazight speakers who are in contact with French as a second language inherited from the colonial era. French also remained a prestigious language at the socio-economic level. The Algerian elites continue to be educated in French, perpetuating *un système à deux vitesses* (a two-tier system).[52] Recently, increasing globalization, the rise of the French-speaking press in the 1990s, and French speeches by President Bouteflika (despite being an excellent Arabic speaker) have revived the debate on the Arabization policy and the role of the French language in Algeria. The overall number of French speakers in Algeria is decreasing, but this issue remains relevant.[53]

The Arabization policy

After Algeria's independence, a dual movement partly explains the tension between languages and the Algerian nation's difficulty managing its linguistic heritage. On the one hand, from 1962 on, the French language rapidly developed due to the population's increased schooling (in the primary, secondary, and tertiary education systems). On the other hand, the Arabization policy was implemented in 1963 with the declaration of Tunis. After that, the decree of May 22, 1964, by President Ben Bella (1962-1965) was the first decree relating to the Arabization of the administration.

Since then, Algeria has adopted dozens of laws on Arabization, but only a few have been fully enforced, such as the law n° 91-05 of January 16, 1991, which aimed to generalize the use of the Arabic

---

[51] Grandguillaume, 1998.
[52] Tessa, 2015.
[53] Lazar, 2014.

language. This law, nevertheless, constitutes an essential text as it excluded the use and practice of French in public administration, justice, the world of education (including universities), hospitals, socio-economic sectors, etc. The Nationalist linguistic policy of Arabization aimed to reverse the balance of power between Arabic and French inherited from the colonial period to make Arabic the dominant language by giving it the status of the only official national language. The goal of the Arabization policy was not to completely eradicate French but to allow the Arabic language to spread progressively in society and to gradually replace the French language in most significant areas of the country, such as higher education (but only partly, with the humanities and social sciences for example).[54] Finally, it is essential to add that the decline of the French language and intellectual production in French is also due to the clashes during the civil war of the 1990s and the exile of many Francophones. The Arabization policy's primary flaw was that despite aligning with the broader identity shared by many Algerians,[55] it did not correspond to Algeria's linguistic and cultural realities.[56]

Indeed, Algerian dialectal Arabic did not exist in the standardized written form of classical Arabic. Moreover, the sizeable Berber population (20 to 25 % of the people in the early 1960s) also spoke Tamazight. Finally, most of the language of instruction was French, a language spoken by almost all political elites. French was also used as the written and ideological language of the revolution (*la guerre de libération nationale*) and the primary language of government and industry. Hence, two problems appeared at the beginning of the Arabization of the country and are still at the center of many Algerian issues today. First, Arabic was seen in the Arab world in the 1960s and 1970s as the language of modernity and progressive politics. In

---

[54] Grine, 2009.
[55] Ruedy, 2005.
[56] Le Sueur, 2010.

Algeria, however, French was the most practical language for technological and scientific progress and rapid industrialization. Second, the large Berber and Kabyle communities saw Arabization threatening their languages and culture. They challenged the concept that Algeria should be exclusively Arab and that classical Arabic should be used in everyday situations (except in the religious sphere).[57] Consequently, this linguistic, cultural, and political crisis continued and erupted periodically in large protests such as the "Berber Spring of 1980," one of the most significant events of post-independence Algeria.[58]

The field of education was the most visible arena in which Arabization happened, and the cultural debate was present. In practice, Algeria completed the Arabization of primary schooling and some higher education sectors (such as social sciences) in 1982. These politics faced considerable staffing challenges, and Algeria massively recruited Algerians and foreigners, considerably lowering teaching standards. At the ideological level, Arabization hardened the distinction between Arabophone elites and Francophone elites, a distinction that the system nevertheless continued to reproduce. The two factions, often portrayed as the advocates of authenticity (using Arabic) versus the advocates of modernity and progress (using French), have also utilized other Algerian languages to further their confrontational agendas, often in the following fashion: "an Arab plus English bloc against a French plus Tamazight plus Algerian Arabic bloc."[59] The replacement of French with English can be seen within this sociological context. During the 1970s, Algeria nevertheless realistically accepted that French would remain an

---

[57] Stora, 2004.
[58] Evans, 2007.
[59] "Un bloc arabe + anglais contre un bloc français + tamazight + arabe algérien." Cited in Grine, 2015.

essential language in the country, including in schools and higher education.[60]

Furthermore, the Arabization policy led to different linguistic and pedagogical decisions in Algeria compared to its Maghreb neighbors, Tunisia and Morocco. In those two countries, bilingualism in Arabic and French was maintained. Moreover, the persistence of a linguistic break between the primary and secondary school systems and higher education remains one of the significant limits to establishing a coherent language education policy in Algeria. Of course, this linguistic divide does not affect the elites who educate their children in French. However, it ultimately serves as a selection process between the university courses taught in French (polytechnic sciences, engineering sciences, medicine, or pharmacy, for instance) and those trained in Arabic (human and social sciences).

Current multilingual practices in contemporary Algeria

Algeria is one of those countries where multilingualism underwent developmental states. First, languages evolved from language contact to an integrative code. This new system, Algerian Arabic, combines components from different languages, namely French and Arabic.[61] French is, therefore, rooted in regional dialects and is becoming more and more Algerian[62] as Algerian Arabic sees an influx of French or Spanish in some areas.

Second, Algeria shifted from de facto multilingualism to official multilingualism. The Berber population resisted the Arabization policy due to the fear of domination by the Arabic-speaking majority. This resistance led to the *"Printemps Kabyle"* (Kabyle Spring) of 1980 and its recurrence in 2001 when more than a hundred protesters were killed. Consequently, Tamazight was granted the status of a national

---

[60] Knut, 2012.
[61] Belfarhi, 2019.
[62] Kourouma, 1997.

language in 2002 and was upgraded to an official language in 2016, with Algeria officially becoming a multilingual country. However, the slow and laborious progress toward a better recognition of Berber culture and language in Algerian society was accompanied by a parallel movement, primarily driven by the state, to replace the use of French with English, as discussed earlier. This approach appears consistent with a historical perspective among Algerian nationalists who want to eliminate the use of French: after gaining political independence from France in 1962, Algeria—according to this particular ideology—needs to be "culturally" liberated from the French language and culture. During the colonial period, the bilingual state of Algeria was considered "circumstantial." Indeed, contrary to what Kateb Yacine said—that the French language is a "trophy of war" or *butin de guerre*—many Algerian statesmen consider French a hindrance to identity development. The use of Arabic might have been the first step of this policy.

In contrast, the use of English, seen as more culturally neutral in Algeria and more practical by younger generations, might be more efficient in that regard. It also holds a global language status and is seen by some as a gateway to modernity and development. As for the Gulf States, more extensive use of English in Algeria could help further a relationship with the United States, following closer ties in the wake of the 09/11 terrorist attacks and the "war on terror." The official diffusion of the English language in Algeria[63] began with the first referendum in 1987, which proposed replacing French with English as the primary language of instruction. This consultation, however, contributed to worrying academics or French-speaking citizens, who feared that the disappearance of French would deprive Algerians of a direct relationship with their past (all the official archives are in French, for example) or other French-speaking and non-Arabic-speaking countries. In recent years, the competition

---

[63] Cordel, 2014.

between English and French for linguistic dominance has overshadowed the competition between Arabic and French.⁶⁴ The competition is, for instance, present in the TV channel appellations, which shows the increasing emergence of the English language in Algerian society.⁶⁵ Nowadays, many Algerians are more interested in Turkish soap operas or American streaming services like Netflix than traditional French television programs. Moreover, younger generations watch fewer French TV channels via satellite and are more connected to social media platforms, such as Instagram and TikTok, where they might converse in English. The spread of English, which began modestly, has been steadily increasing over the past few decades (except during the instability of the 1990s).⁶⁶

In September 2022, President Tebboune announced that Algeria would be pivoting from teaching French to English as a second language in public primary schools during the 2022-2023 school year. However, Algeria will still be the third-largest French-speaking country in the world in 2022, after France and the Democratic Republic of the Congo, with close to 15 million French speakers out of the 321 million French speakers in the world.⁶⁷ Dynamic literature in French also exists, and Kamel Daoud, Yasmina Khadra, and Assia Djebar are among the most famous representatives. This French literature is sometimes "Algerianized," which shows the coexistence of languages in many areas of society. Finally, the francophone media still account for around 30% of newspapers in Algeria. However, French-language publications have been disappearing rapidly for the last ten years (such as *Liberté*, which closed in April 2022 after 30 years of existence).

---

⁶⁴ Belmihoub, 2018.
⁶⁵ Labed, 2015.
⁶⁶ Belmihoub, 2018.
⁶⁷ Observatoire International de la Francophonie.

Researchers have also recently noted multilingual practices as part of the *Hirak* (which means "movement" in Arabic). This vast protest movement started on February 22, 2019, after Abdelaziz Bouteflika announced his candidacy for a fifth presidential term. On that day, protests organized the first nationwide march, and after that, Algerian citizens protested every Friday and every Tuesday. The protests forced President Bouteflika to resign, then focused on demanding the departure of the ruling elite and a transition to more democratic governance. Protesters were a diverse group of Algerian citizens who had been chanting anti-regime slogans, singing, and expressing generalized *ras-le-bol* (fed-upness).[68] The *hirakistes* showed language practices marked by encounters and code-mixing between various languages: Arabic, vernacular Arabic, French, Spanish, and English. In addition, slogans and graffiti are utilized in all the languages in society. It created a linguistic mix characterized by neologisms formed through techniques such as suffixation and prefixation.[69]

In that sense, using words in the *Hirak* context reflected Algeria's linguistic landscape. First, Classical Arabic was prevalent due to its religious and cultural significance. For instance, *bismal-haqq*, meaning "in the name of the law," has been used instead of *bismillah*, which means "in the name of God."[70] Second, Darja, the colloquial Arabic, was widely spoken daily, while French was employed to convey prestige and historical references. English was used to gain visibility, especially on social media, and Tamazight was used on a limited scale in Berber-speaking regions. In addition, these languages were used together, utilizing code-switching techniques. They were evident in oral or written slogans such as *silmiyya, silmiyya, silmiyya*[71]

---

[68] Moussaoui, 2020.
[69] Moussaoui, 2020.
[70] Filiu, 2019.
[71] Leyla, 2020.

(peaceful in Arabic, a slogan also used in other Arab countries). Along with the French slogans, they showcased Algerian humor, for example, *marcher c'est bon pour la santé, manifester c'est bon pour la dignité*, or *ils ont des millions, nous sommes des millions*.[72] The slogan *khawa, khawa* demonstrated a vision of fraternity among protesters, often symbolized by the presence of the Algerian and Berber flags held together in marches. Code-mixing in slogans was also frequent, as in the following: *ni sursis ni mandat, la mafia barra, barra* (*barra* means *dehors* in French).[73]

Lastly, in Algeria, multilingualism is present in music, the topography, and place names. In music, multilingualism is often expressed around themes related to protests and frustrations. For example, Aït Menguellet, Idir, or Djamel Allam sang the revolt of the Kabyle people in Tamazight. At the same time, *raï* singers like Cheb Mami or Cheb Khaled sang in Algerian Arabic about the unhappiness of young people in urban settings. In addition, in Algiers, the three main streets of the center of the Algerian capital all radiate from the Grande Poste. During the French colonization, those streets were Rue d'Isly, Boulevard Michelet, and Rue Sadi Carnot. After independence, the Algerian governments changed many French names of streets, monuments, and cities.

Consequently, the three central streets of Algiers took on the names of revolutionaries: Didouche Mourad replaced Michelet, rue d'Isly became Larbi Ben M'Hidi, and Sadi Carnot conceded its place to the young heroine Hassiba Ben Bouali. While Algerians embraced new names for some streets, such as "Didouche" or "Hassiba," the majority of locals continued to refer to "Rue d'Isly" by its colonial name. This example illustrates Algerian society's multilingualism

---

[72] Walking is good for health, and demonstrating is good for dignity; they have millions, and we are millions.
[73] No reprieve or warrant, out, out the mafia.

and the French language's continued presence in the Algerian linguistic landscape.

For a multilingual education system

In Algeria, French remains the language of the elites and social success. Many private schools use French as the medium of instruction, and the university courses with the most promising professional outcomes are taught in French. This situation encourages a *de facto* establishment of a "two-tier school system" (*une école à deux vitesses*). The massive Arabization naturally leads to Arabized university courses (in human and social sciences and Islamic sciences). These courses mainly lead to civil service or even unemployment.

On the other hand, private schools (officially authorized since 2004) are leading seamlessly to higher education courses in French or even further education opportunities abroad. This problematic situation comes from a lack of linguistic planning based on solid pedagogical research; the *status quo* established around this *système à deux vitesses* stays in place, from which working-class students suffer. Unfortunately, one consequence is that the failure rate in the first year of university studies is very high in Algeria.

After these years of unfinished Arabization, it is clear that the complete replacement of French with Arabic is no longer a realistic objective.[74] However, any solution requires a more harmonious and balanced relationship between all languages in Algeria. It requires a linguistic and educational policy allowing all Algerian languages to contribute to the country's economic development and collective identity. Even Algeria's *de facto* multilingualism has been seen as chaotic, particularly in the educational sector. Some have spoken of "bilingual illiterates" to designate students leaving public schools

---

[74] "L'une est exclue du domaine du développement et l'autre du domaine de l'identité." Cited in Boudebia-Baala, 2013.

without the basic language skills in Arabic or French. Others talk about primary school as the *"fawdamontale"* school (of *fawda*: anarchy in Arabic).[75]

One of the reasons for such difficulties is that after independence, Algeria's conflicting social goals and linguistic features hindered the country's ability to marshal a pool of skilled and trained workers that the development required.[76] Therefore, phasing out French is not the best course of action. Algeria needs to teach English, but it should not replace French. Such a policy may resemble the Arabization policy, which authorities implemented without adequate planning and resources. Additionally, the higher education system and all archives predominantly use French.

Other solutions exist. For instance, an early bilingual education model would allow for a better transition of students from primary to secondary to higher education, thus attenuating Algeria's linguistic rupture. For instance, successive bilingualism (or multilingualism) involves acquiring a second language after initiating the first language's development. For successive bilingualism to be effective, it should also entail additive bilingualism. Additive bilingualism means valuing and nurturing the first language and culture while incorporating the second language. Many experts recommend this approach because it does not create conflict between languages, unlike subtractive bilingualism, which involves diminishing one's language proficiency while learning another language.

There are numerous benefits of multilingualism. For instance, students educated in a multilingual context are better able to learn new languages later[77] and are cognitively more agile and adaptable.[78] They have, on average, better test results and are better able to solve

---

[75] Ahmed, 2015.
[76] Ruedy, 2005.
[77] Madrid, 2011.
[78] Grosjean, 2015.

problems in various situations, while they have greater autonomy than monolingual peers. Their ability to plan, drive, focus, and reject irrelevant information is enhanced.[79] From a socio-cultural standpoint, multilingualism enables learners to fully appreciate the cultural diversity of our world. Students develop greater empathy towards other cultures and a deeper understanding that the world can be perceived and described in various ways. As a result, multilingual individuals can enhance their cultural intelligence[80] – the capacity to navigate different cultures. Hence, immersive multilingual programs are currently expanding worldwide.

Even with the rise of the English language, French still holds an important place in Algerian society. It is an essential language in Algerian society through borrowing spoken languages (dialectal Arabic or Tamazight). Many Algerian citizens are also multilingual individuals (including generations of intellectuals and artists producing in French), and the many media (print, television, radio, or social networks) plead in favor of the durability of French on the Algerian linguistic landscape (despite a reduced footprint). Implementing the early bilingualism model in the school system could facilitate a harmonious coexistence of Arabic, French, Tamazight, and other foreign languages, including English.

Thus, following Arabic-French school bilingualism, from the preschool sector and primary school (at the rate of five to six hours of French per week until the third year of primary school, then at an equal time), English could be introduced from the middle of primary education (at nine years old, up to two to three hours per week). At the *Lycée* level during secondary education, students can learn a new language, which they can pursue further at the university level. In Tamazight-speaking regions, Tamazight could replace French, or Tamazight could be added as a third language, with up to one and a

---

[79] Bialystok, 1999; Bialystok, 2004a; Bialystok, 2004b.
[80] Baker, 2014.

half hours per week starting from preschool. Such a model, which will require the development of new programs, textbooks, and the training of many teachers and administrators, is widely used in many schools worldwide. Following this, students would become trilingual or quadrilingual by the end of their secondary education. Then, with more than fifteen years of French learning, they will be ready to pursue the university studies of their choice in French or Arabic.

Embracing multilingualism: Navigating language policy and identity in Algeria

Multilingual practices in Algeria are both a source of tension and richness. After independence, the government promoted an Arabization policy and an education system aiming to produce a technical workforce that reinforced the Arab-Islamic identity.[81] This policy, a significant change compared to pre-independence, triggered official negative attitudes towards the Berber and French languages. The unfinished Arabization produced mixed results. The education system particularly needs to perform better. Promoting Tamazight as a national language also only resulted in violent opposition, and Algeria still needs to clarify the situation between literal Arabic and spoken Arabic.

Many difficulties in schools come from the fact that "the Algerians write a language that they do not speak and speak a language that cannot be written!"[82] On the other hand, French remains the language of many Algerians, the elites, and social successes. In that sense, we can see that the sequence of unity of the country around one language, Arabic, started to crumble after the protests of 1988 and the decade of the civil war. More recently, the

---

[81] Entelis, 1986.
[82] "Les Algériens écrivent une langue qu'ils ne parlent pas et parlent une langue qui ne s'écrit pas !" Cited in Abid-Houcine, 2007.

plan to increasingly replace French with English is progressing steadily.

In this context, I offer an alternative based on a multilingual Algerian identity and solid pedagogical foundations. Twenty years after returning to Algeria in 2003, I finished my doctorate in Geography and have been involved in multilingual education for almost two decades. I have seen how a global, multilingual education emphasizing critical thinking, creativity, collaboration, cross-cultural communication, and an appreciation of differences is essential to the world we live in today.

Establishing early solid bilingualism (mainly Arabic—French, but in certain areas, Arabic—Tamazight) and introducing English in the middle of primary school would help reduce inequalities and leverage a partially multilingual education system. A more robust multilingual education system based on this early bilingual model will produce citizens who can understand, speak, read, and write fluently in either of their languages. Additionally, multilingualism provides cognitive advantages and social-emotional benefits that foster students' appreciation of differences and the joy of learning.

6. Bilingualism in Arabic language training sets

Zeynep Ertürk
Bogazici University, Turkey

Language learning and teaching has been an area of interest since ancient civilizations, and language has existed with different disciplines in each civilization. For example, while it was accepted as a part of philosophy in Greek civilization, it was seen as a tool facilitating understanding of religious and literary texts in Eastern civilizations.[83] When these language studies are examined under the roof of different disciplines, it is noteworthy that researchers have created a new terminology about language. The verbs in the Akkadian and Sumerian tablets[84] were examined in terms of form, conjugated according to the people, and presented in a specific system.[85] Linguists in this field also studied different dialects of Chinese and revealed information about the sound system.[86] As a result of their research, Indian linguists identified many basic

---

[83] Aksan, 2015; Parlak, 2015.
[84] Sumer is the earliest civilization that has been discovered in southern Mesopotamia south central Iraq between the sixth and fifth millennium BC. The Akkadian Empire, or Akkadian Empire, was the first ancient empire of Mesopotamia after the long-lived Sumerian civilization. As in many other fields, these two civilizations were pioneers in writing. They used cuneiform to record their daily activities on clay or stone tablets. Cuneiform is the earliest known writing system. It is a form of writing that uses a unique approach and has images or letters on it.
[85] Pehlivan and Seçkin, 2020.
[86] Özgen and Koşaner, 2020.

concepts such as grammatical terms, phonetic rules, roots, and stems.[87] In addition, Ancient Greek linguists introduced the concept of gender, which has an essential place in some languages, for the first time.[88] As a result, considering similar studies, it can be said that language's first definitions and determinations were made in the pre-modern period of linguistics.

By the 20th century, language had become a branch of science studied independently. In the early periods, the theory that language is behavior was accepted with the influence of the behaviorist approach. Therefore, repetition and memorization of information came to the fore to learn this behavior, in other words, language. By the 1960s, the theory presented by Noam Chomsky started a new era in language teaching. Chomsky argues that every individual is born with a language mechanism. So, the brain genetically possesses linguistic elements such as phonetics and syntax. Each individual processes this information in the environment in which he was born. With this theory, Chomsky pointed out the source of grammatical knowledge.[89]

The concept of 'generative grammar,' among the commonly used definitions of this theory, aims to describe all the forms of expression that may occur, not just the ones that occurred. In other words, the individual should be able to produce any expression or sentence meaningfully, apart from the patterns he has learned by rote and repetition. Therefore, linguistics should not only examine language structure but also deal with how sentences are perceived and put into function. According to Chomsky, this is possible with human language's 'universal grammar.' According to the universal grammar theory, all human languages have some standard rules.

---

[87] Bloomfield, ty.; Kahrs, 1982; Bronkhorst, 2001.
[88] Parlak, 2015; Kerimoğlu, 2017.
[89] Ertürk, 2021.

Therefore, all languages contain their own universal grammar rules.[90] From this point of view, we can say that the language mechanism in each individual's brain becomes functional when different language data enter into its mechanism. Although these entries are new and varied, they are related. The learning process proceeds by linking and organizing each new piece of information with the previous data.

It is evident that this theory, which Chomsky presented in the field of linguistics, opens a new gateway to the studies that are already done and becomes a basis for future work in the field of linguistics. One of these research areas is comparative linguistics. The effect of an individual's mother tongue or second language on foreign language learning has been the subject of experts' curiosity since ancient times. Therefore, this curiosity has prompted linguists to investigate the interaction between the mother tongue/second language and the target language. These studies have led to fields such as comparative grammar and oppositional analysis. Within the scope of this chapter, the first part contains general information about when comparative linguistics research started and how it developed. The second part will discuss the place of bilingual use in foreign language teaching and the perspective on bilingual use. In the last part, the contents of the existing Arabic language training sets will be examined within the framework of the effect of mother/second language in foreign language teaching.

Comparative grammar-contrastive analysis history and definition

The roots of comparative linguistic studies trace back to the era when modern linguistics first emerged. With the spread of Christianity outside of Europe, the desire of people from different nations to learn the Bible led them to understand the Latin language. Consequently, language education has started to be given core structural features of the Latin language. In addition to Latin, European linguists were

---

[90] Ünal, 2009, p 5-6.

also interested in Greek, Hebrew, and Arabic languages. These developments in the 7th century also opened the gates to grammar book studies for different languages. Books teaching Latin began to be written by linguists in the linguists' language. Researchers have identified similarities between languages due to this research on other languages. Research on these similarities has led to examining languages in terms of origin and has become an instrument in determining language families.[91] In light of all this research, two basic grammar writing styles emerged in the 19th century. The first is 'comparative grammar,' which deals with language families and their origins, and the other is 'historical grammar,' which examines the historical process of language. In this field, essential studies started to attract the attention of linguists such as A. W. Schlegel (1767-1845), F. Bopp (1791-1867), and A. F. Pott (1802-1887). Among these names, F. Schlegel (1772-1892) is the first to use the term 'comparative grammar.'[92] When all these studies are examined, it can be said that the foundations of comparative linguistics studies were laid before modern linguistics.

As mentioned in the introduction, many fields of study have emerged with modern linguistics. One of these linguistics fields is applied linguistics. Applied linguistics studies gained momentum due to the improvements and innovations in foreign language teaching and learning, which attracted attention after the Second World War. Another field studied in the context of applied linguistics is comparative linguistics/contrastive analysis. When we look at the sources to understand whether these two terms are used interchangeably or have different meanings, it is noteworthy that experts do not make any difference between them.[93] For these two terms, which are not separated from each other with clear lines, İşler

---

[91] Burnett, 2013; Kerimoğlu, 2017; Özgen and Koşaner, 2020; Ertürk, 2021.
[92] Kerimoğlu, 2017; Aksan, 2015; Ertürk, 2021.
[93] İşler, 2002; James, 1980; Nickel and Wagner, 1968.

has stated that contrastive analysis is the field of application of comparative linguistics. While comparative linguistics has a more theoretical framework, contrastive analysis is expressed as a concept closer to the field of application (İşler, 2002). In other words, it provides an interface between theory and practice. It uses theoretical data and models about language, but its primary goal is applicability.[94]

Regarding modern language studies, Charles Fries draws attention to the necessity of comparing the target language to be learned with the mother tongue with his comparative hypothesis in his book Teaching and Learning English as a Foreign Language, which he wrote in 1945.[95] Fries says, "The most effective tools are those prepared in the light of the information obtained as a result of the scientific description of the target language and the careful comparison of this description with the mother tongue." In his words, he argues that course materials should be prepared bilingually. Robert Lado is another name who researched the comparative field in the modern period. Lado expressed his views on the subject in his work Linguistic Across the Cultures, published in 1957. As Lado da Fries states, he emphasizes that foreign language textbooks will be prepared with more helpful content due to the comparative research they have carried out between languages. In the following periods, a study comparing different languages was started under the supervision of the Center for Applied Linguistics of the Modern Language Association of America and under the editorship of Charles A. Ferguson. This project compared English, French, Spanish, Italian, Russian, and German languages. During this comparison, both similarities and differences between languages were examined.[96] In the following years, comparative linguistic

---

[94] Gast, 2012.
[95] Ünal, 2009.
[96] İşler, 2002.

studies continued to be carried out by experts in the field. Although the interest in these comparative studies between languages, which gained momentum from the early modern century, was interrupted for a certain period, it is still an area of interest to experts.

Cognitive approach, contrastive analysis, and bilingualism

The definitions of universal grammar and generative grammar put forward by Chomsky, who advocates the cognitive approach in which mental processes are examined in language learning, take us to the first source of the language and reveal the relationship between the languages learned in the learning process. Therefore, we believe that the studies carried out in oppositional analysis can be better understood when attention is paid to the mental connections of both the mother tongue and a foreign language during the learning phase. In the second part, by trying to summarize Chomsky's theories in the field of linguistics within this framework, attention will be drawn to the relationship between oppositional analysis studies. As a result, the importance of using two languages in foreign language teaching will be emphasized.

Noam Chomsky argues that every individual is born with a language mechanism. In other words, just as a child is born with organs such as eyes, hands, etc., he has a biological language ability unique to the human brain. So, what is this innate language ability, and how does it work? First of all, this problem needs to be described. Chomsky described the definition of universal grammar as a description. Universal grammar is a resource that exists biologically in all natural languages and applies to all these languages. Cook says one way to embody universal grammar is to view it as part of the brain.

In other words, we should consider it a mental system similar to our brain's visual system, motor control, and planning system. From this point of view, Cook believes that the concept of learning a language does not fully meet the development of the language; instead, it is more appropriate to use the concepts of growth development. For example, a cell can't learn to become a lung because it grows and develops by realizing its genetic potential with environmental triggers.[97] The language mechanism within the individual is the universal grammar. These universal principles in genetics become visible and grow with the effect of different factors. So, what is the structure of these universal principles? There are two basic structures in Chomsky's theory. These are deep structure and surface structure. Universal principles manifest themselves in contrasting these two structures.[98] The deep structure is the structure that corresponds to the description of the language about sound and meaning.

On the other hand, the surface structure is where the deep structure, sound, and meaning evolve into form through transformation.[99] In other words, the deep structure meets the abstract, and the surface structure meets the concrete. During communication, surface-structured arguments aim to reach a deep-structured meaning.

Therefore, communication occurs because it is mentally observed in a deep structure, even though some structures are not visible in sound and form on the concrete plane or are irregular in syntax. On the contrary, a sentence that conforms to the rules of language as a formal structure (surface structure) may not convey the meaning from the deep structure to the other side. At this point, the context in which the language is used becomes more significant than the language structure. Context is "all of the data related to the non-linguistic social gains, cultural accumulations, experiences, all kinds of information they have gained, and all spiritual experiences of the donor and the receiver." According to Müldür, the surface structure becomes visible as a phenomenon of deep structure in the context of the sentence. Therefore, linguistic context is meant by the concept of

---

[97] Cook, 1985; Chomsky, 1980.
[98] Kıran, 1984; Ertürk, 2021.
[99] Müldür, 2016.

surface structure.[100] At this point, the issue that comes to mind is how deep and surface structures will emerge in foreign language learning.

In this regard, experts have expressed different views on foreign language learning and access to universal grammar. It is argued that a foreign language student has direct access to universal grammar because the mother tongue and the target language have different parameters. On the other hand, some experts argue that foreign language learners start to learn the target language with the parameters of the mother tongue and continue with the principles of the target language when the parameters between the two languages begin to be observed. Some other linguists have stated that someone who learns a foreign language reaches universal grammar through his mother tongue. Lydia White, one of the names who conducted experimental studies on the relationship between universal grammar and foreign language learning, researched foreign language parameters in 1986. In this study on the hidden subject parameter in the mother tongue, the secret subject parameter in their native language was transferred to the target language by the students whose mother tongue was Spanish. However, this parameter was not carried into the target language by the students whose mother tongue is French and do not have a hidden subject parameter in their language. As a result of this study, it has been observed that the students convey the existence or non-existence of the parameters in their mother tongue to the target language as they are.[101] It shows it has reached the universal grammar system with its principles and parameters.

In light of the research put forward so far, It is understood that during the learning of a foreign language, it is necessary to apply the parameters of the previously learned mother tongue or second language to transfer (positive or negative) the data about the language

---

[100] Müldür, 2016; Günay, 2004.
[101] Özen, 2015; White, 1986.

existing in the human mind to the target language, activate and produce it. From this point of view, it can be concluded that comparative studies on languages help individuals to connect and ground the knowledge of the foreign language that they have learned with the help of their mother tongue or second language to universal principles.

The following theory by Lado draws attention when we evaluate the content of the oppositional analysis, which is the application field of contrastive linguistics in terms of what it should be and how it should be).

People transfer the patterns and meanings in their mother tongue and culture and the distribution of these patterns and meanings to their foreign languages and cultures. They do this while actively speaking the foreign language, acting according to their culture, and passively trying to understand that language and culture from the speech and behavior of its owners.[102]

Research indicates that we must consider structural differences and cultural and semantic variations when comparing languages. Lado emphasized that because of these variations, students face challenges and advantages in language acquisition. Following Lado's observations, three prominent perspectives emerged in contrastive analysis:

- The Strong Version (often attributed to Lado): This asserts that identifying the differences between two languages in advance helps students anticipate potential mistakes. The aim is to prepare students for these differences beforehand.
- The Weak Version: This perspective believes that we can't predict all differences between two languages in advance. It recommends addressing challenges arising from these unpredicted differences during the ongoing learning process.

---

[102] İşler, 2002.

- The Moderate Version (introduced by Oller and Ziahosseniy): Based on an English dictation exam for international students at the University of California, this perspective emphasizes the nuanced differences between a student's native language and their target language, noting that learners often mix up these subtle differences. [103]

All three perspectives highlight the process of transferring knowledge from the native language to the target language, debating the extent and method of this transfer. However, it is also crucial to remember that similarities between the two languages significantly facilitate learning. Emphasizing syntax, lexical, and contextual parallels can aid students in processing and producing information. Instead of just cataloging these similarities and differences, the focus should be ranking them based on their difficulty level and then designing course materials accordingly. [104]

Contrastive analysis based on the abovementioned views cannot be limited to comparing the mother tongue and the target language in foreign language learning. On the contrary, reaching all the linguistic accumulations the individual collects in his mind with the target language learned is also possible. Because the foreign language understood can be the student's third or fourth (L3, L4) foreign language, he can also benefit from the different language parameters in his memory while learning a new language. [105] In this regard, Gast even goes one step further and argues that comparative studies are generally concerned with comparing socio-culturally related languages. [106] According to this theory put forward by Gast, restricting comparisons only to languages from the same language family or similar language structures can be viewed with suspicion

---

[103] Lado, 1957.
[104] Aydın, 2010; Dede, 1983.
[105] Esmeray, 2009.
[106] Gast, 2012.

because it is not in line with the nature of language learning. It can be said that such a generalization would not be appropriate for contrastive studies because individuals from many different socio-cultural backgrounds around the world learn languages belonging to different socio-cultures. When learning additional languages, such as a third or fourth language, a student not only relies on their native language but also draws on their experiences from learning a first foreign language. This is because the process of acquiring a first language is often unconscious, making it difficult for learners to recall these early experiences. Therefore, the following words of Esmeray, "a meta-linguistic consciousness (knowledge of a language) that facilitates the process of acquiring languages to be learned later on develops with the 1st foreign language," shows the importance of comparative studies of more than one language.[107]

As all this research revealed, the mental awareness of the individual is positively affected by the reference to both the mother tongue and the second language parameters in foreign language learning. The existence of a first or second language serves as a bridge between universal principles and the target language learned. In addition, it is emphasized that deep and surface structure knowledge of a language and the target language understood can be learned more quickly in the light of the same experiences. In light of this information, oppositional analysis studies are essential in teaching Arabic, as they do in many languages. Studies in this area are not limited to syntax; cultural and contextual language use comparisons have also been made.[108] It can be said that the data obtained as a result of the contrastive analyses affect many factors of foreign language teaching indirectly or directly. By using the syntactic, lexical, and contextual knowledge of the student's first or second

---

[107] Ünal, 2009.
[108] Abushihab, 2015; Al-Saleemi, 1987; Salim, 2013; Aktaş, 2019; Dokuyucu and Akpınar, 2022.

language knowledge, teachers can ensure that the subject is in a more explicit position in the students' minds. In addition, the artificial lesson environment can be instrumental in preparing a more realistic environment close to the natural environment of the language learned because course materials are of primary importance in providing this natural environment. If both audio, visual, and written materials are prepared based on the results of the comparisons, they can significantly contribute to the actual language environment. In particular, it should be designed by considering these contrastive analysis examinations made while creating the contents of the textbooks within the course materials. Due to the importance of the subject, in the last part of this chapter, the contents of the language training sets, which are widely preferred in Arabic education for foreigners in the Middle East, Turkey, and Europe, will be examined within this framework.

Bilingualism in Arabic language training sets

Many factors affect the learning process in foreign language teaching. Among these are many different factors, such as the instructor, the readiness of the student, the environment, the curriculum, and the course materials. Theories put forward in linguistics indirectly or directly affect these factors. Language teachers graduate from the relevant departments of universities within the scope of the curriculum prepared within the framework of these theories. The instructors who graduate from these departments educate foreign language students as a result of the education they receive. All materials prepared for foreign language classes are shaped by the data obtained from the developed theories. Textbooks, which have the most functional role among these materials, are essential in content. Because textbooks are effective course material that directs the teacher, the student, and the course curriculum, they especially appeal to many students who want to study in any educational institution or alone. For this reason, the contents of the textbooks should be prepared by considering the results of the research carried out in the field.

In this section, Arabic language training sets will be discussed in terms of bilingualism or multilingualism, which is the result of the contrastive analysis studies carried out in foreign language teaching within the framework of the cognitive approach, which is the subject of our study. The Arabic language training sets examined in our research were determined from interviews with experts teaching Arabic to foreigners in Turkey, the Middle East, and Europe. These sets, which are widely used in the Arabic education of foreigners in the three regions mentioned: al-'Arabiyye Beyne Yedeyk, Silsiletu'l-Lisân, el-Kitâb fî Ta'allumi'l-'Arabiyye, 'Arabiyyât al-Naas.' It will be examined whether the use of a second language is generally included in the grammar and exercise contents of these sets mentioned above.

El-'Arabiyye Beyne Yedeyk

The *Beyne Yedeyk* series is a teaching set prepared by the Arabic for All Foundation in Saudi Arabia after two years of work—the book's first edition, written by Abdurrahman b. Ibrahim el-Fevzân, Muhtar et-Tâhir Hüseyin, and Muhammed Abdulhâlık Fadl, was published in 2002. Other revised editions were published in 2011, 2014, and 2017. The volume that is the subject of our research is the edition prepared in 2014. When we examine the grammar sections of the book, it has been observed that a second language is not used in both subject and grammar exercises. When we assess the book as a whole, it stands out that the parts covering the other four language abilities do not mention a second language.

Silsiletu'l-Lisân

It is a training set prepared by the Arabic education center al-Lisânu'l-Umm, based in the United Arab Emirates. Its authors; Muhammed Saîd el-Ebraş, Âmir Velîd es-Sıbâ'î and Mümin Tevfîk el-'Ânnân. The set, designed as four levels, consists of two books at each level. When the grammar sections and exercises of the books in this set were examined, it was determined that a second language was not included in the subjects' explanations and the exercises' instructions.

At the same time, when the book is handled with all its parts, it is seen that there is no second language.

Al-Kitâb fî Ta'allum'ul-'Arabiyye

Georgetown University made the first edition of this Arabic set in 1995. Abbas et-Tonsi, Mahmud al-Batal, and Kristen Brustad's last edition of the series, prepared between 2011 and 2013, consists of an Elif-Ba book and two volumes. When the grammar contents and related exercises of both volumes in this set are examined, it is seen that English explanations are included as a second language. The Arabic expressions that are intended to be explained in the grammar sections are given in Arabic, as well as in English as the subject explanation. When defining a concept, if an English term corresponds, it is also mentioned for clarity. The Arabic usages of the examples related to the taught subject are presented with their English equivalents. Some exercises include translation applications from Arabic to English and from English to Arabic. The instructions for the exercises also include English explanations of how the student will progress in practice. In particular, the explanation instructions in all the book exercises, not only about grammar, have been prepared in English. In some reading passages, English translations and Arabic texts are presented side by side. English was used extensively in other language skills and activities. In the exercises and activities on language skills, it is explained in English how the student should follow the process to be followed in detail.[109] Except for the content part of the books, the introduction section of each volume contains statements in English about the book's goal, its methodology, and the procedures teachers and students should follow. On the other hand, the index section has been prepared in Arabic, except for some additional English expressions.

---

[109] Brustad et al., 2013, p.17.

'Arabiyyat al-Naas

This series was written in the USA by Munter Younes and Makda Weatherspoon from Cornell University and Maha Saliba Foster from the University of Denver. The set was first published in 2014 and consists of three volumes. The first volume is prepared as a beginner, the second as an intermediate, and the third as advanced. When the grammar sections in all three volumes are examined, the subject to be explained is explained in English with explanations of Arabic expressions. The instructions for the grammar-related activities have been prepared, especially in English, in the first two volumes. In the last volume, the instructions for the activities were mainly designed in Arabic. In addition, when we consider the content of the activities, bilingual (Arabic-English) applications are also included. When we examine the book, in addition to the grammar sections, it is seen that it is designed in English-Arabic. The book's introduction is available in English and Arabic, while the user manual and section descriptions are exclusively in English.

The crucial role of mother tongue in language acquisition

Throughout my fifteen years of professional life, I have been teaching Arabic to individuals whose mother tongue is Turkish and whose mother tongue or second language is English. One of the general opinions defended by foreign language teaching experts is that the teacher does not use the mother tongue in the classroom during foreign language teaching. However, during this time, in all my classroom practices, I found that students involuntarily compare the universal grammatical structures in every language with their language. Of course, since this comparison was applied amateurishly instead of a scientific framework, it also increased usage errors. Since it is impossible to stop students from comparing the target language they learn with their mother tongue, I thought it should be presented to the students in a more systematic and scientific framework. As a result, the need to research the importance of the mother tongue factor in second or foreign language learning has emerged. In my research, I found that the theory of universal grammar put forward by Noam Chomsky also plays an active role in learning the languages we learn after the mother tongue. Logically, the presentation of these universal language structures to the students in the mother tongue is not limited to the teachers. Textbooks should also support teachers' practices. In this way, the students will reinforce what they have learned in the classroom with the textbooks' lectures, activities, and exercises. From this point of view, in this study, I examined what kind of content they have in terms of mother tongue-target language comparison in Arabic language training sets as a foreign.

Therefore, I chose four Arabic education sets written for non-native speakers. While El-'Arabiyye Beyne Yedeyk and Silsilet'ul-Lisân are prepared for publication in Arab countries, El-Kitâb and 'Arabiyyât al-Naas sets are ready for publication in America. Beyne Yedeyk and Silsilet'ul-Lisân sets are designed to be monolingual (Arabic). Al-Kitâb and 'Arabiyyât al-Naas sets are intended as bilingual (Arabic-English). Since the sets of Al-Kitâb and 'Arabiyyât al-Naas were published in America, it can be assumed that they were prepared by considering the student population whose mother tongue or second language is English. El-'Arabiyye Beyne Yedeyk and Silsilet'ul-Lisân sets are also language sets that are stated to be prepared for non-native speakers. Although published in Arab countries, they may be textbooks by students whose mother tongue and second language are not Arabic in Turkey and foreign countries other than Turkey. Despite this, both sets are entirely prepared in Arabic.

As was determined in the previous parts of the chapter, the student uses the mother tongue/second language parameters at the surface structure level to reach the universal principles in the target language. Because the surface structure is the form of the meanings and expressions in the deep structure transformed into a concrete shape and structure. Therefore, language learning can be facilitated by comparing the minor morphemes that make up the structure of the sentence (if clause, adjective, question sentences, sign nouns, verb, etc.) From this point of view, it can be concluded that using a second language besides Arabic in foreign language textbooks will facilitate teaching. When the results of the research from this perspective are evaluated, it can be said that the Al-Kitâb and 'Arabiyyât al-Naas sets can help, especially the beginners, in reaching the parameters of the target language by using a second language (English) in addition to Arabic. However, considering that the Al-'Arabiyye Beyne Yedeyk and Silsilet'ul-Lisân sets are prepared for non-native speakers, that is, for students who will learn Arabic for the first time, it can be concluded that not using a second language may cause difficulties, especially for beginners in reaching the target language parameters. The learning journey can become even more complicated when considering individuals who want to learn Arabic by themselves without the supervision of a teacher in any educational institution.

This study concluded that the bilingual preparation of course materials is more appropriate regarding the cognitive approach. As a result, anyone who wants to study Arabic can rapidly learn its principles. From this point of view, the contents of the existing Arabic textbooks can be reviewed and evaluated in this context. Revision of these books may come to the fore when deemed necessary. Or it may be possible for content-producing experts to reconsider their newly published books within this framework.

PART 2:
INTERNATIONAL APPROACHES TO ARABIC EDUCATION

7. Multilingualism in Northern Ireland: The challenges and opportunities of introducing Arabic in schools

Rym Akhonzada

While multilingualism has always been an integral part of Europe, Northern Ireland, emerging from a long period of inter-community conflict and civic unrest, has only recently become a noticeably multicultural society. Before this, multi- or bilingual education was primarily evident in the approach to the Irish (Gaelic) language as a curricular second language or in an immersion education environment.[110]

Indeed, in Northern Ireland, languages are not only a means of communication or a linguistic subject but also expand to political, religious, and community life. It is a form of identity, a tool of expression, and sometimes a political identity tool. For example, Irish speakers in Northern Ireland are still campaigning for an Irish Language Act to protect their language rights.[111]

Schools in Northern Ireland, Europe, and other parts of the world face the reality of increasingly diverse classrooms, both linguistically and culturally, due to increased mobility and migration. In Northern Ireland, almost one in every 20 schoolchildren is a 'newcomer,' according to the Department of Education. The speed and extent of the increase in numbers of migrant workers in Northern Ireland – and the sheer diversity of the people involved – pose

---

[110] McKendry and McKendry, 2019.
[111] Mercator European Research Centre on Multilingualism and Language Learning, 2019.

complex challenges for the Government and society alike.[112] One of these challenges is linguistic diversity and maintaining the mother tongue. Schools have made limited adaptations to their policies to reflect the increasing cultural diversity in Northern Ireland.[113]

Within this chapter, I will start by setting the scene about the educational system in Northern Ireland, its changing landscapes, and its effects on the classroom, especially with the recently arrived Syrian refugee pupils. I will then shed light on the recent experiences of introducing Arabic into the curriculum and teaching Arabic to heritage and non-heritage speakers. I will also discuss the strategies, opportunities, and challenges in offering Arabic as a second language (L2) in Northern Ireland schools, focusing on how language teaching dynamics are evolving and the implications on students' (both heritage and L2) motivation and language proficiency levels.

Language, identity, and education in Northern Ireland: Navigating complexities in a divided society

Given the complexity of Northern Ireland's history and religious and political division, it has profoundly impacted the linguistic landscape in Northern Ireland. This is indicated in the debates around the Irish Language Act[114], which created a political rift and was used by some as a tool to advance specific political demands. This has also raised concerns about equality as the Irish language is "perceived to 'belong

---

[112] OFMDFM, 2005b, p.22.

[113] Loader et al., 2023, p.17.

[114] The Irish Language Act for Northern Ireland has been a matter of long-standing debate and contention. The act seeks to provide official status to the Irish language in Northern Ireland, similar to the recognition given to the Welsh language in Wales. The issue is tied up with wider political and cultural debates in Northern Ireland.

to' the Nationalist community and has become a proxy for other cultural issues that have not been dealt with since the peace agreement." [115] As a result, languages are "still seen to be divisive, and identity claims along sectarian lines still mark the languages of Northern Ireland."[116]

Introducing world languages into any classroom has the long-term benefit of creating a welcoming environment and awareness of others. It prepares outward-looking citizens who value cultural and linguistic diversity. This echoes Beacco and Byram's view in the 2007 Council of Europe report on linguistic diversity and plurilingual education that language education can progress beyond being a source of division and be an agent for constructive citizenship. Plurilingualism can be interpreted "as a means of developing intercultural sensitivity and as an intrinsic component of democratic citizenship."[117]

The importance and value of the mother tongue cannot be highlighted better than what Johann Gottfried von Herder has written:

> Has a people anything dearer than the speech of its fathers? In its speech resides its whole thought domain, tradition, history, religion, and basis of life, all its heart and soul. To deprive a people of its speech is to deprive it of its one eternal good... The best culture of a people cannot be expressed through a foreign language; it thrives on the soil of a nation most beautifully, and, I may say, it thrives only by means of the nation's inherited and inheritable dialect. With language is created the heart of a people. *Materials for the Philosophy of the History of Mankind*, 1784.

---

[115] Dunlevy, 2020.
[116] Crowley, 2016.
[117] Beacco and Byram, 2007.

Bilingualism has always been associated with struggle, division, and identity, as is the case for the right of an Irish Language Act in Northern Ireland. Despite continuous efforts to recognize Irish as a second official language alongside English, its popularity and use are still tiny, as only 10.65% of the population claim to have some ability of Irish.[118] This culture of monolingualism, the association of the Irish language with political ambitions, and the skepticism towards the Irish Language Act have impacted language policy and language education in Northern Ireland (NI). Currently, "in the majority of schools in NI, the curriculum is delivered in English. There is also a small but growing Irish Medium Education (IME) sector in which the statutory curriculum is delivered through Irish, adopting a language immersion approach."[119]

Historically, Northern Ireland has been a sanctuary for many seeking refuge worldwide. The recent changes in migration across the world in general and in Northern Ireland in particular have impacted the composition of the society and, as a result, created diversity within our schools. The Department of Education (DENI) defines a Newcomer pupil as one "who does not have satisfactory language skills to participate fully in the school curriculum and does not have a language in common with the teacher."[120] However, although "linguistic diversity is increasingly apparent, and highlighted in political discourse, there does not appear to be evidence of a matching enthusiasm for language learning in the region's schools."[121]

As a result of the war in Syria, "Northern Ireland has welcomed approximately 1,900 Syrian refugees, including almost 700 school-

---

[118] NISRA 2011, 2014.
[119] Jones, 2020.
[120] DENI, n.d., Newcomer page.
[121] Jones, 2020.

aged children and young people, through the Vulnerable Persons Relocation Scheme" in the last seven years.[122]

This sudden influx of newcomer pupils has demonstrated that Northern Ireland's education and schooling system is unprepared to welcome pupils with limited English skills. "School staff have reported a range of challenges including a lack of knowledge and competence resulting in staff feeling overwhelmed and unqualified; social and cultural barriers; a lack of resources; and a lack of training and language barriers."[123] The lack of a diverse, multicultural curriculum, teacher training in diversity and newcomers education, and above all, the lack of language teaching in our schools have put many barriers in accessing the curriculum on the one hand and valuing linguistic diversity and the funds of knowledge the newcomer pupils bring to our schools on the other.

McMullen et al. discuss the challenges and opportunities schools face in supporting Syrian refugee pupils but also highlight that "there has been limited official guidance, policy or research into how schools in Northern Ireland can best support refugee pupils."[124]

It is also important to mention that languages are not taught in Northern Ireland schools until pupils progress to the secondary level (11 years+). In some schools, it is not compulsory to sit the GSCE (General Secondary Certificate of Education) exam in Modern Foreign Languages (MFL) such as French, German, or Spanish. As such, "multi- or bilingual education was mostly evident in the approach to the Irish (Gaelic) language as a curricular second language or in an immersion education environment."[125]

This vacuum of language teaching and attitudes towards learning foreign languages has created a culture of rejection towards

---

[122] McMullen et al, 2021.
[123] McMullen et al, 2021.
[124] McMullen et al. 2021.
[125] McKendry and McKendry, 2019.

language diversity. However, the Good Friday Agreement in 1998 highlighted the importance of languages. The Good Friday Agreement states that *All participants recognize the importance of respect, understanding, and tolerance in relation to linguistic diversity, including in Northern Ireland, the Irish language, Ulster-Scots, and the languages of the various ethnic communities, all of which are part of the cultural wealth of the island of Ireland.*[126]

According to Gallagher and Leitch, Northern Irish teachers lacked awareness of the cultural diversity present in the society[127] as the educational focus has always been on understanding the religious divide between Protestants and Catholics and how identity is developed within these two communities and, as a result, "differences in the region and ethnic minority communities attracted little attention in education or society."[128]

Furthermore, despite the many efforts to integrate newcomers into host schools and acknowledge their cultural and linguistic richness and value, "actual home language support is only provided on an ad hoc basis and varies greatly from school to school."[129]

Arabic in Northern Ireland: The journey

Traditionally, Arabic was not taught in schools in Northern Ireland, the United Kingdom, and Europe. The British Council Report (2016) ignited interest in the Arabic language, which ranked Arabic as the "second most vital language in the U.K." for the future. The report also highlighted the need for more Arabic provision in U.K. schools to meet these needs. Furthermore, on a regional level, Invest N.I.[130] has emphasized the importance of doing business in the Middle East,

---

[126] Good Friday Agreement, p. 21.
[127] Gallagher and Leitch, 2000.
[128] McKendry and McKendry, 2019.
[129] McKendry and McKendry, 2019.
[130] Discover India, Middle East and Africa | Invest Northern Ireland.

which has created an interest in the Arabic language and culture locally.

In 2016, nine schools in Northern Ireland participated in an Arabic language project funded by Qatar Foundation International and the British Council's Arabic Culture and Language Program. These schools that engaged in weekly Arabic lessons include Primary and Grammar schools: Belfast Royal Academy, Methodist College Belfast, St Columb's College in Derry, St Catherine's College and St Patrick's Grammar in Armagh, Saints & Scholars and St Patrick's Primary and Shimna Integrated College in Newcastle. In 2018-2019, two additional schools, Friends School Lisburn and St Dominic's Grammar School for Girls, were added. The overall vision was to allow students to experience Arabic language and culture through weekly Arabic lessons delivered by an Arabic teacher. The classes were aimed at non-heritage speakers with no previous knowledge or connection to the language or its culture because of the student population and the small percentage of Arabic heritage speakers in local schools. However, the population of heritage speakers has grown in recent years due to the arrival of Syrian refugees and other newcomers from different parts of the Arab World. An Arabic scheme of work was developed with the learners' age, ability, needs, and interests in mind, and transliteration along with the Arabic font was used in the lessons. Modern Standard Arabic (MSA) was the medium of instruction, and the Communicative approach was used with a focus on everyday practical language. The choice of MSA is based on the theory that it provides a standard form of language that is uniform across the Arab world. This ensures that learners are exposed to a consistent version of the language, regardless of where they study or which materials they use. Once students have grasped the basics of the Arabic language, they can decide which dialect they would like to learn to further their Arabic language and culture experience.

Two schools (Methodist College Belfast and St Dominic's Grammar School for Girls) have linked Arabic to a particular curriculum area: Arts and business. Linking Arabic to other curriculum areas creates a sense of connection and relevance to future aspirations. "In all parts of the school curriculum, the emphasis now is on the integration of learning—on the links between subjects and the importance of subjects in enabling children to access new meanings and develop generic thinking skills."[131]

In terms of business, a link was made with Invest NI, a regional business development agency, which enabled the students to attend several workshops and a business conference focusing on exports to the Middle East. This gave them a unique opportunity to witness the use and benefits of Arabic in commerce and export, an area relevant to investing in learning Arabic, as highlighted in the British Council report as the language for business, diplomacy, and trade. Arabic for Business workshops were held at Methodist College, Belfast, to highlight the benefits of learning Arabic for inspiring entrepreneurs and those interested in a business career. Young people from schools across Northern Ireland attended the conference. Speakers from the business world and I were invited to speak about their exports to the Middle East and how learning Arabic can enormously benefit future careers.

Alongside the weekly language provision, some cultural activities were introduced to foster a deeper understanding of the language and its culture. Some examples of these workshops included dance, calligraphy (image 2), cooking, quizzes, music, and a trip to the local Arab café (image 1), Islamic Cultural Centre, and Chester Beatty Library in Dublin. The students greatly appreciated and welcomed these cultural exposure activities and trips. They have also raised awareness about Arab culture, a learning opportunity they would have never been exposed to otherwise.

---

[131] Towards an integrated curriculum—CLIL National Statement and Guidelines, October 2009.

Image 1: A cultural trip to the local Arab café

Image 2: Calligraphy workshop

Strategies and challenges in offering Arabic in Northern Ireland

Offering Arabic in post-primary schools in Northern Ireland did not follow the traditional method of language teaching, which mainly focuses on language proficiency by acquiring vocabulary and grammatical structures for exams and where language stands separate from other curriculum areas. It, however, offered diverse opportunities to engage with the students using language content and developing a range of cross-curriculum activities and practical everyday language exposure.

A successful language lesson depends on three factors: the teacher, the learners, the environment, and resources. While these factors are vital, the best outcomes are achieved when all these factors interplay. For example, a motivated teacher can inspire motivation in language learners, and a well-resourced environment can further enhance this language learning motivation.

The teacher

Being proficient in the language and understanding the nuances and intricacies is critical. But knowing the language is not enough. The teacher should also know how to teach. This includes understanding different learning styles, curriculum design, and assessment methods. Furthermore, a passionate teacher can instill motivation in learners, making the learning process more engaging and commitment to learning the language higher.

It is not enough to have a well-planned and well-resourced Arabic language classroom; the teacher plays a crucial role in making that lesson enjoyable and meaningful. The role of a teacher is not only to transmit learning but to motivate, understand, and support the students. The teacher must understand the various motivations driving students to learn Arabic or another second language, whether for professional advancement, cultural exploration, social engagement, or personal interest. This understanding should then inform the development of the language curriculum and the choice of teaching methodologies in the classroom.

The learners

A learner's motivation can be intrinsic (e.g., a genuine interest in the language) or extrinsic (e.g., to get a job or to travel). Motivated students are more likely to engage in the learning process and are committed to attending the language lessons and participating in the learning process.

To motivate learners, the teacher has to be aware of their learning styles. Some might interact better through visual aids, while others might be more auditory or kinaesthetic learners. Recognizing this diversity can enhance the teaching process in the language classroom.

The environment

Access to textbooks, online resources, and multimedia tools can significantly enhance the learning experience. Still, these resources are scarce in Arabic, and we have only recently witnessed several modern resources on the market. In addition, tech tools like language learning apps, online dictionaries, and virtual language exchange platforms can be invaluable in our digital age.

In our enrichment Arabic classes, the students specified their reasons for joining the classes at the start of the program (image 3). Compared to their heritage speaker peers, who have different motivations for learning Arabic, their interest lies in career and travel. Some of the factors heritage speakers identified as vital to them are personal decisions or parental decisions, gaining a language qualification (GCSE and A Level), strengthening their cultural identity and heritage, and their language background is a tool for empowerment (especially for Syrian students who struggle with English.

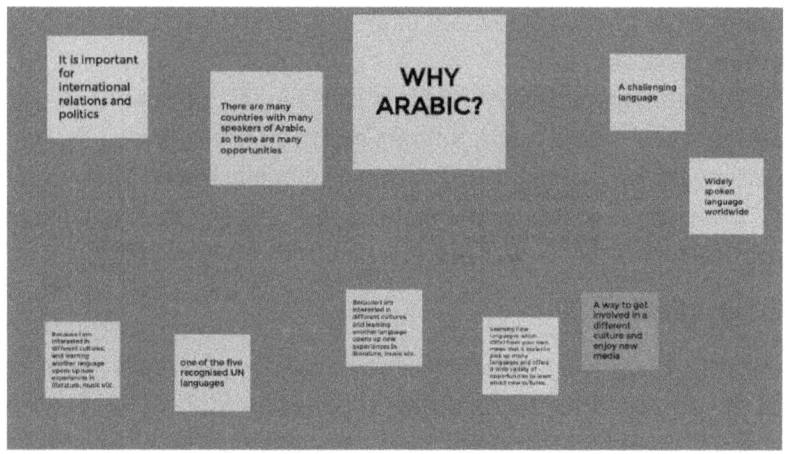

Image 3: Reasons for joining the Arabic program.

Teaching Arabic to non-heritage speakers faces many challenges for teachers and learners everywhere. Motivating and understanding the learners is critical to any successful language lesson, and "their teacher can strongly influence students' motivation."[132]

Some of the challenges we identified with our learners are:

- Writing system and pronunciation are the most problematic linguistic aspects of Arabic.
- Qualification in Arabic for Beginners at A1/2 level.
- There is a need for assessment to measure Arabic language proficiency.
- Frequency of lessons (only 1 hour per week).
- Opportunity to practice the language outside of the classroom.
- Opportunities for cultural experiences are limited in Belfast and non-existent in other parts of Northern Ireland.

---

[132] ALI, 2013.

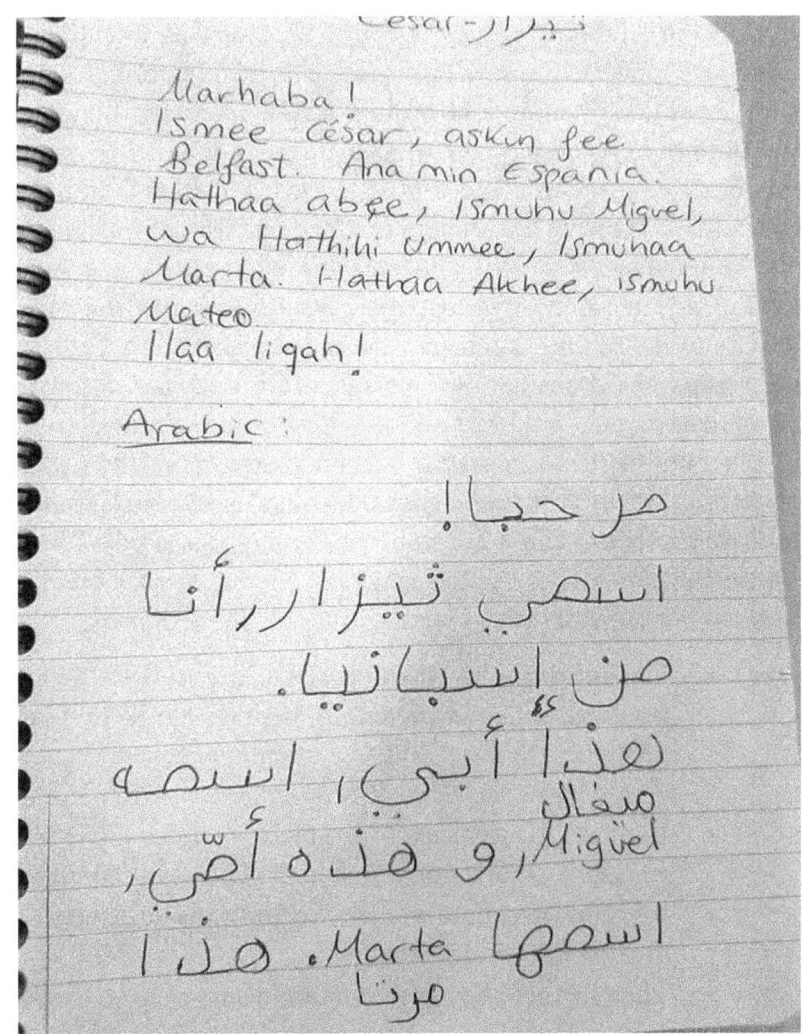

Image 4: sample writing task in transliteration and in Arabic.

Heritage speakers population

Given the increase in the number of newcomers from Arab countries, there was an increased interest from parents and schools in allocating Arabic lessons to heritage speakers to enable them to gain a formal qualification in Arabic (GCSE and A Level). Given their connection with the Arabic language and culture at home, heritage learners attending our Arabic classes use a dialect of Arabic as a medium of communication in the family. They also have different formal Arabic (MSA) writing, speaking, and reading levels. However, they have good cultural exposure because of their frequent home visits, strong community connections, and a good network of friends from the same culture. Montrul (2010) defines a heritage learner as someone from "a linguistic minority who grew up exposed to their home language and the majority language", but because of their varied exposure to their home language, "heritage speakers have achieved partial command of the family language, short of the native speaker level of their parents and peers raised in their home countries."

Like non-heritage speakers' teaching strategies, the Arabic teacher must understand their heritage learners, needs, backgrounds, and learning styles. These are some of the methods used with the heritage learners in our Arabic language lessons at St Dominic's Grammar School in Belfast, where 15 students are heritage:

- Differentiation (different levels) as exposure to the four language skills varies among heritage speakers. Some might be only exposed to a particular Arabic dialect and do not know the MSA.
- Use a project-based approach, which increases engagement and motivation in the language classroom.
- Infusion of culture and the opportunity to strengthen their identity and heritage.
- The balance between communication & grammar, written & spoken, and rehearsed and spontaneous use of language.
- Use heritage learners' fund of knowledge in your classroom to create a sense of belonging.

Creating an engaging and motivating learning environment is vital to the Arabic language classroom as we must equip our students with 21st-century skills and intercultural competence to succeed in today's world. Creativity and flexibility in the teaching environment are essential in the teaching profession and the multilingual classroom. And COVID-19 has shown us that even under severe lockdown conditions, learning can still be interactive, engaging, and relevant using different online platforms.

The road ahead for Arabic language education

Northern Ireland is a unique place with many challenges and opportunities, and although multilingualism has a religious and political divide, the cultural, linguistic, and ethnic landscape of the region is changing. The Syrian crisis has resulted in many refugees making Northern Ireland their sanctuary place since 2015, and as a result, an interest in the Arabic language and culture started to grow. However, despite this public interest, Arabic remains an enrichment subject, and it will take much effort and investment to make it a curricular subject. Furthermore, schools rely heavily on Qatar Foundation International and the British Council funding to offer this program to their students.

It is also worth highlighting that the shortage of trained Arabic teachers remains a significant drawback in expanding the Arabic language and culture program to other areas and schools in Northern Ireland. Furthermore, the lack of modern Arabic resources, both digitally and in books, poses another challenge to teachers and schools.

8. The role of parents and the community in preserving the Arabic language: The case of Qatar Reads

Hanieh Khataee, Qatar Foundation
Fatema M. Al-Malki, Qatar Foundation
Logan Cochrane, Hamad bin Khalifa University

With rapid advancements and changes in technology, innovation, and emerging economies, the English language has become a dominant currency (e.g., in higher education and international business), shaping participation and communication across sectors and populations. Qatar has placed itself on an accelerated path to economic development, and the scale of growth amidst global change and progress has ushered a renewed focus to preserve and deliberately promote the local Arabic language, identity, and culture.

The education model plays a critical role in shaping the developmental trajectory of Qatari children and influencing the adults they become. However, how children and youth see themselves and their relationship with their cultural roots, traditions, and language do not begin and end inside the classroom. Community-based programs have carved out a salient role in responding to cultural and learning gaps, designing interventions that put children and their families at the center of social transformation.

In 2019, the Qatar Foundation launched the Qatar Reads' Family Reading Program to inculcate more interest and participation in reading, particularly in Arabic, among children aged 3-13. Despite the country's high literacy rate[133], personal engagement and interest in reading, particularly in Arabic, was waning. The program was designed to create a reading culture by building reading competencies and fostering reading communities within the country. Recognizing parents' vital role in supporting their children's development, the Qatar Reads program reached the whole family unit, grounded its materials to nurture positive reading habits within the family, and intentionally used reading to promote cultural awareness.

Arabic language—as Qatar's native language—needs active exposure, practice, and application in daily life for confidence and proficiency. If schools place a greater emphasis on English, then the role of parents in helping build Arabic vocabulary and reading engagement becomes more pronounced. Parents who recognized this signed up for the Qatar Reads Family Reading Program and witnessed growth in their children's reading engagement and learning of their culture and heritage.

After an overview of the evolution and success of Qatar Foundation's Qatar Reads program, this chapter will focus on showcasing Qatar Reads' Family Reading Program as a best practice in community intervention models. We will reveal successful approaches to instilling positive reading habits among children, particularly in Arabic. We will demonstrate our ability to create locally relevant learning opportunities and reading content serving a predominantly Qatari-National participation base. We hope the Family Reading Program can inspire and motivate practitioners, educators, policy experts, and advocates to build community-based programming models that provide families with tools and resources to advance their children's reading potential in Arabic. This way,

---

[133] UNESCO Institute for Statistics reports Qatar's adult literacy rate at 93.5% as of 2017.

efforts rooted in community needs are extended further to bolster Qatar's social, linguistic, and cultural advancements.

The role of community programming in Qatar's linguistic and cultural development

Qatar is rich in indigenous knowledge grounded in cultural experience and oral histories. As a society rooted in family-based communities, Qatar has a history of passing language, literature, astronomy, and climate knowledge through these traditions,[134] serving as a solid basis for the country's identity, cultural property, and social progress. Traditional knowledge systems are typically passed down to create cultural coherence and safeguard local practices and ecosystems. Aspirations for national development and economic progress impacted Qatar's preservation of indigenous thoughts and ways of living. New educational demands for English language proficiency were supported to strengthen engagement in global communications and influence participation in international trade and business. Higher education was also prioritized to help prepare Qatar's young adults to transition to a knowledge-based economy and strengthen National capacity development and human capital formation. These advancements impacted the preservation of the Arabic language, particularly reading and writing proficiency.

The public and private education systems follow different curricula, where private schools have traditionally placed greater emphasis on English language instruction and established schools that can also respond to growing expatriate communities. Public schools in Qatar primarily use Arabic; however, National students increasingly gravitate to private schools, resulting in increased challenges to maintaining and promoting Arabic reading and reading

---

[134] Ghanim, 2020.

proficiency among Qatari children and youth. While reforms have been and continue to be made to institutionalize Arabic language learning, other community-based efforts have been mobilized to respond to this pressing and growing gap.

In Qatar, out-of-school community programming can be an essential vehicle to help children overcome challenges and participate in learning opportunities that better use their discretionary hours. Instead of additional screen time, children can be exposed to activities that build social and emotional competencies, improve their physical and mental well-being, and better prepare them for the school environment.

In 2017, the Qatar National Library opened to the public so that people of all ages and abilities could participate in and embrace lifelong reading and learning. The library features the latest technology in Qatar Foundation's Education City while promoting Qatar's history and Arab culture through its rich heritage collection. The library houses over one million books and holds an extensive digital catalog with the world's largest digital heritage archives in the Middle East. It also offers various community activities that nurture learning, cultivate curiosity, and strengthen community engagement. This library is widely used, although the children's library has a higher engagement with expatriates than national children.

Qatar Reads—a National Reading Campaign—was designed in 2016 to spearhead a cultural shift through reading. In 2019, Qatar Reads launched community programs as a holistic response to building reading engagement, attracting different target audiences to cover the entire lifecycle of an individual and their reading aspirations. The program was rooted in shifting the perception of reading as a chore to an intrinsically desirable habit. As a community-based effort, it took the act of reading outside the formal education system. It extended it to the home or social environment, creating intergenerational interactions within and among communities.

The program was specifically tailored to the national context, aiming to increase national participation, especially since frequenting libraries and possessing home libraries were existing barriers to reading. Qatar Reads aims to make reading relevant to everyone, irrespective of their literacy level and current association with reading for personal pleasure. It also strives to remove any barriers to reading while increasing access to materials and building desirability. Through its multi-pronged programming approach, Qatar Reads' Mommy to Be focuses on early learning and care; the Family Reading Program makes learning engagement among children and their families; Read to Lead reaches adults in the workforce; and the School Membership program increases the provision of reading materials available in local public schools. Qatar Reads runs with One Book, One Doha—a national campaign that enhances engagement in Arabic literature, bringing together all communities and multi-sectoral stakeholders to read and engage with one iconic piece of Arabic literature annually. Each targeted effort takes reading outside traditional learning environments, promoting renewed enthusiasm through self-prompted learning.

Drawing on its extensive community reach, Qatar Reads ensures reading materials and community engagement opportunities are informative, educational, and culturally relevant. Beyond linguistic or cognitive improvements, it provides room for cultural reflection and representation, creating opportunities for participants to see their lives mirrored in the reading material. As a community intervention, it enriches the learning experience by allowing personal and cultural representation and growth.

Qatar Reads' Family Reading Program: Enabling access and opportunity

Children's acquisition of vocabulary, reading competencies, and overall interest in reading for pleasure is deeply influenced by the extent to which parents themselves read and role model to their children, the availability of books in the home environment, and reading engagement between parent and child. "Children listening to a reading aloud of a picture book are roughly three times more likely to experience a new word type that is not among the most frequent words in the child's language."[135] The books parents read to children expand their linguistic capabilities beyond everyday spoken-language exchanges. Irrespective of a family's educational attainment or socioeconomic status, home libraries shift children's perceptions and influence participation in reading for personal development and pleasure. The Family Reading Program facilitated these habits in the home environment in Qatar.

The subscription-based program initially launched with 92 children enrolled and has grown over four years to represent 1,100 children ranging from 3 to 13 years of age. 70% of participating children are Qatari Nationals, and 30% are from the expatriate community, with the majority (70%) attending private schools. Families were mobilized through country-wide marketing campaigns and informal outreach efforts across communities. The program requires a nominal fee with costs primarily subsidized by the Qatar Foundation to encourage access across all family income levels. Each subscribed family receives a Qatar Reads mailbox, allowing monthly packages to be delivered straight to the home. This feature stands out in Qatar's absence of a postal delivery system, creating a visual symbol in households' neighborhoods that value reading. Currently, 700 Qatar Reads mailboxes cover over 40 zones across the country.

Each child subscribed to the Family Reading Program has an online profile clustered by one of seven age groups. This allows parents to identify their child's correct reading level quickly. It enables the program to curate age-appropriate content and distribute materials to girls and boys by age and reading proficiency. Parents determine whether children receive books entirely in Arabic, English, or both languages. Currently, 22% of families receive reading materials solely in English, while 64% receive a split in the provision of Arabic and English, and 14% receive materials in Arabic only. This data signals an expressed interest among families in nurturing

---

[135] Massaro, 2017.

and elevating reading engagement in Arabic. Qatar Reads increases the presence of Arabic language resources in the home, tailored to the interests of the modern community, and enhances children's opportunities to experience life through the lens of Arabic language and culture.

Monthly reading packages include two books, corresponding activity sheets, and local comics. Curated content centers on culturally and socially relevant monthly themes, helping children learn about an issue or concept. Parents are also provided talking points to help their children engage critically with the reading materials. Content themes aim to build awareness across relevant matters and, where possible, are tied to critical events taking place within the country, such as Qatar's National Day, Autism Awareness Day, and Sports Day, to name a few.

Thematic content creation is integrated into its approach, aiming to build knowledge rooted in a locally relevant context while strengthening children's social and emotional competencies. For example, the theme of sustainability drives awareness of the importance of biodiversity and waste reduction while promoting personal environmental stewardship rooted in values of social responsibility and empathy. In this way, the program goes beyond literacy attainment, helping to cultivate character development rooted in attributes that are core to preserving Arab cultural identity.

Along the program's learning continuum, exclusive subscriber-only community events are held several times a year, enabling applied learning against the reading themes. These events provide opportunities for young readers to build interest-based bonds of friendship with children outside their existing social circles or classrooms and help families expand their social networks. Drawing on the theme of sustainability, children and families were invited to participate in a beach clean-up event organized by Qatar Reads and

Youth 4 Environment[136] to drive applied learning and collective action against a pressing and tangible concern. Creative and experiential approaches to learning help transfer reading content for children and bring concepts to life. These community-based events add relevance to the reading experience and promote children's self-reflection.

As well as activities, storytelling sessions are a pillar of Qatar Reads community events and participation. While the program encourages and facilitates reading aloud at home between parent and child, it also ensures the availability of storytellers for subscribers, a critical component to mastering reading.[137] Events are designed to initiate conversations that make reading topics enjoyable and understandable for children. A theme on animals led to discussions on veterinary methods and Arabic heritage at Qatar Foundation's Al Shaqab, a leading equestrian center, with free daily horse-riding lessons. Among all these activities, a storytelling activity was featured to link books to these different channels of learning and heritage-based activities.

Culturally rooted Arabic reading materials are sourced by Qatar Reads through collaborations with publishing houses. Qatar Reads establishes relationships with publishing houses to augment the demand for the provision and availability of high-quality, updated content in the Arabic language. Since 2020, a pool of 12 Arabic

---

[136] An environmental association in Qatar focused on creating a movement in support of achieving the goals of Qatar's National Development Strategy and the Sustainable Development Goals.

[137] Sonnenschein and Munsterman, 2002.

publishers[138] has been identified to expand both publishing capabilities and increase the availability of Arabic reading materials in Qatar and across the region. This has led to purchasing over 150 Arabic language titles per month, with quantities averaging 100 per age group. Due to this concentrated demand, Qatar Reads is also driving regional publishing trends and accelerating the availability of culturally relevant content that has been noted to restore and preserve language and culture.[139] Qatar Reads focuses on reinvigorating the production of Arabic language resources to ensure continuity in its preservation and to enrich children's connection to their native language.

Arabic books are generally perceived as more complex to source and difficult to verify in content quality and design. As part of its efforts to increase Arabic literary supply, Qatar Reads established 'Stories to Go,' which supports local literary voices and artists in building content in the form of visually appealing and easily digestible comic strips. The comics are built into the monthly package provisions with Qatari protagonists, allowing readers to see their culture and themselves in print, elevating cultural representation within localized content. Stories to Go is bilingual, enabling English-language speakers—within Qatar Reads and the broader community—to learn about Qatari identity and culture with archived content openly available to the public on the Qatar Reads' website.

---

[138] Qatar Reads collaborative publishers: Scholastic English USA, HBKU Press Arabic Qatar, Noon Books Arabic Jordan / Canada, Al Salwa Arabic Jordan, Al Yasmine Publishers Arabic Jordan, Asala Publishers Arabic Lebanon, Dar Al-Hadaek Arabic Lebanon, Kalimat Arabic UAE, Dar Rosa Arabic Qatar, Dar Napja Arabic Qatar, Bedaya / QDB Arabic Qatar, Dar Al Watad Arabic Qatar, Ilyas and Duck Arabic Qatar / USA the latter was translated to Arabic exclusively for Qatar Reads and coupled with one year of content for the Stories to Go.

[139] Romaine, 2007.

The content of the Family Reading Program packages is carefully curated to reflect local context and identity. This is, at times, further enhanced with the inclusion of supplementary materials. For example, a collaboration with the Qatar Foundation and the University College of London helped promote Qatar National Day by creating a series of dialect cards entitled *Qatari Heritage Words* to promote the Qatari dialect. The cards were multilingual—Arabic, French, and English—allowing readers to learn new vocabulary across multiple languages. *Ali's New Thob* comic was disseminated to create positive associations with local culture and norms, and *Eco-adventure* promoted the protection of Qatar's mangroves and their significance to preserving biodiversity. Inclusion and accessibility through sports were also addressed, emphasizing the social value of equitable access to recreation while encouraging representation of Qatari girls in sports through *Basketball with Sara*.

Qatar Reads' materials frequently reference Islamic values. During Ramadan, children receive advent calendars featuring lanterns, puzzles, excerpts from the Qur'an, and other toys or learning tools to generate excitement and enrich the learning experience during the holy month of Ramadan. The concept was brought to life through a collaboration with local artist Fatima Al Mesnad and a local graphic design company, Render. Stories to Go features titles such as *Fahad's Eidyah* and *Eid Prayer,* which are resources typically shared during Islamic festivals or rituals and supplemented with Makkah-themed crafts. Beyond the month of Ramadan, children learn about financial literacy, tolerance, and compassion, all rooted in promoting Islamic values. One theme, Entrepreneurship, featured financial management and project starters for children, complemented by an exclusive Arabic language book on *zakkat* with a visit and storytelling led by the author. This allows children to take Islam beyond specific rituals and learn its application in everyday life.

The Family Reading Program proved to be such an efficient tool for cultural promotion that it was used as a vehicle for cultural exchange in the Year of Culture[140] in 2021. It was designed to enhance cultural relations between the United States of America and Qatar. Qatar Reads shared 800 bilingual reading packages to Washington DC, reinforcing Qatar's history and culture, and 12 students from Qatar Foundation schools joined to encourage the habit of reading with other participating children. Through its activations at the Year of Culture, Qatar Reads promoted Arabic and elevated the value of reading and writing in Arabic among non-native Arabic speakers. Through the 'I Love Reading' traceable Arabic bookmarks and coloring sheets featuring the Doha skyline, international community members were exposed to Qatar and the beauty of its culture and language. One participant shared her experience on social media: "As an Arab living in America, I am always looking for ways to develop the Arabic language for my daughter because our Arabic language is our inheritance, our history, and I'm very happy with this activation."[141]

Our collective impact

To understand the benefits of the Qatar Reads Family Reading program on its participants, Qatar conducted an evaluation in partnership with Hamad Bin Khalifa University at Qatar Foundation. A thorough literature review, measurement framework, and ethics review underpinned the study. The survey was administered in Arabic and English to participating parents, requesting responses and reflections on each child.

The findings were positive and encouraging, revealing that well-designed community programs can yield intended results, such as improving reading habits and children's confidence, and unintended

---

[140] First launched in 2012, Year of Culture is an annual bi-lateral exchange of culture and creativity. It is an opportunity for Qatar and a select country to come together to celebrate their cultures and heritage and deepen mutual understanding across nations through a year of cultural programming.
[141] Qatar Reads, 2021.

results, such as strengthening family bonds. The findings confirmed what research data has proven all along, that with more books at home and reading engagement, children have a better attitude toward reading and improved reading aptitudes.

For Qatar, it was increasingly promising that the Family Reading Program has many Qatari children and families, representing 88% of total program participants. This is particularly encouraging given the program's emphasis on tailoring its approach to meet user needs and successfully promoting the Arabic language and Qatari culture and identity, helping serve its intent and reach the national population and creating an ability to fulfill a niche demand.

Qatar Reads also increases reading engagement among families, where 70% of parents reported spending more time reading with their children. This strengthens family bonds and provides children with positive role-modeling, creating beneficial associations with reading and helping them form healthy habits at an early age. Equally important is that 81% of children reported reading *more* after joining the program. Children receiving Arabic content is significant in ensuring increased engagement with the Arabic language and cultural content, helping strengthen cultural identity and culturally rooted knowledge and behaviors.

The evaluation solidified that the Qatar Reads Family Reading Program was well-designed and confirmed that reading leads to discovery, exchange, exploration, and transformation. As a vehicle for social transformation, Qatar Reads has enormous potential to influence children's developmental and learning trajectories, where nurturing and cultivating a child's love for reading influences how they interact with and understand their social world.

The transformative impact of Qatar Reads on children's development and cultural identity

Reading is a powerful tool for children, helping develop critical social competencies and lifelong learning skills and behaviors that enable growth and self-discovery. Reading creates a foundation for inquiry, self-confidence, problem-solving, and necessary thinking skills. For Qatar, this program helps build the next generation, which carries the program's core values: read to create, debate, discover, and think. In the case of the Family Reading Program, children and families read to transform.

The act of reading is evolutionary, enabling both personal and cultural development. As a community response, Qatar Reads has successfully created pathways essential to children's development and identity formation where they see their history, current reality, and identity in their native tongue. The journey of Qatar Reads is motivated by children's curiosity and the impetus to honor Qatar's cultural and linguistic roots. The program will continue to create opportunities for children to achieve their full potential anchored in understanding their language and culture. It will help children to confidently participate in their cultural environments, carrying the legacy of the Arabic language: a prominent and distinct representation in the literary world.

9. Arabic dual language immersion programs in U.S. public schools

Robert Slater, American Councils for International Education
Gregg Roberts, American Councils for International Education
Carine Allaf, Qatar Foundation International

In 2019, the American Councils Research Center (ARC) at the American Councils for International Education, in partnership with Qatar Foundation International (QFI), embarked on a study designed to understand better public or public charter Arabic Dual Language Immersion (DLI) programs in the United States.[142] QFI commissioned this study to explore the characteristics of four Arabic DLI programs and how they are situated within the greater DLI programs across the United States. The first program at PS/IS 30 in Brooklyn, NY, began in 2013.

This has been followed by three other programs: Baltimore International Academy (BIA) in Baltimore, Maryland; Arabic Immersion Magnet School in Houston, Texas (AIMS); and the Elizabeth Learning Center in Los Angeles, California (ELC). As this chapter is published, an additional program will open in New York, and a handful of others are in the planning stages. In this chapter, we will explore the qualitative findings from this study—specifically

---

[142] QFI has assisted in the development, implementation, and support of these four initial programs. External involvement in the development and proliferation of dual language programs, like that of QFI, is not unusual. For example, the French embassy in collaboration with the FACE Foundation has for years actively promoted and funded numerous French DLI efforts across the U.S., particularly in Louisiana, New York, and Utah.

those from surveys and interviews with teachers, parents, and administrators.

Arabic dual language programs

Although Arabic is the fastest-growing language in the United States and the fifth most spoken language in the world, there has been no significant growth in dual language programs involving Arabic. This is particularly evident given the considerable increase in DLI programs nationwide, particularly in Spanish, Chinese, and French. There are only four Arabic DLI programs in the United States. Explanations for this lack of growth vary.

There is significant growth in the number of Arabic speakers in the United States. We know Arabic is the second most spoken home language for English learners in U.S. schools, ranking only behind Spanish. About half of these speakers are concentrated in four states that have the highest populations of Arab Americans: Michigan, Illinois, New York, and Virginia. Yet the four Arabic DLI programs are in California (Greater Los Angeles), Maryland (Baltimore), New York (New York City), and Texas (Houston).[143]

The study focused on the four public and public charter school Arabic DLI programs in the United States. Table 1 offers a glance at each school (as of April 2023), and a brief description of each Arabic DLI program follows below.

---

[143] OELA [Office of English Language Acquisition]. 2019. Fast facts: The top languages spoken by English Learners ELs in the United States.

PS/IS 30	**AIMS**	**ELC**	**BIA**
Brooklyn, NY	Houston, TX	Los Angeles, CA	Baltimore, MD
Kindergarten to grade 8 (K-8) public school. Arabic DLI in grades K-5. Language other than English (LOTE) in grades 6 to 8. Established 2013.	PreK-8 magnet school. Arabic DLI in grades K-8. Established 2015.	K-12 public school. Arabic DLI in grades K-5. Established 2016.	K-8 charter school. Arabic DLI in grades K-7. Established 2013.
Side-by-side model in grades 1-5. Stand-alone in K and Grades 6-8.	PreK-2: 60/40; side-by-side immersion model. Grades 3-5: 40/60 three teachers. Grades 6-8: 30/70 Arabic LOTE: Additional conversational Arabic is an elective.	Two-way 50/50 immersion model; Stand-alone Teacher Model.	Total language immersion model in the early grades. Grades K-5 Arabic; Stand-alone Teacher Model until Grade 2, where English LA class is introduced with a separate teacher 1-hour a day.
Priority is given to English Language Learners (ELLs). The majority of the students come from Arab homes.	In 2019, roughly 20% of the schools reported coming from an Arabic-speaking background. No priority; magnet school.	Most students speak Spanish at home, and some are heritage students. No priority.	Over 95% only speak English at home/Title I targeted assistance. *(Title I: Funds to aid students in need).* No priority.
Math, science, and Arabic Language Arts (LA) in Arabic.	Arabic LA, science, and math are offered in Arabic.	All core subjects are in both languages, including math, science, social studies, and physical education.	K-1: all core subjects (LA, math, science, social studies) are in Arabic only. English introduced as students go up to grade 2 onwards.

PS/IS 30 Brooklyn, New York (PS/IS 30).

PS/IS 30 was the first Arabic DLI program. PS/IS 30 is a public New York City school that enrolls students from its neighborhood catchment. It officially began in 2013 with one kindergarten class. Like most DLI programs nationwide, they advanced to the next grade level each subsequent year. The PS/IS 30 program is a two-way immersion program. It strives to ensure that half of each classroom comprises Arabic-proficient students and half of English-proficient students, keeping with NYC's Department of Education policy. PS/IS 30 uses a side-by-side model in which students have one teacher for the Arabic portions of the day (math, science, and Arabic language arts) and another for the English portion of the day, except for kindergarten, where one teacher teaches in both languages.

Arabic Immersion Magnet School, Houston, Texas (AIMS)

AIMS began its program in the fall of 2015. It is an all-school Arabic immersion program, the only public school of its kind in the country. It has recently started its middle school with plans to continue through grade 8. It is not a 50/50 program, with a limited number of students who report speaking Arabic at home. AIMS uses a side-by-side teacher model with Arabic instruction in language arts, science, and math and another teacher instructing in English. As a magnet school, students from throughout the Houston Independent School District can apply to enroll.

Baltimore International Academy, Baltimore, Maryland (BIA)

BIA is a charter school that offers immersion programs in Spanish, Chinese, Arabic, Russian, and French. Arabic was the most recent addition in 2013. As a school that draws on an almost entirely African American population, 95% of students speak English at home. The BIA model only offers intensive language (Arabic) kindergarten and grade 1 instruction. English is then introduced from the second grade for an hour a day, with its usage gradually increasing as the students enter higher grade levels, currently offering up to grade 8.

Elizabeth Learning Center, Los Angeles, California (ELC)

ELC began its Arabic DLI in the fall of 2016 with one kindergarten class. It now extends through grade 5. At ELC, priority for enrollment is given to students who live within the school's attendance boundaries. ELC draws on an almost entirely non-

Arabic-speaking student population; instead, its students are from Spanish-speaking homes. Because of this, the program is a one-way model, beginning with a 70/30 split between Arabic and English in kindergarten and moving toward 50/50 in grades 3 and above.

Insights from dual language immersion programs: A teacher survey analysis across four schools

Teachers from across the four schools were surveyed to identify classroom approaches and strategies used in the four DLI programs. The analysis below focuses on a summary of findings for all schools. The survey was distributed online to all DLI teachers in these four schools in December 2020 and focused on six key topics:

1. Minutes of Arabic Instruction and Teacher Characteristics.
2. Instructional Strategies and Time.
3. English Language Learners (ELLs) in the Classroom.
4. Professional Development.
5. Principal and Additional Classroom Support.
6. Teacher Pathways and Years Taught.

A total of 21 DLI teachers responded to the survey:

BIA	5 out of 7
AIMS	7 out of 12
ELC	3 out of 4
PS/IS 30	6 out of 7

The most notable among the findings are the following:

- 60% of teachers focused on language arts, 45% on math.
- 18% on social studies and 28% on science.
- Almost all teachers are native Arabic speakers, with 50% using modern standard or academic Arabic in their teaching and 50% using their dialects. It is interesting to note that in the 2018–2019 school year, there was only one non-native Arabic teacher in the four Arabic DLI programs.
- Teachers reported focusing on the following skills: 60% on listening, 23% on reading, and 15% on writing skills.

The most important instructional strategies cited were:

- Language and content objectives.
- Providing language support.
- Requiring language production.
- Almost all Arabic DLI teachers reported having received professional development.

Exploring family choices and perspectives in Arabic dual language immersion programs

With an expanding array of dual language programs available in many school districts, families can choose whether to enroll their children in DLI and which language they want. The decision is influenced by critical factors, including the heritage of the parent(s) and school district rules about enrollment (geographical boundaries, language background, etc.). It is essential, particularly for a language like Arabic, to understand why families choose to enroll their children in Arabic DLI.

The parent survey was sent to all email addresses of parents whose children were enrolled in the Arabic DLI programs, as provided to the research team by each school. Responses were received from 123 total parents:

AIMS	68
BIA	18
ELC	16
PS/IS 30	21

Parental motivations and perceptions:

A series of questions were asked about the motivation behind enrolling children in the Arabic program and parental perceptions of the program. Parents ranked the four most important reasons for enrolling their child in the Arabic DLI program in the following order:

- The perceived opportunity for high-quality academics.
- The opportunity for bilingualism.
- The academic and career advantage.
- The opportunity to communicate with Arabic speakers.

Several additional questions shed essential light on parents' perceptions and attitudes toward the program. The chart below summarizes the responses to the questions.

These responses provide critical insights into the motivations and perceptions of the four Arabic DLI programs. To further explore the responses to the parent survey, we held online (Zoom) conversations with a limited number of parents from AIMS and PS/IS 30. These conversations served to reinforce the responses to the survey.

Statement	Strongly Agree	Agree	Neither Agree nor Disagree	Disagree	Strongly Disagree
The faculty and staff have been successful in promoting diversity and understanding among the school community.	53%	37%	6%	3%	0%
I am satisfied that the Arabic program is teaching my child necessary subject matter.	50%	44%	3%	3%	0%
I feel that my family is valued by the school.	50%	41%	6%	3%	0%
I would recommend the Arabic DLI program to other parents.	68%	27%	5%	3%	0%
Studying Arabic is important for my child because it will enable a better understanding and appreciation of the world.	79%	18%	3%	0%	0%
Studying Arabic is important for my child's future career.	62%	21%	17%	0%	0%
Studying Arabic is important for my child because it will make them smarter.	41%	32%	27%	3%	0%
It is important for all children to study their language and cultural heritage.	72%	19%	7%	2%	0%

There is little data about parent motivations from other schools or districts.[144] However, we know that with DLI programs, heritage/family background, along with the perception that DLI programs offer essential opportunities for academic achievement, are critical factors in decisions made by parents. This suggests that parents' answers are relatively consistent with the perceptions and motivations of many parents who enroll their children in other language DLI programs. However, some important caveats to our analysis of parents' motivations and perceptions (for Arabic DLI specifically) emerge from the survey responses and conversations.

Many parents seem to recognize the importance of Arabic as a world language, particularly in Arab culture and politics. Several parents expressed a commitment to Arabic tied to their hopes and expectations that the programs would enable their children to be 'better citizens' and contribute to a 'better world.' Parents appeared animated and highly committed to this. It is also important, if not critical, to attract parents who value the importance of Arab cultures and the Arabic language because of their heritage. In conversations with parents, it became apparent that household decisions were influenced by the Arabic-speaking background of at least one parent, especially in the case of a place like PS/IS 30.

It is important to note that many of the households interviewed speak English, even though at least one parent is likely proficient in Arabic. This is vastly different from the conventional two-way DLI program, where many children come from non-English speaking homes, and the parents' motivations are to maintain their home language (such as Spanish) while providing children with a perceived opportunity to achieve academically in English. Regardless of the program's structure (e.g., two-way, one-way, 50/50, 80/20), the Arabic DLI programs seem to address the values of learning Arabic, with English learning a lesser concern. An exception to this might be

---

[144] See for example: Parks, 2008.

the ELC program, where children come from Spanish-speaking homes and are challenged to learn Arabic and English. PS/IS 30 is also unique. Although most students come from Arabic-speaking homes, they are not necessarily proficient in Arabic or English at the onset of their schooling.

It is also important to note that parents expressed concerns about the capacity of the programs to continue beyond elementary school even though both AIMS and BIA have grades six to eight (and PS/IS 30 offers it as an additional language in middle school). With an apparent longer-term commitment to learning the Arabic language and culture, conversations with parents suggested a concern that Arabic would not be effectively sustained through middle school and high school. We should add that this is no different from other DLI programs where issues of enrollment and curriculum structure have challenged schools after elementary school.

Leadership perspectives on the success and challenges of Arabic dual language immersion programs

Studies of DLI have generally pointed to the critical role that leadership plays in successfully implementing programs. In December 2022, questions were sent to each of the school principals. The questions were answered in writing in two cases, and in two, they were discussed during a virtual meeting. These responses and interviews are not attributed directly to the respondents, who were told no direct quotes would be used. This analysis provides generalizations across the four programs drawing from these four responses.

Motivations for Arabic-speaking parents to enroll their children in the program

There was consistency across the four respondents in describing motivations. Arabic-speaking parents want a 'safe place' for their children to learn the language and culture. Many pointed out that the programs presented an opportunity to learn Arabic without the social pressures and biases often associated with the language and culture. Consistent with many parents who enroll their children in DLI, they want their children to improve their Arabic language skills. One of the respondents indicated that approximately half the students are in the program to learn Arabic without a 'religious' component, while another half were there because they have not grown up speaking Arabic.

Motivations for English-speaking parents

Like most DLI programs, English-speaking parents seek academic opportunities and cultural diversity. The administrators reported that parents are seen as responding to the evidence that learning two languages helps their children advance academically, be better citizens, and understand other cultures more. Additionally, it was pointed out that Muslim parents (not necessarily Arabic-speaking) are motivated to immerse children in the Arabic language and culture. Again, like many DLI programs, effective marketing and providing information on the strengths and capabilities of the program increase parents' interest in enrollment. In the case of one school, BIA, it is apparent that as an IB school that focuses on languages, parents select it because of the multiple perceived academic benefits to their children in a city where the local schools might not be seen as providing the same opportunity.

Consistent with the responses to the first two questions, the respondents agreed that enrolling in the program provides an opportunity for children to be multilingual, global citizens, and college and career-ready. It was noted that in some cases, recent immigrants from Arabic-speaking countries see the program as necessary because the students can begin studies in their native language and learn English at a somewhat slower pace. It was also noted that parents see the Arabic program as a 'niche' opportunity and are intrigued by the incorporation of language and culture.

Each program is unique in the approach it takes to recruiting students. Parents seek to enroll their children in some places, like PS/IS 30, where Arabic is a high-priority language. DLI might be an important motivation in other areas, regardless of language. In cases where the program is a 'magnet' and applications are accepted across the school district, Arabic might not have been the first choice, but parents wanted DLI for their children regardless.

Administrators reported that, generally, parents consider a school's standardized test results a critical factor in deciding about schools. The evidence that children enrolled in Arabic DLI have equaled or exceeded student performance across the district is not lost on parents seeking strong academic opportunities for their children.[145] Coupled with the dual language opportunity for Arabic-speaking children or English language learners, the academic achievement records of these programs are significant motivators for parents.

Navigating district support for Arabic dual language immersion programs

Support from the respective districts is uneven at best. Respondents reported that budgets are challenging and securing financial support from the district is a significant task. One respondent indicated little support besides encouragement and acknowledgment of the successes achieved. We should note some important issues involved with district support. Our conversations clearly show that financial and program support from QFI is instrumental in the success of many of the programs. It is not clear that these programs would survive without QFI support. While we cannot assert from our data that the programs benefit from the extensive support (across all programs in terms of professional development and, in some, financial support), it is difficult to imagine that these programs would be as effective or

---

[145] Although this chapter does not discuss this aspect of the research, in almost all cases the programs reflect the results of major studies of DLI that confirm that students enrolled in DLI are achieving academically as measured by state assessments. See Steele et al. 2017.

successful without it. It is also important to note that Arabic DLI must compete with other DLI programs for support in many districts. In many districts nationwide, multilingual support is mainly identified for Spanish, with enormous student numbers and demands. As a perceived 'niche' program, Arabic DLI must compete for attention and funds like other smaller programs.

Enrollment challenges and opportunities

Like many other DLI programs, these programs experience significant challenges: enrollment, space, and teacher workload. Each school has significant enrollment challenges. In the case of two programs, enrollment targets have not been met. In one case, grades are combined to sustain the program. In another case, enrollment has been sufficient to maintain each grade, but the targeted number of students has not been achieved. Middle school enrollment remains a significant challenge that might threaten the program's viability at that level. Middle school program sustainment is subject to several vulnerabilities, including alternative opportunities for children beyond elementary school, defining curriculum and developing instructional materials at this level, and state requirements for another curriculum that eliminates instructional hours in Arabic. Lower student enrollment in middle school significantly threatens the viability and sustainment of the Arabic DLI programs beyond the fifth grade. Both schools with middle school programs are currently (as of summer 2023 when this report was written) experiencing challenges with the continuation of Arabic DLI.

One school identifies space as a significant challenge. While enrollment numbers would support two classes per grade, space in the school does not. As an alternative, they have structured a side-by-side model that requires teaching two classes on different grade levels instead of two classes on the same grade level. This stresses the teachers significantly because they teach two separate grade levels.

This leads to the last major challenge identified: teacher workload. All administrators reported that developing and maintaining classroom curricula and materials burdens the teachers enormously.

Adapting to unprecedented challenges: The impact of COVID-19 on Arabic dual language immersion programs

The arrival of COVID-19 in early 2020 was an unanticipated and significant handicap. Planned research strategies had to be dramatically altered. Direct and personal contact with school officials and parents became impossible over a protracted period, particularly impacting data collection and planned focus groups and surveys. Data collection was delayed and thwarted, especially in New York City, where the student data collection requirements levied by the New York City Board of Education were already burdensome and became more so during COVID-19. Plans for in-person focus groups with parents were changed to virtual formats and meetings with teachers and school principals. An unintended advantage of the survey approach is that we were able to reach a broader cross-section of families. To supplement the survey, the research team held virtual focus group discussions with several parents from AIMS and PS/IS 30. We could carry out this research during incredibly challenging times because of the extraordinary commitment of each school's leadership teams and the help of each district. As a result, the research also took much longer to complete.

Across the nation, however, COVID-19 was a significant challenge for DLI programs because of the loss of direct contact with teachers while maintaining learning in two languages. One administrator described the impact as 'devastating' and indicated that COVID-19 created a significant learning gap in children's English and Arabic skills. We should note that this is not inconsistent with reports now being received on the impact of COVID-19 on student achievement, generally, and on DLI programs across the country. Like many DLI programs, the administrators referred to the resilience and dedication of the teachers, and many doubted that the Arabic DLI programs would have survived without their commitment.

Advancing Arabic dual language immersion: Insights and reflections

The analysis presented in this report provides essential insights into Arabic DLI in the four public school programs. We have gained significant insight into each of these programs. This helps us better understand what is needed to build and sustain Arabic DLI in the U.S. By examining all four programs, we hope to advance our understanding of the current state of Arabic DLI and the potential to maintain and expand programs.

We can speculate (and confirm from surveys and interviews) that parents identify DLI programs and seek to enroll their children in them, and this appeared to be no different for Arabic DLI. Given that these four programs are all in major cities with unequal opportunities for achievement and success, parents often see DLI, in this case, Arabic, as an oasis in a generally underperforming public school system. When taken together with self-selection, where more competitive parents might actively seek out these programs for their children, it is unsurprising that the four Arabic DLI programs might attract students more likely to succeed.

What we learned from this study leads to another essential generalization about Arabic DLI programs. Arabic is distinctive in that it attracts two types of parents who enroll their children. The first is heritage families who seek out these programs as opportunities to provide Arab culture and Arabic language for their children. As we saw in the parent survey responses and conversations with parents and school leaders at PS/IS 30 and AIMS, maintaining cultural and linguistic heritage is perhaps the most critical factor in enrollment. These two programs draw heavily from a population committed to providing their children with this opportunity. The second is simply the idea of a better education—ELC and BIA present other motivations. Many Spanish-speaking ELC parents seek Arabic as an opportunity for their children to get a better education and be trilingual. BIA parents identify with the Arabic DLI program at the school for several reasons. It is clear from the surveys and interviews that Arabic is frequently not the first choice of parents, who might prefer to enroll their children in the other BIA DLI programs such as Spanish, Chinese, Russian, or French. Arabic is sometimes selected as a default if there are no spaces in the other languages. This tends to show the need for more information on the importance of Arabic DLI specifically and the utility of Arabic.

It is also worth noting that in three locations—Houston, Los Angeles, and New York City—parents could consider enrolling their children in a large array of dual language programs across multiple languages. It is a very competitive enrollment environment. Many of these programs are open to students from across the school district, although parents living in a specific catchment area are often given priority. With high student enrollment percentages, Arabic must compete among other highly attractive languages, including Chinese, French, and Spanish. Program placement within a district becomes paramount, particularly for Arabic, where the appeal might be more limited than other large-enrollment languages. For example, by locating an Arabic program in a predominantly Spanish-speaking area, ELC has limited enrollment opportunities. It is important to note that the two more established programs, AIMS and PS/IS 30, draw from a broader population of Arabic speakers and heritage families, mainly due to their locations in Houston and New York City, respectively. Neither has experienced serious enrollment issues in elementary school, although, like many DLI programs, both certainly struggle to deliver programs in middle school.

Our parent surveys and interviews also provided additional insights into the decision to enroll in Arabic. Where Arabic is selected, there seems to be a conscious effort to engage their children in what some parents perceive as an important world language and culture. Parents often referred to their commitment to building character and cultural diversity in their survey responses and conversations, including those who do not speak Arabic at home.

Conversations with administrators suggest another potential conundrum for Arabic programs. There appears to be little proactive support in each district for curriculum development and teacher professional development specific to Arabic. General DLI professional development opportunities are available to all teachers, but programs can struggle to achieve without clear strategies for delivering Arabic dual language instruction. Unlike languages, where there are multiple programs within the district, Arabic teachers are likely to suffer from a lack of opportunities to engage with other teachers of Arabic. This lack of support has significant implications for QFI's role moving forward. QFI support has played a major, if not pivotal, role in the success of these programs to date. QFI's role in funding and academic/professional development support for these programs makes an enormous difference in their capacity to sustain and succeed. Annual teacher training efforts for Arabic teachers, sponsored by QFI, provide a vital lifeline for professional development. Pedagogical support provided through QFI by some of the best DLI experts has contributed to the quality of the programs. Without such support, it might be difficult for these programs to establish and maintain their high academic standards. Teachers devote extensive time translating content lessons and creating Arabic lessons aligned with needed standards. School leaders worry about burnout. It is, again, hard to imagine that these programs would be able to sustain their levels of success without QFI's active role.

Replication of these successful programs, particularly PS/IS 30 and AIMS, seems to be the model to adopt. These are essential programs in cities with significant populations motivated to study Arabic. Yet, the expansion of Arabic DLI in the U.S. faces considerable challenges. Two-way programs like those in New York and Houston might be difficult to replicate without identifying school districts with substantial Arabic-speaking populations and English-speaking populations both eager to enroll in Arabic as opposed to other languages. Parents have more choices with the proliferation of DLI programs across many districts and states.

10. "Mama, are you speaking Spanish?" Experience of parents developing their children's standard and colloquial Arabic

Aishah Alfadhalah
Kennedy Krieger Institute

A personal journey through standard and colloquial Arabic

I remember the first time I thought I was not good at Modern Standard Arabic (MSA). You would wonder, if I were a native speaker born in an Arabic-speaking country, how could I not be fluent in my language? Arabic has two main variations: MSA, fuS-Ha, and regional dialects. MSA is the formal language used in books, media, and legal documents. On the other hand, Arabic dialects are informal languages that are used within a specific region or country.

We must understand the subjective distinction between a language and a dialect to understand the Arabic language. From an English speaker's perspective, you might think a language is a collection of dialects that can understand each other in terms of intelligibility. Yet, in many different languages, that is not the case. Some mutually incomprehensible dialects are under the same umbrella of one language. For example, Mandarin and Cantonese are considered two different dialects of Chinese. However, Mandarin and Cantonese have more significant differences than Spanish and Italian. The Arabic language has approximately 30 distinct dialects. The colloquial form of Kuwaiti Arabic differs from that of Jordanian Arabic. The Arabic language is used to unify cultural identity despite the vast linguistic differences across the dialects and MSA.

I grew up in Kuwait City. I have only heard MSA on TV during the news segment, and I have seen it in books. I used colloquial Kuwaiti Arabic to argue with my sisters, negotiate with my parents, make friends, and re-tell my grandmother's stories. I have attended public elementary school. Only the Arabic teacher spoke MSA. The teachers spoke in their colloquial tongues for the rest of the classes. I have one teacher who spoke colloquial Egyptian Arabic and another who spoke Palestinian colloquial Arabic. The Arabic teacher called my mother, stating that I seemed to have difficulty with MSA grammar, structure, and pronunciation. From that day on, I would stay silent in my checkered white and blue uniform. Avoid being asked to answer in a language that is supposed to be mine. My ears never found MSA in conversations over tea and mingling in the grocery store. The Arabic teacher would ask us to recite poetry in MSA from memory. I stood in front of the class, reciting the poems of Al-Mutanabbi. Suddenly, I forget the words I memorized repeatedly in the kitchen, on the drive to school, and before bed. The words slipped from my mind like sand slips between the fingers of your hand. I viewed MSA with fear, a language I could not reach. In elementary and middle school, I rarely understood the layers of the meaning of stanzas I recited in front of the class in MSA. I only knew the surface, and I could not see the depth. There was an unfortunate tension between my two tongues: MSA and colloquial.

Kuwaiti is what I truly knew intimately. The uniqueness of substituting the /ch/ sound with a /y/ and /q/ to /g/. The vocabulary stems from French ([əsʕən.sʕeːr], elevator), Persian (rıznamə] calendar), English ([wajır] wire), and Turkish (ʃoːrbə], soup), representing all the movement that happened into our land. I rediscovered MSA in high school when I started reading my great grandfather's book about comparing idioms across Middle Eastern dialects. The book was written in MSA. Since then, I have discovered MSA by reading my great-grandfather's books and Arabic literature. MSA has given me access to more vocabulary and shades of feeling. In MSA, there are 11 words for 'love' and hundreds of words for 'camel.'

Since the first grade, we always had an English class at school, once or twice a week for an hour per class. I had to increase my

English proficiency in high school because English is the language of mobility in higher education. British English is taught in public schools in Kuwait due to the traces of British colonization. When I came to the United States for college and moved throughout, I realized there was no such thing as Standard English. Linguistic differences are equal, but domination is not. Though diverse dialects exist, they are all beautifully complicated and continuously evolving. The first state I settled in was Milwaukee, Wisconsin.

I often understood what people literally said but could not grasp the meaning conceptually. There were many standard American ways that I did not know of. I didn't realize that the English vowels could throw me off, and I struggled with words such as bag or bagel. The fact that people would say, "How are you?" and keep walking was odd to me. I didn't know that the National Football League meant only teams within the U.S., and I didn't know what cheese curds were. I had a hard time forming friendships with American natives. I often felt it was because of my frequent questions after any comment or joke (what do you mean?). The majority of my friendships were with other international students. After a few years, I started feeling confident in English. However, I was learning Spanish by then and was at the start of another complicated learning experience.

After being in the U.S. for ten years and feeling fully immersed in English, I moved to Baltimore, Maryland, in 2015. My fascination with dialect has flourished. The dialects in Baltimore are varied and rich in culture and history. The differences across the east and west sides of the city, its pronunciation amongst people, and the divide between Blacks and Whites as the red lines of the city were so profound. As much as language can connect us, it also has the ability to divide us. It is the reality of the effects of hierarchy and superiority. I see language as a reflection of our experiences and the structure of our thoughts or how it shapes our perceptions. I feel that Kuwaiti colloquial is the language of stories over tea, rhyme songs, humor, and loud family gatherings. English is the language of structure, objectivity, and the future tense. Spanish is the language of passion, intimacy, and present tense. MSA is a universe I am still exploring, giving me labels of experiences that my other tongues lack.

Parent as an Arabic language support

I started working with Arabic-speaking patients as a trilingual speech-language pathologist at Kennedy Krieger Institute in 2015. I noticed the decay of Arabic (MSA and colloquial) through the generations of the Arab diaspora in the U.S. Once, a Syrian mother told me that she spoke MSA to her child and that he responded by asking her, "Are you speaking Spanish?" The family has been displaced from their home country, Syria, to the U.S. for five years at this event. The child was eight when he thought his mother spoke Spanish to him. However, the mother reported speaking Syrian Arabic to her children most of the day. At that moment, when she spoke MSA and her child did not understand her, she realized her children did not recognize MSA. The mother asked me how to support her child's Arabic at home. That question reminded me of my journey with standard and colloquial Arabic. I grew up in an Arabic-speaking country with access to books, media, and individuals to learn MSA, and I still struggled. This Arabic-speaking child grew up without access to bilingual schooling and with a limited Arabic-speaking community and resources. In 2018, I started a journey to research and support parents to develop their children's Arabic (both MSA and colloquial).

Multilingual caregivers face unique challenges supporting their children's home language learning due to language dominance of "standardized English" over other dialects and languages and the lack of support from schools and limited linguistic community to practice the language.[146] Most immigrant students in the U.S. lose their home language and shift entirely to English by the third generation.[147] The study below explores the impact of providing

---

[146] Tadess, 2014.
[147] Wilder, 2014.

explicit guidance for Arabic caregivers on their ability and desire to support their children's learning. An online six-week caregiver workshop was created to share with caregivers the importance of maintaining the home language and providing language strategies for them to use with their children. The study investigated the relationship between intervention in the home language and caregivers' increased knowledge of home language usage and language strategies with their children. The study participants comprised four Syrian Arabic-speaking mothers with children in K-5 Baltimore City schools.

Importance of maintaining the home language

All mothers in the intervention expressed the importance of using and maintaining the home language. The component that emerged from the qualitative data that explains why caregivers maintained the home language was culture, which is a collective of characteristics and knowledge of a particular group of people, encompassing language, religion, social habits, and identity.[148] In the pre-intervention survey, mothers were asked why it was essential to maintain Arabic with their children. Mothers reported the importance of using Arabic due to their Islamic religion, communicating with immediate and extended family, and belonging to the Arab identity. After the intervention, mothers kept the same rationale for maintaining Arabic with their children, with the additional emerging reason for the importance of bilingual language development. In the post-interview, two of the mothers stated the following comments that highlight the advantage that a bilingual child might have, "a person when he/she knows two languages is two people with two brains," and "excel in his life for being bilingual and understanding different perspectives." In the first session, the mothers were presented with information regarding transferring skills

---

[148] Archer, Francis, and Mau 2010.

across languages in bilinguals. Literacy skills in the home language cannot be transferred to the second language if the home language has not been developed adequately.[149]

Students with high oral and literacy proficiency in their home language do better in their second language literacy and metalinguistic awareness.[150] Skills that students acquire in the home language are found to transfer to a second language, especially if the concepts relate to cognitive-communication functions (e.g., inferencing, narration, compare and contrast, etc.).[151] A strong foundation in the first language supports the development of a second language.

Overall, caregivers maintained the same rationale in teaching their children Arabic throughout the intervention due to connecting to their cultural heritage, encompassing religion, communication, and identity. For two caregivers, an additional rationale has emerged: if their children maintain Arabic, they might develop bilingual cognitive advantage (e.g., perspective taking). Bilingualism was beneficial in linguistic domains (transfer of skills) and cognitive domains such as attention, working memory, and cognitive flexibility.[152]

Approaches to teaching Arabic to their children

The second theme in the data collected during the intervention indicated that mothers changed some approaches to teaching Arabic to their children. In the pre-intervention qualitative data, two of the four mothers reported using tutors when asked, "How do you support your child's Arabic language development" (e.g., "Arabic

---

[149] Baker and Wright, 2021.
[150] Skutnabb-Kangas and Mohanty, 1995.
[151] Cummins, 2008.
[152] Blumenfeld and Marian, 2013.

language private teacher" and "Enroll in courses to strengthen the Arabic language"). However, in the post-intervention, all caregivers stated strategies they could implement directly with their children, such as reading and telling stories. In addition, mothers reported increased intentionality in working directly with their children. The intervention might have resulted in the mothers feeling empowered to apply evidence-based strategies and not only depend on external sources such as tutors to develop their children's language.

In the post-intervention interviews, mothers reported acquiring new knowledge to support their children at home. For example, one mother reported building on homework the child brings from school and practice and explaining the same academic concepts in Arabic, e.g., "If they take a topic in school, they talk about it in Arabic (present it to me)." Another mother mentioned using extension and expansion, two strategies covered in the social language session ("Correct their grammar through modeling or encourage them to reflect on the sentence they said."). Increasing mothers' knowledge of using evidence-based strategies with their children might have been empowering for the mothers. Mothers do not necessarily need to be bilingual to positively support their children's academic learning and second language acquisition. Mothers can use their linguistic resources (the home language) to support their children.[153]

---

[153] Nguyen, Shin, and Krashen 2001.

Table 1. Mothers' quotes – home language importance.

	Mothers Quotes
Pre-Intervention Survey *Culture*	"Because my mother tongue is Arabic." "To communicate with us and with the family well, to develop a way of understanding." "Because it is our original language and so he can communicate with us." "Because it is my native language."
Post-Intervention Survey *Culture*	"It is our mother tongue and the language of the Qur'an so that the child can communicate with the mothers." "Because it is the language of the civilization that we have come from, in addition to it being here, we speak it, so why not take advantage of it?" "Because it is the language of communication between them and relatives in Arab countries." Post-Interview: "Very important. First, I love the Arabic language. It is their culture and their religion." "Does not feel he is not understood or not understanding people around him. To communicate with family when he goes visit. "Because we are Arab and Muslims and to connect with family in Syria."
Post-survey/Interview *Bilingual Advantage*	"Excel in his life for being bilingual and understanding different perspectives." "My grandmother used to say a person, when he/she knows two languages, is two people with two brains. It is important for my children to be bilingual."

Mothers reported intentionality in developing their children's Arabic language. For example, one mother stated. "You open my mind. I used to think I am only going to develop their English" and "Intentionally spending the majority of the day in Arabic." This intentionality of maintaining and developing the home language might have resulted from the mother's understanding of the benefits of extending the home language to second language acquisition.

Table 2. Mothers' quotes – knowledge of strategies.

Components	Mothers Quotes
Increased application of evidence-based language stimulation strategies.	"If they take a topic in school, they talk about it in Arabic (present it to me)."
	"When I explain a word in Arabic, I explain it in Arabic instead of using English translation."
	"Correct their grammar through modeling or encourage them to reflect on the sentence they said."
	"Storytelling to improve language development. The difference between formal and informal language."
Increased intentionality of Arabic development	"You open my mind. I used to think I was only going to develop their English."
	"Intentionally spending the majority of the day in Arabic."
	"I have taken the first step to maintain Arabic with my children."

Application of evidence-based strategies to develop Arabic

The third theme that mothers indicated from the data is the application of the language stimulation strategies discussed in the intervention. The qualitative post-interview has displayed the following components in applying the mothers' language strategies in the intervention with their children.

There was a difference in the reception of children from their mothers' efforts in maintaining the home language. Younger children (K-5) were more receptive and interested in using Arabic. Language shift is a common phenomenon reported in minority-majority contact situations. *Language shift* refers to the changes in language use across time and generations. The process in which the immigrant community uses the language across various contexts or more frequently as children increase contact with the majority language, especially in school, is a move toward adopting the majority language as a means of communication. There are discrimination and stigmas associated with speaking a language other than English in the U.S.[154] Therefore, older children may prefer to speak the dominant community language to avoid discrimination.

Family isolation and mothers being the primary keepers of Arabic exacerbate the language shift, reducing opportunities for individuals to use the home language across contexts. Mothers reported their husbands speak Arabic to their children. However, the mother reported that the husbands are the primary breadwinners and work most of the day. All the mothers in the intervention were stay-at-home mothers. The mothers felt they were the primary individuals to teach and maintain Arabic in the household. High-quality language exposure entails the use of the language in social interactions.[155] Opportunities to interact with multiple speakers in

---

[154] Deaux, 2006.
[155] DeLoache et al., 2010.

various contexts have been linked to vocabulary learning in bilingual children.[156] Therefore, family isolation and lack of opportunities to use the language might cause language loss.

The most valuable strategy the mothers reported is the distinction between formal and formal Arabic. The Arabic language has two main variations: Modern Standard Arabic (MSA), also referred to as *fuS-Ha,* and regional dialects. MSA is the formal language used in books, media, and legal documents. On the other hand, Arabic dialects are informal languages that are used within a specific region or country. Mothers felt more confident maintaining the dialect, which is grammatically and structurally different from MSA.[157] As a result, mothers outsourced teaching formal Arabic to tutors and reading books (e.g., Qur'an).

---

[156] Hoff and Core, 2013.
[157] Farghaly and Shaalan, 2009.

Table 3. Mothers' quotes – application of strategies

Components	Mothers Quotes
Age differences in the receptiveness of the strategies. Specifically, preschool and elementary children enjoyed the play-based strategy and were more receptive to using and learning Arabic.	"They like it—especially the young ones. The older ones in high school do not respond. They want to play video games and be with their friends. The younger ones have less homework from school, so we have more time to play in Arabic."
The strategy that mothers felt most helpful was the usage of formal language.	"To use formal Arabic and correct their grammar through modeling or encourage them to reflect on the sentence they said."
Family isolation limited the usage of Arabic.	"We do not have a community here to use Arabic with. I do not have a car to enroll them in Arabic classes, for example, or activities outside the house."
Mothers used more dialect/colloquial Arabic than formal Arabic.	"I feel confident they will speak our dialect, but I am not sure how they will be proficient in formal Arabic. They can read the Qur'an, but I do not think they understand it fully."
Mothers were the primary teachers of Arabic in their children's environment.	"Their father works all the time. Through the phone, when we talk to the family."
	"Myself. Online tutoring is one time per week for 30 min and focuses on reciting and reading the Qur'an. Husband speaks all in Arabic."
	"My husband used to explain concepts in English but now in Arabic. We remind each other to speak in Arabic all the time. You know, sometimes it is hard when we are tired."

Addressing the need for comprehensive support in preserving Arabic language and literacy among immigrant families

The fourth theme is the support mothers reported they need to continue maintaining Arabic usage and literacy with their children. Although mothers reported benefits in terms of increasing intentionality of the use of language strategies, their children's frequency of usage of Arabic did not change across the term of the intervention. The lack of progress might be due to the small sample or language development taking more than six weeks. The qualitative data shows that mothers need support beyond their individual effort to maintain the language, which may contribute to the no-change in the quantitative data.

Table 4. Mothers' quotes – support needed.

Components	Mothers Quotes
Teaching literacy in Arabic (spelling, writing, and reading)	"Differentiating between alphabets through presenting two letters and asking them to point. Slowly putting two alphabets together and identifying the sounds."
	"How to teach them Arabic writing and reading."
Increased opportunities to speak Arabic outside the house.	"Mainly, the children use Arabic to talk to family back home or to us. Between each other they code-switch between the two languages. Again, with other Arab children, they speak all in English."
	"It is Arabic at home and online tutoring, but all English in the community. Sometimes, we interact with other Arabic families, but it is like once a month."
School environment that encourages multilingualism.	"Bilingual schooling"
	"Use Arabic at home"

The focus of this intervention was on oral language rather than literacy development. Mothers reported that they must know how to teach literacy, spelling, and writing in Arabic. Students with strong reading skills in their home language also have strong reading skills in their second language.[158] Additional intervention focusing on literacy development might be needed to support mothers in teaching reading and writing to their children.

Language loss occurs mainly in contexts where minimal support is provided for the home language. Thus, due to the sociolinguist environment, factors such as different values are placed in a minority-majority language dichotomy. This is typical for immigrant communities that speak a different language than the host country's. The language disparity between the home and second languages is due to reduced home language usage across domains.

Exploring the dynamics of language, power, and identity: Insights from Syrian emergent bilinguals and their families

We need to understand the power dynamics of language in the historical and current context of race and socioeconomic status. The sample of the study consists of emergent bilingual students from Syrian background and their mothers, who are disadvantaged by lacking the (a) dominant language (e.g., English) proficiency and (b) access associated with socioeconomic-related services (e.g., bilingual schooling). They are subjected to raciolinguistic ideologies, which refer to the relationship between language and race that reflect their marginalized experience in preserving their home language (Arabic).[159] History has indicated a bias for the mainstream society (English), which stems from colonial roots. This tends to isolate those whose ethno-racial and sociolinguistic backgrounds do not conform to the dominant culture.[160] School and home practices are microcosms of the greater societal ideologies.

---

[158] August, Shanahan, and Escamilla, 2009.
[159] Alim, 2016.
[160] Flores and Rosa, 2015.

All the mothers who participated in the intervention highly valued maintaining the Arabic language at home. Mothers indicated that they supported the home language to connect their children to their cultural heritage and to gain a cognitive bilingual advantage (e.g., flexible thinking). Mothers reported increased awareness of the benefits of bilingualism and language transfer of skills, which may have contributed to their empowerment to use the linguistic resource Arabic to support their child's overall language development. All mothers in the intervention were the households' sole "teachers" of Arabic. Mothers also reported limited opportunities to use Arabic outside the home, which may contribute to the mothers feeling that maintaining and developing the home language is their responsibility alone.

Mothers reported differences across their children's ages regarding their perception and willingness to use Arabic. Older children might feel language power dynamics since school and their peers use mainly English, which may cause them to be less interested in maintaining Arabic.[161] Another critical barrier to home language development is the limited opportunities to use the home language outside the home environment. For example, mothers indicated that their children mainly use Arabic with the immediate family, but when these same children meet other Arabic-speaking children, they tend to speak English. This is an example of raciolinguistic ideology that is reflected in the school and culture of marginalizing minoritized languages.

Since Arabic is a diglossic language, the mothers in this study felt more comfortable teaching their children informal Arabic than formal Arabic. Despite the emphasis on colloquial language, mothers reported that teaching standard Arabic is vital so their children get access to knowledge in written form in Arabic.

The fourth theme emerged from mothers' comments about the resources needed to support their children's Arabic language

---

[161] Menken and Kleyn, 2010.

development: strategies for formal language literacy, school programming to support multilingualism, and opportunities to use the home language across contexts and speakers. Support from the community in terms of school, social opportunities, and parent education is needed to maintain and develop home language in emergent bilingual students.

Mothers reported a lack of support from the school in maintaining the home language. In the U.S. education system, children are immersed in a majority language with limited support and exposure to their home language. The dominance of a monolingual model originates from a culture of colonization.[162] This is referred to as subtractive bilingualism when the second language acquisition comes at the cost of losing the home language.[163] The barriers of limited context, people, language power dynamics, and lack of school support might all contribute to a home language loss.

To prevent language loss, schools and communities need to support the development of students' home language. Dual-language schooling has effectively eliminated the academic opportunity gap between emergent bilinguals and their peers. Emergent bilingual learners take an average of six years to reach grade-level achievement if they start in Kindergarten in quality dual-language schooling in both the home language and the second language with at least half of the instructional time in their home language. Emergent bilingual students require longer, seven to ten years, to become fluent in English if they have not had the opportunity to receive instruction in their home language.[164] Many emergent bilingual students in this situation do not reach grade-level achievement. The school system often refers to them as "long-term English learners." Students in dual-language programs have higher academic achievement and engagement with the learning process than their emergent bilingual

---

[162] Motha, 2006.
[163] Valenzuela, 1999.
[164] Collier and Thomas, 2017.

peers who are not in dual-language classes.[165] High-quality, long-term bilingual programs close the educational gaps between emergent bilinguals and their peers after five to six years of schooling.

When bilingual schooling is not possible, we can implement practices that support students' home language in the classroom. Translanguaging is an effective classroom strategy that can be used to encourage multilingualism. *Translanguaging* pedagogies are instructional approaches that enable students to fluidly use their linguistic repertoire in ways that reflect how bilingual people naturally use language. Examples of translanguaging in a classroom may include students inspired to create stories with bilingual characters, engage in peer-to-peer conversations in the home language, and collaboratively translate (from English to the home language).[166]

Many immigrant communities establish community-led supplementary educational programs to maintain the home language. These programs can be on the weekend or during the week after school hours. These schools were found to play a central role within the community by functioning as an essential place for socialization for children and their families.[167] These programs can provide children additional opportunities to use Arabic outside the house and with peers their age.

All caregivers can support their children's literacy and language development, regardless of their educational background and English literacy. Teachers can help caregivers by encouraging them to read and engage their children in stories using the home language. Also, teachers can send what the child is learning about in class to the parent to reinforce learning using the home language. Teachers and researchers are encouraged to continue emphasizing the positive implications of caregiver interventions in increasing caregiver

---

[165] De Jong and Howard, 2009.
[166] García and Lin, 2016.
[167] Alsahafi, 2017.

knowledge and using evidence-based strategies. Dual-language schooling, inclusive language practices in the classroom (e.g., *Translanguaging*), weekend/weekday home language programs, and caregiver support might be more effective and holistic when used together to develop students' home language. These are possible solutions that can be used by schools and teachers depending on the resources available in a particular context.

11. Unveiling the shared heritage of Arabic and Amazigh

Mohamed Foula

Exploring the linguistic interplay: Arabic and Amazigh in the heart of Morocco

Venturing into the rich landscape of linguistic diversity, this account is informed by nearly two decades of my experience teaching Arabic to non-native speakers, with a particular emphasis on the Demnate region of Morocco. The Tachelhit dialect of the Amazigh language is prevalent in this area, providing a distinctive vantage point for examining the mutual influences between Arabic and Amazigh cultures. My journey to uncover the shared linguistic heritage between these languages culminated in creating a lexicon that connects two thousand roots, showcasing the profound interconnections that blur the lines of linguistic identity. Delving into authoritative texts such as Ibn Manzur's *Lisan al-Arab*, this investigation goes beyond academic interest, aiming to deepen our comprehension of how these languages intertwine and their collective impact on educational approaches and cultural viewpoints. The discovery of approximately ten thousand shared terms enhances the learning experience. It stands as a tribute to the longstanding tradition of linguistic intermingling fostered by centuries of shared living spaces and interactions.

This methodology has enriched my teaching practices and served as a vital tool in psychologically bridging the gap between Arabic and Amazigh for learners, reinforcing the notion that these languages share a multitude of linguistic roots. My research has identified about two hundred fundamental linguistic roots, each giving rise to several words and cumulatively contributing to a remarkable ten thousand shared terms. These terms often mirror each other phonetically and semantically, further highlighting the linguistic synergy between Amazigh and Arabic.

The relationship between the Amazigh and Arabic languages is marked by fascinating linguistic connections, especially evident in the realm of linguistic borrowing, a common phenomenon when languages or dialects coexist within a specific geographical area, intertwined by shared territories, trade, and social ties.

Predominantly spoken across North Africa and parts of the African coast, the Amazigh language, often classified under the Indo-European family, appears markedly different from Arabic to its native speakers. Nonetheless, this discussion seeks to illuminate the deep-seated similarities between these languages, challenging the traditional classification of Amazigh as non-Semitic and inviting a reconsideration of the impact of colonial-era linguistic studies on our understanding of the region's language dynamics.

Exploring pronominal echoes: Tracing Arabic and Amazigh pronoun parallels

In Arabic, the plural possessive pronoun "نا" plays a crucial role in denoting ownership, transforming "book" into "our book" as "كتابنا." This linguistic feature showcases the nuanced complexity of Arabic possessive structures. Intriguingly, the Amazigh language adopts a similar phonetic element, "ن," in its possessive pronouns, yet it extends its usage across singular and plural forms. For instance, the singular possessive form in Amazigh is expressed as "لكْتَابْنُّو" for "our book." In contrast, the plural takes on a slightly different form, "لكْتَابْنَّغْ," with the "غ" morpheme suggesting plurality. This consistent presence of the "ن" sound in Amazigh's possessive pronouns, regardless of number, mirrors the linguistic pattern observed in French, exemplified by "notre livre" for "our book," where a singular possessive form encompasses a plural notion without altering the pronoun.

The table below elucidates the parallel structures and shared phonetic elements in the pronoun systems of Arabic and Amazigh, underscoring the linguistic bridges that connect these two rich languages. This comparative analysis highlights the shared linguistic heritage and points to the broader Afro-Asiatic language family's intricate tapestry, offering insights into the historical and cultural exchanges that have shaped these languages over centuries.

Pronouns in Amazigh and Arabic

Pronoun Meaning	Arabic	Amazigh	Note
Dual & Plural (First Person)	نحن (We)	نَكُن	Both have the ن sound consistent
Singular (First Person)	أنا (I)	نْك	Both have the ن sound consistent
Singular (Third Person)	هو/ هي (He/She)	نْتَّ/ نتَّ	In Arabic: Speaker pronouns. In Amazigh: Absent pronouns
Dual & Plural (Third Person)	هما، هم/ هما، هن (They)	نُتْن/ نُتْنت	In Arabic: Speaker pronouns. In Amazigh: Absent pronouns

Both Arabic and Amazigh mark femininity with the letter تاء. In Arabic, ذال is replaced by تاء to indicate feminine forms, as seen in الذي becoming التي and هذان turning into هاتان. Amazigh, on the other hand, keeps the دال and appends تاء, transforming وَد into تد to denote femininity.

Unveiling gender markers: The articulation of femininity in Arabic and Amazigh

In Arabic, femininity is often marked by the elongated 'Alif' or the 'Taa marbouta.' However, there are exceptions where one has to refer to a dictionary to determine gender. For example, the word البئر (the well) is feminine, as mentioned in the Qur'an verse وبئر معطلة (Al-Hajj, verse: 45). In Amazigh, femininity is indicated by adding two 'Taa's, one at the beginning and one at the end. For example, تَسْدَلْت (head cover). It is also noteworthy to mention the similarity, if not the exact match, of the Amazigh root word to the Arabic root سَدَل which means "to cover," as in أَسْدَلَ الستار (he draped the curtain).

Comparison between the linguistic roots in Arabic and Amazigh

Now, we present examples of similar words, some of which are similar in pronunciation and meaning, others only in pronunciation:

- أَبَر: In colloquial Arabic, it is لِيبْرَا, used for sewing. It is suggested that the term is inspired by a natural resemblance, namely the "scorpion's sting." In the *Lisan Al-Arab* dictionary, it is mentioned: "The scorpion's sting: what it stings with." In Amazigh, it is إبْريت, meaning "it hurt him." The one who is hurt by the scorpion's sting is referred to as من أَبْرته العَقْرب.
- أَبِر, أَبَار: In Arabic, it is the person who waters the palm trees. In Amazigh, it is أسَرَّار. A phonetic correspondence exists between the beginning "Hamza" in Arabic and the ending "Ra" in Amazigh.
- أبْرار in Amazigh describes animals, particularly horses. In Arabic, it is أبرش, which means speckled.
- يأجور: In colloquial Arabic, it is الياجور without the "Hamza." This omission is expected in the Maghreb. In *Lisan Al-Arab*, it is mentioned that ياجور refers to clay cooking used for construction.
- أتَّى: In Amazigh, إطَّايْت means followed him or chased him away. In *Lisan Al-Arab*, it indicates making way for water flow.

Mosaic of Tongues 163

- أَخَر: Common in colloquial Arabic and Amazigh, but its use came later in Amazigh. It is used as آخِرُ ثَمَن in colloquial Arabic, and لْخَّرْ نُوَاوَال in Amazigh, meaning "last word".

- إد: Used in Amazigh both as a descriptor and a verb. The verb إد means went. As an adjective, it describes someone who lost his mind. In *Lisan Al-Arab*, it is mentioned: أَدَّ فِي الأَرْض: went.

- أُودُم: In Amazigh, it means face/faces, whether it is a person's face or the surface of something. In classical Arabic, a similar term for surface is أديم, like the earth's surface.

- أرث: In the Sous region of Amazigh, إثْرَات means to overcome. In another dialect of Amazigh, it is إرَّات. The term suggests the economy of linguistic expression. In *Lisan Al-Arab*, أرَّثَ means to cause discord among people.

- أزم: In Amazigh, the word for lion is إزْم (Izm). In the Arabic lexicon, الأَزْم (Al-Azm) refers to a forceful bite with the whole mouth or specifically with the canines. The canines are called الأَوَازِم (Al-Awazim). It seems the term transitioned from referring to the canines to the animal itself, or vice versa, which is difficult to explain.

- In the context of fasting, the Amazigh say أُزُومْغ (Azumgh), meaning fasting. The similarity between the term for fasting and the Amazigh term is evident. The 'Z' sound may stand for the Arabic 'S' sound, which we don't need to affirm here. In Arabic references, الأَزْم (Al-Azm) can mean "abstinence from food." Arabs used to refer to a single meal a day as أَزَمَة (Azma), suggesting the person is heeding the advice of Harith bin Kalda to Umar when asked about the ideal diet: "It is al-Azm," which means not introducing new food to a stomach that still has food.

- أزو: The Amazigh say أزّا (Azza), which is a sensation in the throat due to stomach acidity or something similar. In Surah Maryam (19:83) in the Qur'an, it says, "Did you not see that We sent the devils upon the disbelievers, tormenting them with azza?" The Arabic lexicon explains الأزو (Al-Azwo) as distress or discomfort.

- The Amazigh use أَزْوُو (Azwu) to denote the movement and speed of the wind. It is known that facing such wind would make one shrink and huddle to preserve body warmth and reduce the wind's impact. The Arabic lexicon suggests that آزَانِي means "he embraced me." This illustrates the causative relationship between the Classical Arabic and Amazigh terms: the former is the result, and the latter is the cause.

- أسف: In Amazigh, أَسِيف' (Asyif) means river. In the Arabic lexicon, الأَسِيف'(Al-Asyif) refers to a barren land that doesn't yield crops or a thin land that hardly produces anything. The commonality is the land; a river is on the land, and its flowing water doesn't allow plants to grow, showing the semantic closeness of the two terms.

- بقل: لْبَقُّول (Lbaqqoola) in colloquial and Amazigh refers to a dish made from the first sprouts of the legume plant. The Arabic lexicon describes بَقَل (Baqla) as "appeared" or "emerged." The relationship is about appearance; the dish is made from the first sprouts of the legume. Further support is provided from the Arabic lexicon: any green plant emerging from the ground can be referred to as بقل (Baql), and there are references to the term meaning "leg" or "foolish," but any green plant is referred to as "Baql."

- أبوقال (Abuqal): In Amazigh, it refers to the head. The head attracts attention in a human being, as it is the most important part that should be visible. In colloquial Moroccan Arabic, a person is also described as بُوقال (Buqal) as a euphemism for foolishness. In *Lisan Al-Arab*, باقل (Baqal) is mentioned as the name of a man who is used as an example of someone with a defect, العي (al-'ayy), which refers to a lack of intellect.

- بقي (Baqi): It remains the same in both languages. In Moroccan colloquial Arabic, it is باقي (Baqi), and in Amazigh, it is اِبْق (Ibqa). Its presence starts from reception until the very end.

- بكر (Bakr): It refers to a type of fig in both Amazigh and Moroccan colloquial Arabic known as ْلْباكور (Lbakour). It is what appears first from the fig tree. In *Lisan Al-Arab*, الباكور (Al-Bakour) is described as the early or quickly realized. It also states that الباكورة (Al-Bakoura) means the first fruit. For speakers of either language, the term ْلْباكور (Lbakour) can sometimes be derogatory, referring to a young person who hasn't yet experienced much of life, likened to a fruit that ripened too quickly.

- دكل (Dakl): In Amazigh, it is أَمْدَكُّل (Amdakul). The prefix أم (Am) denotes the agent noun form, which is an additional form. The word means friend or companion. In *Lisan Al-Arab*, to be affectionate or indulgent with someone is expressed by the verb تَدَكَّلَ عَلَيْهِ (Tadakkala 'alayhi). How can a friend not be lenient to another?

- دلح (Dalh): دَلَأْح (Dallah) and تَدَلَّاحْت (Tadallahat) refers to the watermelon. *Lisan Al-Arab* mentions it in relation to something heavy with water. The fruit is known for its high water content. In Amazigh, اِدْلَح (Idlah) refers to a man walking aimlessly, moving here and there. Due to its heavy load, the *Lisan Al-Arab* notes a slow-moving animal, and an aimless walker's pace is often slow since he isn't rushing toward any particular destination.

- دلس (Dals): In Amazigh, it is تِلَّاسْ (Tilas), which means darkness. Lisan Al-Arab defines الدَّلَس (Al-Dalas) as darkness.

- عبر (A'bar): عْبَرْ / إِعْبَر (A'bar/I'bar) means to measure distance or cross over. *Lisan Al-Arab* defines it as crossing a river, a path, or the side of something. It might also mean making the right choice, the one who looks at something and deduces from it. It is as if the act of observing eventually leads to making the correct decision. لْعَبْرَت/لْعَبْرَ (L'abra/L'abrat) relates to measurement, its weight is between 16 and 18 kilograms.

- عرج (Arj): أرْجْدال/لْعْرَج (La'raj/Arjdal) means limping or a person who limps. In Amazigh pronunciation, the only missing letter from the Arabic word is ع ('Ain). The word might also have a combination of two words رجْل (Leg) and أعرج (Lame).
- لْعْزيب (La'zib): A summer camp for livestock herds, where they move to higher mountain areas with abundant pastures and cooler temperatures. The term relates to someone staying with his livestock away from people in pasture lands. It is an area with abundant forage, and العزيب (Al-'Azib) refers to camels or sheep that stray away from their herders in the pasture. The commonality is the act of moving livestock to distant lands with abundant forage.

Navigating the linguistic labyrinth: Unveiling the shared heritage of Arabic and Amazigh

This chapter concludes an intricate exploration of the linguistic landscapes where Arabic and Amazigh converge, revealing a complex web of shared lexicon, evolving semantics, and cultural interplay. Through examining terms ranging from human anatomy, like أبوقال (head), to natural phenomena, such as بكر (a type of fig) and دلح (watermelon), we uncover the dynamic nature of language as it crosses cultural thresholds and adapts to diverse contexts. The analysis illuminates how words can shift in meaning, enriched by their usage in varying scenarios, thus painting a vivid picture of the interconnectedness of language and culture. The recurrent invocation of *Lisan Al-Arab* cements the historical depth of these linguistic ties and enriches the discourse with authoritative insights. This chapter, therefore, is not merely an academic inquiry but a cultural voyage, unraveling the intertwined narratives of Arabic and Amazigh languages and celebrating their shared heritage and mutual influences.

12. Learning Arabic outside the Arab world: A language of identity that opens doors of opportunity.

Sarab Al Ani
Yale University

Who is a heritage language learner?

The answer to this question is a complex matter that carries a lot of ambiguity and generalization. In most cases, it depends on the purpose behind defining it, whether that purpose is political or historical, considers the repercussions of the educational process and curriculum development, or focuses on the learner's identity and social status.[168] Therefore, when definitions try to outline the profile of a heritage language learner, these definitions are criticized for either being too inclusive or too exclusive, depending on that purpose.[169] For instance, in 2001, Valdés defined a heritage language learner as someone raised in a home where a non-English language is spoken and either speaks or understands that language.[170] However, he revisited this definition in 2005, proposing a broader, more inclusive definition, stating that a heritage language is not used by the majority of the community for daily communication but is used by societal groups known as minorities. Therefore, the descendants of this language who are interested in studying, maintaining, and revitalizing it are heritage language learners.[171] Montrul agrees with this broad definition, adding that a heritage

---

[168] Hillman, 2019.
[169] Hillman, 2019.
[170] Valdés, 2001.
[171] Valdés, 2005.

language learner who grew up with the heritage language is now a conscious individual seeking to learn or relearn it, aiming to improve their current performance level.[172] A deficiency in knowledge and performance in the heritage language arises because the learner grew up in a community where the home language differs from the external community language, likely due to them and their family being immigrants to that community or country.[173] The American Council on the Teaching of Foreign Languages generally describes heritage language learners as those who begin their language studies with what the Council refers to as "kitchen language."[174] They start their language studies with a cultural foundation, but their proficiency in communication might be minimal or nonexistent. The Council adds that there's another group among these learners that can communicate using one language dialect and are proficient, in addition to their knowledge of the standard or formal dialect.

The previous definitions mainly focus on two critical aspects of defining someone as a heritage language learner: the cognitive and performance level in the language and belonging to a specific group (minority). At the same time, there are broader concepts in determining these conditions; perhaps the most famous is the concept proposed by Van Deusen-Scholl, which is based on the idea that a heritage language learner is anyone who sees a cultural connection to a specific language, regardless of their actual knowledge of that language, which can sometimes be nonexistent.[175] In an interview with Scalera, Webb says that heritage language learners have a personal or emotional connection to a non-English language since there's a strong bond between them and that language.[176] For

---

[172] Montrul, 2010.
[173] Montrul, 2008.
[174] American Council on the Teaching of Foreign Languages, 2006.
[175] Van Deusen-Scholl, 2003.
[176] Scalera, 2011.

Fishman, there is enough for a familial connection between the learner and the language they study to consider them a heritage language learner.[177] In their article, Hornberger and Wang agree with Fishman's idea about the family connection, adding that the connection might extend beyond the immediate nuclear family.[178] Meanwhile, Carreira focuses on the identity factor, saying that heritage language learners form an incredibly diverse group whose members share one characteristic: their linguistic or affiliative need to learn a language connected to their family background. These needs arise from their limited exposure to that language during their formative years, pushing them to pursue learning it in structured lessons.[179]

The status of the Arabic language in the United States

The Arabic language in the United States has witnessed a notable increase in the number of students wanting to study it over the past two decades, even though it is one of the less commonly taught languages in terms of the number of academic institutions that offer it.[180] Welles documented in 2004 the leap in the number of students studying Arabic in educational institutions in the United States from 5,500 students in 1998 to 10,584 in 2000, which is more than double. This increase surpassed other less commonly taught languages in the United States, such as Chinese or Japanese. This growing ratio was not limited to institutes and universities alone. The number of children studying Arabic in private and public primary schools also saw a similar rise. Greer & Johnson, in 2009, pointed to the presence of about 50,000 students studying Arabic in the United States. Some believe that this increase came as a result of the rise in the number of Muslim and Arab immigrants to the U.S. due to globalization

---

[177] Fishman, 2000.
[178] Hornberger and Wang, 2008.
[179] Carriera, 2004.
[180] Husseinali, 2010 ; Furman et. al, 2010 ; Rhodes and Pufahl, 2010.

policies, the invasions of Iraq and Afghanistan, and the repercussions of the September 11 events and the Arab Spring.[181] These factors collectively led to an increased interest in Arabic as it became a vital language for national security.[182] The 2010 American Community Survey results confirmed that Arab immigrants increased by 76% compared to 1990.[183] This growth presented several challenges to those in the field of teaching Arabic. The first challenge was the rapid and widespread establishment of new programs teaching Arabic in American universities and colleges.[184] For example, these programs increased by 82% between 1998 and 2000[185], and this number continues to grow.[186] The second challenge is to effectively create these programs to meet the diverse needs of this growing number of learners, with their varying objectives, motivations, desires, and backgrounds.[187] From the above, it is clear that the reasons that led to an increase in the number of students wanting to study Arabic in the U.S. also resulted in their diversification. They are a mix of students studying it for the first time and others with some prior connection (learners of heritage Arabic).

Who is a heritage learner of the Arabic language?

From the above, it is clear that Arabic language learners are generally a large and diverse group that has expanded in the United States over the past two decades. The same applies to learners of heritage Arabic. As we saw in the definition of heritage language learners above, there are broad, inclusive definitions and others that are less inclusive, just as is the case with the concept of heritage Arabic learners. For

---

[181] Abourehab and Azaz, 2020; Husen, 2011; Al-Batal, 2007; Ayouby, 2007.
[182] Al-Batal, 2007.
[183] Zabarah, 2015.
[184] Al-Batal, 2007.
[185] Al-Batal and Belnap, 2006.
[186] Wahhan et. al, 2014.
[187] Al-Batal, 2007, Al-Batal and Belnap, 2006.

example, Albirini believes heritage Arabic learners are students who have enrolled in Arabic classes in American universities and institutions.[188] They are of Arab origin, coming from families that migrated to the United States from Arab countries, and speak one of the many dialects of Arabic. When Ibrahim and Allam surveyed to understand the composition of heritage Arabic learners, they found it divided into four sections.[189] The first section includes learners whose parents are of Arab origin and who heard or learned one of the Arabic dialects at home. In the second section, there are learners with only one parent of Arab origin, and they did not speak Arabic at home while growing up. Muslim students from non-Arab countries formed the third section of this group; they know Arabic from learning the Qur'an but do not use it for communication. Temples describe them as learners of heritage religious language. The fourth and last section includes Arab learners who live in Arab countries and come from Arab families. They constantly speak one of the Arabic dialects at home. Still, they completed their primary education in international schools, so they did not get a chance to learn Modern Standard Arabic (MSA). Thus, we see a clear difference between the two definitions.

Albad tried to define heritage Arabic learners, considering their knowledge of MSA specifically, given that most Arabic classes in the United States teach MSA, not the dialects.[190] This categorization resulted in two groups: learners who know Arabic in one of its dialects but have never studied MSA, and the second group includes non-Arab Muslims who only know Arabic from the Qur'an. The study conducted by Husseinali concluded by combining heritage Arabic learners from non-Arab Muslims and heritage Arabic learners of Arab origin into one group, as he believes they all have a cultural

---

[188] Albirini, 2014.
[189] Ibrahim and Allam, 2006.
[190] Albad, 2016.

affinity for the Arabic language.¹⁹¹ Engman arrived at a similar conclusion as Husseinali, stating that there are prominent shared cultural resources between heritage Arabic learners from non-Arab Muslims and heritage Arabic learners of Arab origin.¹⁹²

What are the motivations for learning Arabic as a heritage language?

De Bot believes that the motivations behind learning a language and the learner's perception of that language are the foundation for the entire learning journey.¹⁹³ All learners of the Arabic language, regardless of their types and attitudes, hold a positive view of it, its speakers, and their culture.¹⁹⁴ However, two primary motivations drive foreign language learners to study them.¹⁹⁵ The first type is integrative motivations, which stem from the desire to communicate with the language's speakers and connect with their culture. The second type of foreign language learning motivation is instrumental, driven by the learner's desire to utilize the language for future employment. It is essential to distinguish between the motivation to learn a foreign language and the orientation toward understanding it. Gardner and MacIntyre clarified that the orientation to learn a language involves the goals that motivate someone to learn a language.

In contrast, orientation encompasses continuous, strenuous efforts in the learning journey of that language. The motivations (i.e., reasons) that drive learners to study foreign languages include reasons for travel, political reasons, getting to know other cultures, securing a job, and the learner's cultural identity.¹⁹⁶ Husseinali's study

---

[191] Husseinali, 2006.
[192] Engman, 2016.
[193] De Bot, 2007.
[194] Naji, 2021.
[195] Garmner and Lambert, 1972.
[196] Husseinali, 2006.

revealed that learners of Arabic as a heritage language have more reasons to study Arabic due to their identity. Dhahir also agreed, emphasizing that learners of Arabic as a heritage language possess a more significant passion that drives them to continue learning the language that brings them closer to their identity, culture, and religion, in addition to their desire to learn Arabic for future employment.[197] Zabarah concluded in her study that when discussing the reasons, motivations, and orientation to learn Arabic, all language learners refer to their communication with Arabic speakers.

Regarding learners of Arabic as a heritage language, Zabarah believes there's a fundamental difference between them and those who learn Arabic as a foreign language.[198] Namely, the previously mentioned Arabic speakers are close family members or friends who form an integrated support system that is not available to learners of Arabic as a foreign language. It is evident from the above that learners of Arabic as a heritage language have unique characteristics compared to their peers who learn Arabic as a foreign language regarding their motivations, orientation towards it, and the support they might receive from their families and friends.

Learners of the Arabic language as a heritage language: Requirements of the educational process.

Now that we know who the learners of the Arabic language are and how they differ in their divisions, motivations, and orientation toward studying Arabic, it is no longer difficult to understand the existence of specific educational requirements accompanying them. They have a strong sense of identity and thus have more significant social motivations than career motivations,[199] especially given their

---

[197] Dhahir, 2015.
[198] Zabarah, 2015.
[199] Husseinali, 2012.

increasing numbers over the past two decades.[200] At the same time, learners of Arabic as a heritage language show more interest in improving their communication abilities in Arabic than in learning about the culture of Arab countries, which they feel they are somewhat familiar with.[201] For the same reason, the study by Trentman concluded that the opportunity to study Arabic in a program designed for Arabic studies in an Arab country (in summer, for instance) provides the most suitable circumstance for these learners to perceive their need to learn both culture and language, especially when they face situations that compel them to use Arabic and interact with its speakers, where their identity becomes part of that interaction.[202] As for the Muslim learners of heritage Arabic, they are more interested in learning about their religion than the language itself.[203] Despite the diverse backgrounds, dialects, and motivations of learners of Arabic as a heritage language, Albirini found that the extent of their use of Arabic at home is the only significant factor affecting their Arabic learning, regardless of other factors.[204] Thus, we can conclude that those exposed to Arabic at home and who can practice it there will be better able to learn it more efficiently, and they are also more likely to retain it for a more extended period.[205] At first glance, some might think that segregating learners of Arabic as a heritage language in separate classes because of their unique characteristics might be the best approach. However, the study by Azaz & Abourehab advocated for their integration with other Arabic learners, noting that this could enrich Arabic language classes, particularly since some of these learners' knowledge of spoken Arabic dialects can be a valuable resource for accessing

---

[200] Azaz and Abourehab, 2019.
[201] Husseinali, 2012.
[202] Trentman, 2015.
[203] Husseinali, 2012.
[204] Albirini, 2014.
[205] Husseinali, 2012.

Modern Standard Arabic if utilized optimally.[206] Thus, Azaz & Abourehab believe that the most pressing need is to develop programs to train Arabic language teachers to deal with learners of Arabic as a heritage language to ensure the best outcomes. Although Zabarah emphasizes that placing learners of Arabic as a heritage language in separate classes is the ideal situation,[207] she also agrees with Azaz & Abourehab that integrating them with the rest of the learners requires significant teacher training to serve both groups fully, especially since separating these two types of learners is often not a feasible option for schools and universities.

Redefining Arabic language education for heritage learners in the U.S.

Heritage learners of the Arabic language in the United States constitute a large and diverse group. Their numbers have grown over the past decades and continue to expand daily. Some speak one of the Arabic dialects at home, while others do not. Some are of Arab descent, while others are connected to Arabic through religious ties, having been introduced to it through their knowledge of the Qur'an. They all share a cultural bond with the Arabic language and its culture. Still, their motivations and orientations to study it may differ somewhat, not to mention how these motivations and orientations differ from those looking at Arabic as a foreign language. In most American institutes and universities, heritage learners of Arabic are merged into a single class with learners of Arabic as a foreign language. This merging decision might either enrich the educational process or hinder it.

Considering all the factors and circumstances surrounding heritage learners of the Arabic language, it becomes evident that academic institutions in the United States need to pay close attention

---

[206] Azaz and Abourehab, 2019.
[207] Zabarah, 2015.

to this segment of learners and their needs, significantly as their numbers are continually growing. Perhaps the best starting point for these institutions is to provide and allocate more training for teachers of the Arabic language, aiming to equip them with the appropriate tools and educational plans. This will enable them best to serve the needs of heritage learners of Arabic more suitably while maximizing the benefit for their peers studying Arabic as a foreign language.

PART 3:

ARABIC IN THE GLOBAL CONTEXT

13. Arabic in the digital era: Reaching a new concept of language

Hossameddine Abouzahr,

The Living Arabic Project

Standard Arabic (SA) now enjoys many high-quality digital learning tools, but dialects remain limited in the digital education field. However, this poses risks to literacy in Arabic, be it SA or dialects, and the ability to pass on Arabic. Arabic is characterized by diglossia, a split between everyday spoken dialects and the formal SA. It requires unique learning tools to build a solid basis in the mother tongue and dialects and facilitate learners bridging from their mother dialect to SA. Digital tools can support these efforts by adapting already available platforms and material to dialects, helping children bridge from their mother dialect to SA by raising awareness of diglossia and phonological and morphological differences between dialects and SA, and finally by building skills of code-switching and control that are particular to a diglossic context.

Technology can change the playing field

In recent years, we have witnessed increased usage of dialects in social media, private messaging, and even in the publishing of books. Although there remains resistance to using dialects in education, technology has again been gaining acceptance in media targeting youth, including books, graphic novels, and movies translated into both SA and the Egyptian dialect. However, the current material being developed seems to fall into the binary of either SA or dialect; particularly when considering education, the question of how to build tools that promote a multilingual education system seems largely ignored. As such, a sense of conflict between dialects and SA remains, and the literacy gap created by the current exclusive focus on SA in education shows no signs of being alleviated.

Using digital tools to develop new educational models specific to Arabic's diglossic situation can help close the literacy gap by acknowledging dialects in the education system and building on them to teach SA. Reviewing literacy statistics for Arab countries, Riham Shendy shows a considerable gap in literacy rates between Arab countries and their peers. She further summarizes the literature about the detrimental impact of teaching exclusively in SA on literacy and not acknowledging the mother tongue, that being dialects, highlighting the fact that it affects "phonological awareness, morphological awareness, phonological representation, word decoding, reading fluency, and letter naming" and noting that this negative impact is "greater for families of lower socioeconomic standing."[208] Digital tools, if developed correctly, allow for the quick development of educational platforms that can then be replicated and adapted to different contexts based on dialect and other factors.

Digital tools can also achieve a new language concept by showing SA and dialects in a complementary, supportive relationship rather than a competitive one. In multilingual societies across the globe, educational systems that acknowledge the mother tongue and work with it have been shown to improve literacy in the mother tongue and any future languages learned—the latter in Arabic's case, including SA.[209] Ministries of Education in the Arab countries, though, have refused to adopt any such approach, primarily because of a deep-set belief that teaching in dialects or even acknowledging them as languages will undermine SA, which is seen as holy and politically crucial because of its relationship to the Qur'an and Arab nationalism. Anthropologist Niloofar Haeri further notes that Arabs' blind praise of SA, with few able to master it, and the

---

[208] Shendy, 2022.
[209] Saiegh-Haddad and Spolsky, 2014; Myhill, 2014.

negative perception of dialects results in Arabs looking down on themselves (Haeri, 2009). Digital platforms that balance between SA and dialects and use them to reinforce one another can encourage Arabs to embrace dialects rather than reject them.

Arabic education in the tech world

There are many apps now available for Arab children, although most, if not all, of them are designed exclusively in SA. Some of the best apps include Antura wal-Huruf (*Antura and the Letters*) and It'am al-Wahash (*Feed the Monster*), designed to introduce children to basic letters, sounds, and first words through simple games.[210]

Several reading apps also exist for Arabic, unsurprisingly focused on SA since there is almost no children's literature in dialects. Many of these, such as *Nahla wa Nahil*, require a paid subscription. The app *Manga al-Arabiyya lil-Sighar*, which the Saudi Research and Media Group produces, includes original Arabic comics and translated material. Outside of apps, several online resources post reading materials, such as the United Arab Emirates *Board on Books for Young People* on Instagram, which posts readings of children's books.

There are also more comprehensive platforms that include a variety of material such as books, educational games, and videos, such as *Arabee*, *I Read Arabic*, *3asafeer*, *Kutubee*, *KamKalima*, and *Alefbata*, as well as bilingual-focused platforms such as CALEC's *Read in 2 Languages*. These platforms are relatively high quality but require a subscription for full access. In conversations with the author, the founders of *Arabee* and *I Read Arabic* acknowledged the lack of material in dialect. However, Little Thinking Minds has mentioned possibly creating some material in dialects.

---

[210] Norwegian Agency for Development Cooperation, 2017; Qualey, 2020.

Technology can open doors

From the above overview of digital learning tools for Arabic, it is clear that it is not the lack of tools per se that is the problem, but rather the lack of tools that address the underlying challenges of diglossia by building up a solid foundation in learners' mother dialect, bridging to SA, and teaching skills necessary to operate in a diglossic society. The following are three main approaches that can be used to generate learning tools designed for Arabic's diglossia. They capitalize on two critical aspects of technology: the ability to provide dynamic platforms so that content can be developed for multiple dialects quickly and at a low cost and the ability to put SA and dialects on par with each other to improve bridging between them and reduce bias in favor of one or the other.

Facilitating content creation in dialects

Those critical of using dialects in education often point to the plethora of dialects and the difficulty of creating material in each one as an insurmountable obstacle. No matter what final educational model is used, the first step in any multilingual approach to Arabic education is generating content in dialects and SA, and modern technology provides several avenues to achieve this.

A great way to start is to adapt existing tools to Arabic's complex diglossia by generating word lists that can be used with available applications such as flashcards, card matching games (like *Memory* and *Concentration*), and word jumble games. Apps like *Quizlet* and *AnkiApp* can be used for flashcards, and apps like *MyMemo* allow users to create their decks for card matching. The technology for many of these games exists, and some even have user-friendly versions that do not require coding knowledge to add new words. However, there is a lack of prepared word lists that can be used for dialects, putting the burden on users to develop everything from scratch. There is even a lack of authoritative sources on many dialects, much less word frequency studies by grade level. The most recent effort to overcome this is led by Arabic professors Geri

Atanassova, Laila Familiar, and Rasha Soliman to rate Arabic vocabulary according to Common European Framework of Reference (CEFR) proficiency levels. Currently, though, the plan is to provide a starting point of SA vocabulary that can then be adapted to dialects by individual instructors.

Word lists go beyond the early years of literacy and can be applied to various other situations, one of the most relevant being games. For example, tabletop and computer games such as Dungeons & Dragons (D&D) have become popular among Arab youth. However, when playing with Arabs, Arabic Professor Alexander Magidow noted that most of the specialized terms of monsters, weapons, and technical moves were used in English, so he started a D&D group by translating D&D rules and terms created by Ahmad Aljabry. The same professor has also translated part of an alternative set of rules known as Dungeon World. These game rules can be adapted to specific dialects, making them better fit with each region's distinct culture.

Making the best use of word lists requires gathering them in one place. A repository of word lists with the apps they work on or games they go with would go a long way to ease the burden on teachers and learners of creating their learning materials. Additionally, if machine translation technology was developed for inter-dialect translation, it could quickly translate most word lists from dialect to dialect.

Similar to changing word lists in a single program, video material can be dubbed into multiple dialects, which is more accessible than creating original content for each dialect. Whereas some entertainment (not geared toward education specifically) videos are now being dubbed into SA and the Egyptian dialect, there is no effort to dub into other dialects to expand the reach of videos. Simple educational videos such as the SA series *Adam wa Mishmish*, which was a significant success and has received more funding[211], lend themselves well to being dubbed into multiple dialects.

A more challenging approach that can yield massive amounts of material in dialects is to make a concerted effort to "localize" early learning material into dialects via machine translation so content producers do not have to recreate the wheel in each country. This localization process is a well-developed field and is used on even complex material such as video music lessons—where the software must differentiate between the spoken instruction and the actual music and transcribe and translate only the former— and so could easily be adapted to early literacy material.

However, this requires developing machine translation technology to translate between SA and dialects. Machine translation tools are being developed for dialects, such as Shaheen, developed by Qatar Computing Research Institute, and even Google Translate, which can handle some dialect terms now. Still, currently, neither tool allows a user to specify the input or output dialect. Nonetheless, the technology is moving in the right direction. Suppose more dialect data were made publicly available. In that case, there are enough open-source neural machine translation systems that tools could be adapted specifically to the education sector and to creating learning material in multiple dialects, perhaps even targeting subdialects.

Bridging from dialects to SA

A method shown to improve literacy in SA is building directly on learners' knowledge of their mother tongue and transferring that knowledge to SA, which might be called bridging. A World Bank report also notes that morphological awareness "helps children make links" between their mother dialect and SA.[212] One study showed that even "explicit knowledge and awareness of diglossia" was

---

[211] Wamda, 2021.
[212] Gregory et al., 2021.

enough to improve literacy.[213] This approach inherently makes sense: you must know where you are starting to reach your final destination. New digital tools can be built around bridging and supporting creative assessments to give a clear picture of what learners need to focus on.

Even for the early years of education, a flashcard app that includes the word in SA, a dialect, and an audio recording could help learners build upon words they already know. Primary learning material could also be done in both SA and dialect, with the teacher walking learners through the differences and similarities. Here, technology can again play a role. Sophisticated reading apps for some languages already allow learners to select specific words to hear the pronunciation. An additional recording of the word in dialect could be added, or what the equivalent word in dialect would be in cases where it is not simply a phonological difference. Once learners start to understand the phonological and lexical links, morphological awareness could also be taught, although teachers would have to be wary of not making lessons too grammar-intensive.

This author's work on *The Living Arabic Project* shows that dictionaries are another avenue to bridge between dialects. Modern technology allows for the easy display of multilingual dictionaries compared to print dictionaries, and apps could be built to enable users to search in SA, at least one dialect, and perhaps a third language such as English. Dictionary apps built for children can be a constant companion to young learners, who can quickly look up and compare words between their parent dialect and SA. The main challenge for such a tool is that dialect dictionaries are few and far between and are not written for children; Arabic-Arabic dialect dictionaries tend to be written from the perspective of cultural history and etymology and are written as SA-dialect dictionaries, whereas learners need both SA-dialect and dialect-SA to go back and forth

---

[213] Khamis-Dakwar and Makhoul, 2022.

between the two. Moreover, these tools are mainly in print, outside a few sites like Mo3jam.com, built on crowdsourced contributions. Dialect-English dictionaries are better designed for education, but they target adult learners and lack SA. The idea of a dictionary is just a starting point for an app allowing students to access a wealth of knowledge. The technology is available for features like adding images and audio and for students to interact with the app verbally, ask for definitions or grammar questions, and receive an answer comparing SA and a dialect.

Another innovative approach would be to develop what is known as a bilingual writer corpus, such as the Zayed Arabic-English Bilingual Undergraduate Corpus (ZAEBUC), which contains "comparable texts in different languages written by the same writer on different occasions" in ZAEBUC's case that being essays in English and Arabic from mainly freshman Emirati students. The corpus can be used to compare how students write in two languages, such as the complexity of sentence structure and differences in vocabulary, and how students' background impacts their writing in different languages. If such a database were developed for students writing in dialect and SA, it could be an assessment tool to give insights into where students need to improve and how to transfer their knowledge of one language to the other.

Teaching control and code-switching

Given the high degree of interaction between dialects and SA, an essential skill for learners is control and code-switching, meaning the ability to alternate between dialect and SA depending on the situation. Unlike a monolingual society, a multilingual context requires learners to know when each language is appropriate, when mixing multiple languages may be right, and how to capitalize on that to speak most effectively. With the exclusive emphasis on SA in education, this skill is overlooked and not even recognized. It is seen most clearly in live media, where many speakers feel the need to express themselves in SA but do so with mixed results. Some can do so fluently and effectively, whereas others struggle, resulting in a hybrid of the mother dialect and SA that depends on the speaker's level of control.

One potential educational tool is chatbots, such as Botta, that can understand and differentiate between different dialects and SA.[214] For instance, scenarios could be set up where learners interact with the bot in either dialect, SA, or a hybrid. When experimenting with Botta, it exhibited the ability to recognize a user's dialect, opening up the possibility for the bot to give feedback to learners. A concerted effort could also be made to develop a virtual assistant like Apple's Siri to interact with children in Arabic. Educators and parents have reported the positive impact of children's interaction with virtual assistants, particularly those with special needs and ESL students.[215] The challenge in Arabic would be gathering enough data to enable the virtual assistant to interact in dialect and SA. The recent release of Maqsam, a voice-to-text app that can transcribe dialect text better than Google's and Microsoft's apps, sets the foundation for successfully building such apps. One user who tested Maqsam stated that it could even transcribe former Libyan dictator Muammar Gaddafi's February 22, 2011 speech in which he vowed to hunt down protestors "inch by inch, house by house, and home by home."[216]

The recent evolution of large language models, such as OpenAI's ChatGPT and Google's Bard, that mix chatbots with Generative pre-Trained Transformers (GPTs) shows the potential technology offers and its shortfall. In tests with ChatGPT, it can respond well in SA, offering an excellent tool for practicing Arabic. However, it constantly reverts to SA when trying to communicate with it in a dialect.[217] Hence, not only are students unable to use this new era of AI-powered chatbots to practice dialects, but critical skills

---

[214] Abu Ali and Habash, 2016.
[215] Newman, 2014; Istrate, 2019.
[216] Drissner, 2023.
[217] Schor, 2023.

such as code-switching are not available. Moreover, OpenAI does not seem focused on languages besides English, even significant languages like Spanish,[218] so any efforts to better enable these large language models to work in SA and Arabic dialects must stem from outside the company.

A large undertaking would be to develop an app that lets learners practice their pronunciation to work on differentiating between their mother dialect and SA, helping them develop finer phonological control and also aiding them in transferring their knowledge of words they already know to SA.[219] English already has interesting apps that enable learners to improve their pronunciation, such as *Say It: Pronunciation*, which was developed by Oxford University Press and allows learners to record themselves saying a word and then compare the waveform of the recording with that of a native English speaker. The idea is relatively straightforward and could be adapted to Arabic dialects and SA, helping learners differentiate between two pronunciations of the same word, such as qara'a (قَرَأ), meaning to read, and various colloquial pronunciations. A more complex task would be to develop an app like *ELSA Speak* for Arabic, which allows users to record themselves saying words and then uses AI to analyze the recording and give feedback on moving their lips and tongue to improve their pronunciation. Any such app, though, should not focus on simply "correcting" students' pronunciation to SA; instead, it would require the option to work in dialect and SA and remind kids when to use one or the other.

---

[218] Dave, 2023.

[219] Since the writing of this chapter, the Qatar Computing Research Institute released a mobile app called QVoice (qvoice.qcri.org), which is currently freely available for download and use. The app allows users to hear a word and then record themselves saying it. It then provides basic advice on pronunciation, such as where the speaker said the letters correctly and where he / she mispronounced it.

Overcoming challenges

In recent years, a growing number of digital and non-digital educational materials have been made available in SA. The question, then, is how to overcome the barriers that prevent adapting current materials into dialects and create new ones. There are two main technological challenges facing Arabic: lack of good data for dialects and lack of standardized writing systems for dialects.

Good data for big data technologies

Access to data remains the most significant obstacle facing the development of sophisticated tools that rely on extensive data, such as AI. Whereas SA has abundant content, dialects are less lucky, and the lack of data means that Arabic will be left behind as new technologies that rely on big data are developed. While Arabs show little interest in reading in SA — many Arabs do not seek reading as a pastime, and in 2019, UNESCO estimated that only 6,500 new books were published across the Arab countries[220]—they are sidelining their dialects and preventing material from being developed.

Strict copyright laws also cause a lack of good data. Professor Nizar Habash, who heads New York University Abu Dhabi's computer science program, highlighted just how dire this predicament is: whereas SA has millions of words documented, organized, and annotated in a way that an AI program can digest, the Egyptian dialect has only 400,000, Levantine dialect only 50,000, and Gulf dialect only 200,000. To gather the data for the Gulf dialect, Habash's team was fortunate enough to find non-copyrighted text in the form of 1,200 romantic novels written by anonymous women.[221] Fortunately, even with these relatively small sets of data, dialects can

---

[220] Steward, 2019.
[221] Zacharias, 2020.

start to catch up by using what is known as transfer learning from SA and other dialects.

Content creators and official bodies dealing with copyright can also look into making data more accessible. While protecting artists' original material is essential, granting access to texts in ways that can help develop new databases without harming the artists is vital for the future of the language.

Standardizing dialect writing systems

Another hurdle that shows how neglected Arabic dialects are is that no standardized writing system exists. Instead, when people write in them, such as on social media or in the few books published in dialect, they write as they see fit. A single word like بقى (said ba'a, baga, or baqa, depending on the dialect) might be written بقى, بقا, بكا, بأه, or بگا —any way the writer wants, and sometimes one author will use multiple spellings in the exact text.

While standardizing writing systems for multiple dialects might initially seem daunting, setting clear criteria can facilitate the process. For his work on numerous dialect dictionaries, this author developed a writing system that capitalizes on the similarities between dialects and SA when possible but included phonetic notes to clarify the pronunciation so that it is easier for learners to transfer their knowledge from SA to a dialect while still learning the phonetic differences. Hence, a word like بقى would retain its SA spelling, with readers reading it differently based on the dialect. Another helpful addition that some texts use is superscript characters, such as a qaf with a hamza on it to show that it is a qaf in SA but is pronounced as a glottal stop in that context (as in بقٔى). Capitalizing on the overlap with SA allows the code to be designed so that SA can analyze the data better. Even without emphasizing the similarities between dialects and SA, a standardized writing system would put data in a more programming-friendly form and make it more readable to learners.

Embracing dialects: A new horizon for Arabic language education

Cultural aversion to teaching in dialects remains the most significant barrier to developing educational tools—digital and non-digital. Whereas the authors of a 2021 World Bank report titled "Advancing Arabic Language Teaching and Learning" acknowledge that SA is no one's mother tongue, they disregard the proposal of teaching Arab children to first read in their mother dialect before SA because "significant attitudinal changes would be needed for this."[222] However, technology has opened a lot of new spaces where dialect is used, most prominently on social media but also in videos, books, and private chats and messages, which may signal a change in Arabs' attitude toward the usage of dialect.

Governments, stakeholder organizations, and individuals can make inroads into changing this negative perception by raising awareness about the benefits of teaching in the mother dialect and that teaching learners basic literacy in their mother dialect can strengthen literacy in any other language learning, including SA. In other words, awareness campaigns should focus on the benefits of teaching initial literacy through dialects, and the fear that teaching dialects will harm SA is misplaced. There will continue to be resistance to the idea, especially initially, but finding receptive communities for pilot projects would also go a long way to alleviating fears and showing the effectiveness of an alternative model. Funding bodies could also look into supporting projects to generate content in dialects. Even small-sized grants for authors and publishers to create content in dialect or translate already available materials into dialect are a simple way to make books, games, and apps.

Technology, though, may be the main game changer in Arabic education. With previously unimaginable platforms now at our

---

[222] Gregory et al., 2021

fingertips, new digital tools offer new ways for learners to engage with Arabic and enable us to envision Arabic as a constellation of dialects with SA rather than merely SA imposed on, and even trying to eliminate, people's mother dialects. While the first steps are always challenging, the benefits are more than worth it: better literacy in SA, stronger connections with our cultural roots through language, a sense of pride in both our mother dialects and SA, and the ability to pass on and share all forms of our language.

14. Voices of home: A multilingual journey

Marina Chamma

Before he started the class and while everyone eased into a cross-legged position, my yoga teacher always took two to three minutes to share his spiritual pearls of wisdom. From centering one's awareness at the moment to boosting positivity and appreciating life's small blessings, the pep talk is something I try to carry with me long after the class ends, or at least until the next one. Being in Beirut, the talk is in Arabic. The class is conducted in English, with occasional Arabic commentary throughout the practice and sprinkles of Sanskrit to denote the original name of the yoga poses. Before the class starts, I often overhear two long-time students discussing their day and eagerness for the class. Although they converse in Arabic, it is in French that they genuinely express their admiration for the teacher and how practicing yoga with him has impacted their lives.

When I think back to this scene, it is hard not to view it as a quintessential Lebanese "Hi, kifak, ça va?"[223] moment. If we include Sanskrit, four languages were present in less than an hour within a 200-square meter space. Everyone understood each other, and perhaps due to the uplifting yoga ambiance, it didn't come across as pretentious as it might in different contexts. But one thing was certain: just a few years ago, I wouldn't have understood the Sanskrit, might have been bemused by the French conversation (though that might still be true today), and wouldn't have been able to answer

---

[223] A stereotyped Lebanese greeting "Hi, how are you? All well?" denoting a local habit of mixing languages in the same sentence, in this case English, Arabic and French.

questions about a downward-facing dog in Arabic before assuming the pose. Language is essential, even when exercising the body and mind.

Learning Arabic abroad

Born and raised by Lebanese parents abroad, multilingual learning was a given. English was the first language I began to speak, read, and write in. Being part of a French and Arabic-speaking family, French was also integral to our communication. Arabic came third in the order of languages I learned. Only in my later childhood did I begin to speak it fluently. Despite this, it is hard not to regard it as my mother tongue.

Arabic is my parents' primary language and was always dominant at home. While it wasn't my first language—based on the traditional definition of a mother tongue—it surpassed any other language I would learn. "The vagueness of this term has led some researchers to claim," Nike Pokorn says, "that different connotative meanings of the term 'mother tongue' vary according to the intended usage of the word."[224] To this day, I often pause when asked about my native language. But if I were to single out the language that connects me to my family and roots, Arabic has always been my mother tongue.

Apart from the emotional and philosophical ties we have to a language, a certain level of fluency is necessary to consider it an additional spoken language, let alone a mother tongue. Many children of emigrant and expatriate families can confirm that mastering Arabic is often challenging when residing in non-Arabic-speaking countries. During the 1980s and 1990s, when the internet and instant communication seemed like concepts out of science fiction movies, my parents depended on Saturday schools (when available) and occasional homeschooling to teach me the basics.

---

[224] Pokorn, 2005.

A short two-year stay in Lebanon gave me my first (and only) formal academic introduction to the language. Although brief, the experience was valuable, helping me grasp the basics of reading and writing. My spoken Arabic improved, and I incorporated new vocabulary I acquired from being around Arabic speakers. Sometimes, as my father sipped his morning coffee or prepared for work, he would listen to the poetry of Said Akl or Michel Trad from a small radio cassette, narrated by an acquaintance. He listened so frequently that I memorized much of it, even if I didn't understand its meaning then. However, whenever I inquired, he would recite it in its original form, then simplify the Arabic so I could understand. Meanwhile, as my mother tried to get me to focus on my homework, her exasperation, primarily in Arabic, at my continual distractions also helped expand my Arabic vocabulary. While these instances added joy and created fond memories of my interactions in Arabic at home, it was through such daily engagements that I continued to enrich my Arabic wherever I went.

What is certain is that speaking Arabic abroad allowed me to hide behind the *daads* and the *ayns*[225] when I wanted to. It often placed me on equal footing with locals in countries where I didn't know their language, and they couldn't even guess mine. This provided me with an advantage when I could understand them, and they had no inkling of my origins or what language I was speaking. Haven't you ever felt a mischievous delight in speaking another language—regardless of your proficiency—that no one around you comprehends? The fun ceases when you return to an environment where everyone understands you, and language is no longer on your side.

---

[225] The fifteenth and eighteenth letters of the Arabic alphabet with possibly no equivalent in any other language.

The mother tongue in the motherland

When I returned to Lebanon over fifteen years ago, my spoken Arabic was proficient, but my reading and writing skills needed improvement. Engaging with Arabic on various fronts—socially, in daily interactions, and professionally—I revisited the fundamentals taught years prior, combined with what I had gathered over time.

Like other countries in the Levant, Lebanon boasts a trilingual society. A blend of historical, demographic, and socio-economic influences has enabled French and English (often both) to be widely spoken. Generally, this multilingualism offers broader opportunities locally and globally and fosters global openness. However, such linguistic diversity has its nuances.

It soon became apparent that: (1) being a "native" Arabic speaker is a relative term; merely being born and raised in a country doesn't guarantee fluency in its language; (2) many individuals might use two languages daily, but that doesn't necessarily mean they are fluent in either; and (3) perceptions about the Arabic language, its role as a primary mode of communication, and the apparent need for proficiency in it vary widely.

The stories stemming from these realizations are diverse. They range from university graduates unfamiliar with reading the Arabic script to the cringe-worthy experience of hearing individuals speak a foreign language they believe they've mastered. Even more striking is the belief held by some parents—often passed down to their offspring—that mastering the Arabic language isn't worth the effort and might only harm a child's academic average. Living in Lebanon as an adult may shed light on the fact that (1) while Arabic was spoken everywhere, not everyone had a deep understanding of their so-called native tongue; (2) even with bilingual education, fluency in a second or third language wasn't always a given; and (3) the value placed on the Arabic language was influenced by factors like regional origin, religion, socio-economic standing, ties to other countries, and one's level of attachment to Lebanon, which can sometimes be tenuous at best. This linguistic landscape proved intriguing for educational and anthropological studies. My objective was distinct: to claim polyglot status and genuinely earn it. By then, I had added Spanish and Portuguese to my linguistic repertoire, leaving only Arabic to master.

I persisted from noting new words in a vocabulary journal to gratefully acknowledging corrections in my speech. Reading was challenging and often time-consuming. I would frequently halt mid-read, occasionally out of sheer frustration. To solidify my commitment, I pursued private Arabic lessons after work. I owe much to Istez Farid Mrad, who welcomed me into his home for lessons, patiently covering verbs, grammar, and spelling. Our writing exercises, typically describing vacations, diverged slightly: I wrote about business trips instead of sunny family getaways, the more familiar topic for school-aged students. Although our sessions were cut short by my professional and personal commitments, I remain thankful for his guidance and, in hindsight, proud of my dedication.

Although learning is an ongoing and never-ending process, especially in languages, the hard work paid off at that point. I became fluent in my mother tongue and, dare I say, spoke better and more eloquently than many so-called native speakers. The commitment notwithstanding, Arabic isn't an easy language. However, it somehow felt that Arabic was always 'in me,' so all I needed to do was unearth and make the most of what I already knew. Arabic had finally been genuinely reinstated as my mother tongue.

Arabic beyond communication

My parents' insistence on Arabic being spoken at home and all their efforts to teach me when no other formal schooling was available was essentially about forging an indispensable anchor and connection to the motherland. This wouldn't have existed had I maintained a shallow relationship with the language, limited to being fluent in *habibi*, *masare*, *tabbouleh*, and *hommos*.[226] Not only by living abroad but also as a daughter of diplomats—constantly moving from one country to another during the first 20 years of my life—my parents understood that without this linguistic connection, Lebanon could never be a place I could identify with, feel I belonged to, or even call home one day. As much as a so-called Lebanese identity was (and remains) a fluid, controversial, yet indispensable concept, my parents managed to forge a link, for better or for worse, between their 'citizen of the world' daughter and the motherland through language itself.

Throughout the years, the essence of this connection has fluctuated from feeling a deep sense of belonging, attachment to, and involvement in socio-economic issues to feelings of apathy, detachment, and utter indifference to everything related to it. Language has allowed me to have a complete and unfiltered account of the zeitgeist. During times of political and socio-economic upheaval—more often the norm rather than the exception in Lebanon—reality hits differently and much stronger in its original form, expressing anger, pain, surrender, despair, rage, and loss. Little is left to chance, and nothing is lost in translation. When understood directly from the source, pain has a way of being slightly more painful.

Multilingualism today

Whether stemming from colonialism or the region's dynamic relationship with the West, multilingualism is an essential characteristic of Arab societies, especially Lebanon. More recently, various factors have emerged that play a vital role in perpetuating the treasure of multilingualism many take for granted, including emigration and linkages to the motherland, increased travel,

---

[226] Arabic for "dear," "money" and the ubiquitous staples of Lebanese cuisine are examples of some of the few basic words that second or third generation Lebanese who don't speak Arabic are usually familiar with.

education abroad, and the demands of socioeconomic globalization and technology. Multilingualism is an opportunity that should be nurtured and constantly taken advantage of, if only for the increased opportunities it presents, but never at the expense of one's native language, as has often been the case in recent years.

The vestiges of colonialism may also account for the historical lack of interest and nonchalance towards the Arabic language for many. At the same time, in countries like Lebanon, the educational system and how Arabic is taught—predominantly uninterestingly, using outdated textbooks and methods—is also to blame for perpetuating this experience. However, the recent "revival" of Arabic has opened the door for a renewed relationship between the language and its people. From the use of Arabic writing and calligraphy on t-shirts, re-acquaintance with Arabic music (traditional old school and new inspired by Western genres), all the way to increased Arabic content on social media (written in Arabic or using the Latin script), Arabic has become "cool" and even perceived as less threatening to the outside world. If anything, this should pave the way for the younger generation to re-appropriate their language while adhering to the traditions of multilingualism for its invaluable social, cultural, and economic considerations.

By the time I was back in Beirut, I was already a fluent polyglot with close encounters with Japanese and German, which I didn't pursue further. In such places as culturally and linguistically diverse as the cities I was lucky to call home—such as Rio de Janeiro, Santiago, and Tokyo—speaking the native language meant that I wasn't considered nor felt like an outsider (except in Tokyo), managing to make the most out of my time there. In the short term, language was a matter of communication, a way to make daily life easier, and a window to a deeper understanding of the country. In the long run, it is an unbreakable bond to the culture and history of these countries and regions and the human links created. The compliments on my Arabic fluency, comprehension, language consistency, and even enunciation always brought me the greatest joy... and still do.

"To possess another soul"

Charlemagne is reputed to have said that "to speak another language is to possess another soul," implying that language isn't only about another option to communicate but a new vision towards life, or perhaps another life altogether. The Arab World and Arabic speakers worldwide have always been predisposed towards multilingualism—whether historically, culturally, or geographically—and continuing on this trajectory today shouldn't be a matter of debate. What should be the best and most effective ways of pursuing multilingualism? The challenges will always remain, whether learning another language for practical or personal reasons, but the prospects are unquantifiable, just as possessing another "soul" would be.

During one of his pep talks, my yoga teacher quoted 10th-century poet Abu al-Tayyib al-Mutanabbi, also known as the Arabic Shakespeare. I don't remember the exact quote, having heard of the poet but never read his poetry, but I seem to recall it had to do with gratitude and perseverance. While the quote fits well within the context, a yoga class was undoubtedly the last place I thought I would be introduced to medieval Arabic poetry. But before I had the time to ponder on al-Mutanabbi's words, it was time to get back on our feet in English, put our hands to heart in Sanskrit, and raise our hands to the sky in Arabic.

15. The language I knew without knowing

Hakim Benbadra

As far back as I can remember, I knew how to count in Arabic. Wahed, djoudj, thlatha, etc. However, I don't recall ever learning it. It felt like these words were a part of me as if they had been with me since immemorial times. I knew several other words, and they seemed innate. Yet, verbalizing them was always a challenge. As an adult, I realized that this probably meant I was spoken to in Arabic as a newborn and later as a child. Indeed, my grandparents and my father primarily communicated with me in Arabic, specifically Algerian Arabic. Only in adulthood did I understand that we spoke the Oran variant of Algerian Arabic and that Algeria had other regional dialectal groups. This revelation occurred during an extensive journey through the vast landscapes of the largest country in Africa.

Algerian Arabic (darija)... It is a long story. Throughout my teenage years, I resisted this language. Initially, it was out of reluctance, especially since my father believed it should come to me naturally. Later, I felt alienated by French society, which viewed it neither as a beautiful language nor as a worthy one—much like many non-European languages. Nor did they recognize it as a language at all, deeming Algerian Arabic a mere dialect and not a language in its own right.

One day, I realized that this language was part of my heritage. How could I reconcile not speaking my ancestors' language? Isn't language a cornerstone of identity? Not speaking it created an identity crisis for me. How could I deeply understand this country without its language guiding me? Speaking a language represents a way of thinking and positioning oneself in the world and in relation to others. On the cusp of my extensive journey to Algeria in 2018, I made peace with my ancestors' tongue. Through this chapter, you will journey through my personal experience with Arabic multilingualism as a Franco-Algerian.

Childhood & adolescence

I was born in France to Algerian parents. The unique aspect of my family background is that my father was born in Algeria and lived there for a significant portion of his life before settling in France. My mother, on the other hand, was born in France to Algerian parents. Algerian Arabic permeated my childhood, whether with my maternal grandparents or my father, as they mostly spoke to me in Arabic. That's why I knew many words in Algerian Arabic as a child.

Yet, as far back as I can remember, I understood my father's language but rarely spoke it, which frustrated him. He would address me in Arabic, and I would respond in French. I was in a situation of imperfect multilingualism; I was fluent in French but uncomfortable with this guttural language I was supposed to speak. Over the years, I realized I wasn't alone in this situation; many children of immigrants in France were in this imperfect bilingual scenario, understanding their parents' language but replying in French, often influenced by their parents' origins from former French colonies.

Growing up, I don't recall my teachers emphasizing the value of mastering a non-European foreign language. How often was I told Arabic wasn't a beautiful language during adolescence? How often was I told that Maghrebi Arabic sounded like an argument language? Suffice to say, it didn't inspire me to speak a language that I knew but didn't truly understand. In the French context, identity plays a significant role. Mastery of one's native language is perceived as a sign of non-integration into French society rather than a value addition for young children and teenagers of non-European origin. Unbeknownst to me, my relationship with Algerian Arabic was entangled in an identity game that was beyond my understanding.

I rejected Arabic during my teenage years. I didn't want to speak a language that was viewed negatively. I felt frustrated for not being able to speak my father's language. How many times was he surprised that I didn't know certain words? I recall the day I decided to stop trying to speak Arabic, even though I was making an effort. That day, I must have been around ten years old. My father asked me to fetch chairs (kresa in Arabic) from the room, but I only knew the singular version of a chair (kursi). Not grasping his request, I remained silent, which annoyed him. From then on, I refrained from speaking Arabic, feeling it wasn't for me.

The French integrationist approach, which places a burden on immigrant children with the supposed need to assimilate into a nation where they were born and raised, didn't help either. My mother spoke only French to me even though she was fluent in Arabic. This was the case for other immigrant children, too. I could have lived my life without really speaking Arabic. From childhood to late adolescence, my relationship with Arabic was complicated. That was until I went to Abu Dhabi for a semester abroad. Everything then changed.

Adulthood—Classical Arabic

I had the opportunity to study in Abu Dhabi for a semester and eagerly took it. I was thrilled to spend a few months in an Arab land, reconnecting with the Arabic language I had ignored until adulthood. I quickly learned that the Arabic spoken in the United Arab Emirates differed from what I was familiar with. I also experienced the depth and richness of the Arabic language. Vocabulary nuances, sentence structures, and word meanings varied depending on the speaker's nationality: Egyptian, Moroccan, and Lebanese, to name a few. I discovered the beauty of the Arabic language and decided to use my time in the Emirates to learn Classical Arabic.

At that time, I only understood Algerian Arabic and was unfamiliar with other Arabic forms. I saw Classical Arabic as a bridge between my linguistic heritage and the broader Arab world cultures. I dived headfirst into learning "fos3a" Arabic. Within a month, I enthusiastically learned to read and write in Arabic—a joyous milestone in my relationship with the language. Arabic calligraphy became familiar again, reconnecting me to a centuries-old bond between my family and this language.

Being a diligent student, I took pleasure in reading anything at hand to practice my newfound Arabic reading skills: newspapers, signboards, you name it. Learning classical Arabic became an advantage in my aspirations to work in international relations, and mastering this language seemed like the perfect tool for connecting with people from the Arab world. Stepping outside France allowed me to better appreciate the wealth of my Algerian linguistic heritage. I began to see beyond a monolithic identity that only defined me as a Frenchman of Algerian origin. I could fully embrace my Algerian identity as a remnant of the past and a living, evolving identity. Away from Paris and its gloomy skies, I found reconciliation with the Arabic language. In this journey of rediscovery, the languages of others would play a significant role, particularly the neighboring Italian language of France.

Adult—Other languages

During a year-long study stay in Italy, I came to master the Italian language. My stay beyond Piedmont allowed me to view my identity with fresh eyes and realize that I knew more about the country of the locals than my own. Initially, I was surprised when people thought I was Italian, meaning I looked European—something that seemed impossible in France, where my social identity was Arab. Or at least, that's the image the French society projected onto me. I quickly understood that many Italians looked like North Africans due to geographical proximity. I made rapid progress in my proficiency in Italian until I spoke it fluently.

By mastering Italian, I felt I was validating what my father always said about Arabs and our tendency towards multilingualism. He constantly praised the potential for polyglossia that the diverse phonemes of the Arabic language allowed. I discovered that I had a knack for languages and moved away from the idea that, as a Frenchman, I was likely to only ever speak one foreign language, English, with a heavy French accent. At that point, my Arab side took over, and within a few years, I became a polyglot, fluent in six languages. My experience with the Italian language had been the catalyst for my polyglossia.

During this year of studies, I also immersed myself in local culture. Out of curiosity, I seized every opportunity to visit other cities and regions of the country: Lombardy, Umbria, Sicily, Rome, Veneto, Apulia, and many more. I roamed the Italian boot alone or accompanied by other exchange students like myself. I marveled at historical buildings, the culinary diversity, and the country's artistic heritage. By the end of the year, I had visited a large part of Italy. I understood the culture better and had an excellent geographical knowledge of the country. It was then that I realized my ignorance about contemporary Algeria.

Even though I knew the geography of my ancestral country in theory, I had no practical knowledge beyond the family village. I didn't truly know how modern-day Algerians lived, thought, or dreamed, yet I knew this about the Italians. This realization was the final push I needed to apply for my Algerian passport, which I did at the end of my Erasmus stay. It took a few more years and another year living in Germany, where I learned another country's language and customs again. All of this brought me closer to the deep-seated need within me to go to Algeria, to connect with my Algerian side, and to begin my Algerian project, which would evolve into a backpacking tour of Algeria, seeking out positive initiatives but mainly in search of myself.

Adult—Trip to Algeria

Five years after my Italian experience, I mustered the courage and decided to visit Algeria in January 2018. I will never be grateful enough to Rafik, a man from Algiers I met a few months prior, who was the final catalyst I needed for this journey to the roots of my identity. Methodically, I approached my Algerian re-education as if I were heading to an unknown country. I read numerous Algerian authors, watched Algerian movies, explored Algerian music, and talked about Algeria with every Algerian I met (including my family) to hear their views on the country.

And what about the language in all of this? I understood that Algerian Arabic was my heritage, but I had to start from scratch to build a solid foundation. Treating it as if I was learning a new language seemed obvious. I grabbed a modern Algerian dialectal Arabic manual to refresh my knowledge and quickly realized I knew this language better than I thought. It was there, deep inside me, waiting patiently for the attention I had given to Italian, German, and English. I also forced myself to communicate only in Algerian Arabic with my father and grandparents, the only family members who spoke to me in this language. It was challenging! How many times did I stumble over certain words? How often did I feel embarrassed not to speak it as fluently as my ancestors? I was fortunate because I got to practice in a supportive environment. I could make mistakes, knowing they wouldn't judge me.

I left for Algeria with a decent language proficiency, which allowed me to communicate and understand my family there. I surprised them; they expected me to speak only in French. I felt a particular pride. Finally, I was no longer fumbling with Arabic. I could admit that I spoke it imperfectly but was on the path to fluency. As I traveled through Algeria over the following months, I began to master this simultaneously foreign and familiar language, discovering the incredible diversity of my country. The dialects differed by region, and I learned many new words, forming my version of Algerian Arabic—a mix of all regions and encounters across the country. By the end of this journey, I understood all the accents and dialects of Algerian Arabic. I was proud. I could confidently say I was fluent in Arabic, naturally using words from every region. This journey reconciled my identity.

Discovering modern Algeria, I found much more than I expected when I arrived in Oran that January. I encountered a great and culturally rich nation linked to my ancestral history. Through this Algerian journey, which took me over 15,000 kilometers and introduced me to remarkable people, I discovered my Algerian side—a part of my unfamiliar and not fully understood identity. This trip enriched me immensely. Today, I feel actively connected to Algeria, no longer passively. I live my Algerian identity, understanding what being Algerian means without neglecting my French heritage. This Algerian essence complements me, shaped by my overseas experiences.

Finding my voice: The journey of identity and language across cultures

My relationship with a language I knew but didn't truly understand had its ups and downs intertwined with my identity journey. Being born in France didn't make this easier. In a country that primarily valued French culture and identity, embracing my Algerian heritage was challenging. This changed with my trip to the United Arab Emirates, where the refreshing Gulf breeze was a balm. This experience allowed me to reflect on my multifaceted identity. I read *In the Name of Identity: Violence and the Need to Belong* by Amin Maalouf, a powerful example of Arab multilingualism. This Lebanese-born author joined the French Academy, bringing his linguistic and human experiences. Learning new languages, mastering them, and living them was unmatched wealth. These foreign languages brought me closer to the familiar Algerian Arabic. As Nelson Mandela said, you must speak their language to reach people's hearts. Speaking Arabic connected me with my heart, my father's, and my grandparents'—people I deeply loved. I knew my mother's heart through French but had spent much of my life distant from the hearts of my close relatives. My Arabic multilingualism experience was deeply personal, diving deep into myself, those I loved, and a nation with both painful and exceptional history.

Arabic was the most beautiful stranger in my life. As I turned 25, Algerian Arabic became integral to me, reconciling all facets of my identity. It was the missing piece at the intersection of language, history, culture, and identity. The subsequent years allowed me to shift from Western ethnocentrism, which predominantly influenced

Western European languages. I learned Amharic in Ethiopia, began studying Swahili, and traveled to Egypt and Tunisia to immerse myself in other Arabic cultures and dialects. I was surprised to understand Tunisian Arabic and adapt to Egyptian Arabic easily. I was pleased when others recognized my Algerian heritage and how I spoke Arabic in these brotherly nations. Now, I am eager to explore more Arab countries, immersing myself in their cultures and dialects. Languages are a treasure. Each language offers a unique worldview. I am grateful for my life experiences and look forward to future adventures.

16. Arabic for all, why my language is taboo in France—an interview with Nabil Wakim

Fabrice Jaumont

The Center for the Advancement of Languages, Education, and Communities

Teaching the Arabic language in France presents a multifaceted challenge, primarily due to the national education system's limited focus on this linguistic demand. Consequently, parents frequently resort to religious institutions like mosques for their children's education, where the curriculum predominantly revolves around religious texts, lacking a vibrant and engaging approach to language learning. This situation raises an important question: how can we enhance the appeal of languages, heritage or foreign, to young learners and ensure they align with the cultural milieu in which these children are growing up?

To explore this complex landscape, Nabil Wakim, author of *L'arabe pour tous, pourquoi ma langue est taboue en France* (Arabic for All, Why My Language Is Taboo in France), published by Éditions du Seuil, embarked on a journalistic exploration to shed light on the contentious nature of Arabic language education in France. His inquiry delved into the varied stances of government officials regarding this issue, including ministers and presidents. Wakim's investigation goes beyond mere journalistic inquiry, weaving in his personal narrative alongside those of a diverse group of individuals— ranging from artists and former government officials to journalists and immigrants who have transitioned to parenthood in various communities. Released in 2020, his book has garnered a wealth of feedback from parents deliberating on how to pass on their heritage, be it Arabic, Breton, German, or other languages, to their children, highlighting the universal challenge of language transmission in multicultural contexts.

Language education is a profoundly emotive topic that frequently ignites passionate discussions. The involvement of teachers and parents is often intense, underlining the significance of practical concerns such as hiring, training, and ensuring a consistent educational journey. In France, the recruitment of Arabic language instructors remains notably scarce. However, there is potential to adopt the model used for English by employing language assistants to bridge this gap. Moreover, maintaining educational consistency is vital for students committed to learning a language over an extended period. It is essential to nurture their interest without obliging them to study a language that doesn't captivate them. Addressing the continuum issue is also fundamental, as well as ensuring that language learning opportunities are readily accessible at all educational levels, from primary to high school.

Conversations across cultures: Nabil and I discuss Arabic language learning in France

Fabrice: I wanted to congratulate you on this book that I devoured in a very short time. I couldn't put it down; I found many exciting things in it, especially this fight for our children. That's what I wanted to talk about to start our discussion. Nabil, can you tell us a little bit about what motivated you to write this book? Is it a personal story, a family story?

Nabil: Yes, this book is called *L'arabe pour tous, pourquoi ma langue est taboue en France* (Arabic for all, why my language is taboo in France). There are two threads inside, both intimate and political. It is personal because I tell my relationship with the Arabic language. I was born in Lebanon and came to France with my parents when I was four. Arabic is my mother tongue, but somewhere between the ages of 4 and almost 40, I lost it along the way. I wanted to investigate why I had lost my mother tongue. In fact, the book was nearly called "How I lost my language"!

There is also a political aspect that concerns the social debate in France on the place given to languages in general and Arabic in particular. This is one of the primary motivations of the book. Another motivation is to become a father; I want my daughter to speak Arabic because it is part of my cultural heritage. However, I realized it wasn't easy to transmit a language I did not speak. This led me to question myself and to write this book.

Fabrice: In the book, there are parts about linguists, bilingualism, and children's ability to learn languages, which I found fascinating but also a barrier for many parents in learning and teaching languages to their children. This point is critical, especially since I have noticed a growing interest in bilingualism in France and the United States, and more and more parents are interested in this issue of bilingual education. But it is above all a feeling that parents have, how to transmit their language to their children, that is the starting point of many parents who are reading this interview.

Nabil: It is important to understand that you can lose your language. For a long time, I lived with the idea that I had the Arabic language stuck somewhere in my head and that I just had to find the magic formula to be able to trigger the Arabic language. But the linguists I consulted explained to me that it wasn't like that at all. Of course, you can lose your mother tongue.

Fabrice: Do you speak Arabic, and if so, how did you come to learn it?

Nabil: Indeed, I speak Arabic. I talk about it a bit in my book. I learned Arabic from my grandmother, who often reminded me of it. So, the language was part of me, and I still practice it quite regularly.

Fabrice: You mentioned that the Arabic you spoke and understood was a home Arabic, a domestic Arabic—Is that common in all families?

Nabil: Yes, I think that exists in all families and for all languages. The Arabic that I spoke was an Arabic that was limited to everyday life. It was limited to a specific lexical field, such as food, tidying the room, etc. If I hear these words in a movie, for example, it evokes something for me. But it is more difficult for me if I have to talk about more technical subjects in Arabic, like in my job as a journalist in the energy sector.

Fabrice: It can be a challenge, indeed. But you seem to have a particular curiosity about the language.

Nabil: Yes, I have always been curious about the language. But there's always this idea of working, maintaining, and improving my Arabic to make it more alive.

Fabrice: Your book talks about a funny experience when returning to Lebanon often. Can you tell us more about it?

Nabil: Yes, that's true. My first stop is immigration. These agents looked at my passport and talked to me in Arabic to see if I spoke the language. I have this anxiety that I don't know Arabic, even though I know the language well enough to say that I don't speak it very well. But I'm quickly exposed, which often leads to a conversation in Arabic. But I am not able to hold a very long conversation.

Fabrice: You are fluent in French, Spanish, and English, correct?

Nabil: Exactly. I lived in the United States. My daughter was born there. And now, there's a question of whether she should learn English or Arabic first because those two languages are part of her history. However, children choose what they decide to keep or not, and it is a challenge for us as parents to give them the tools to make those choices with awareness and freedom.

Fabrice: Indeed, language learning can open up many opportunities. And Arabic is a language rich in history and culture.

Nabil: Absolutely. Arabic is the fifth most spoken language in the world, with more than one million speakers in the United States.

The subject of teaching Arabic in France is complex. Teaching modern languages, except for English, is problematic in France. However, teaching Arabic is particularly badly considered and suffers from a lack of means and attention. Only 0.2% of students in France learn Arabic as a foreign language in middle and high school, which is very low.

There is a paradox in the teaching of Arabic in France. On the one hand, Arabic is often poorly regarded and considered a language of poor class in schools attended by the children of immigrants from the Maghreb or the Near East. On the other hand, France has a strong tradition of learning Arabic in elite classes, in schools such as Sciences Po, Polytechnique, or certain large Parisian high schools.

The lack of intermediaries between these two extremes is a significant challenge. There is a lack of teaching Arabic as a standard living language that would open doors not only to the descendants of Arabic-speaking immigrants but to all those who want to learn the language. Learning Arabic can offer incredible opportunities, not only culturally but also professionally, in terms of friendship and love.

Fabrice: Arabic language instruction is more widespread and highly regarded in the United States. There are bilingual programs in Arabic and English in public schools, such as the Khalil Gibran School in Brooklyn. However, even in the U.S., bilingualism differs from one community to another, and there may be resistance or prejudice.

Therefore, ways should be found in France to promote teaching Arabic as an everyday living language and preserve this linguistic heritage. This would require investments and a change of mentality so that Arabic is no longer considered a low-class language but a language rich in history and culture, spoken by millions worldwide.

Nabil: In France, the teaching of Arabic is in bad shape. Teaching modern languages, in general, is difficult, except for English. Only fourteen thousand students in France currently learn Arabic as a second language in secondary school, which represents

0.2% of the students. France has a particular paradox because the Arabic language taught to the children of immigrants from the Maghreb, or the Near East, is often poorly considered as a language of poor class in schools that are not necessarily of good quality. On the other hand, "elite" Arabic is taught in certain grandes écoles and preparatory schools, where the elites are prepared.

There is a real need to teach Arabic as a standard living language, which would open doors not only to Arabs and their descendants but also to all those who want to learn. Teaching Arabic is possible in France, as it already exists in secondary schools with bilingual classes from the 6th grade, where French students can learn Arabic and English.

However, the opening of Arabic classes is not always well accepted by all. Some campaigns, sometimes online, are led by local elected officials or school principals who fear they will have a different population in their schools. It is, therefore, essential to do pedagogical work to find agreement and open classes.

There is also a problem of stereotypes and xenophobic amalgams around the Arabic language in France, linked to caricatures that still exist and that often stem from complete ignorance of what the Arabic language is. Parents are sometimes afraid to speak Arabic to their children, to transmit it, for fear of being discriminated against or categorized.

Fabrice: Bilingualism is no longer considered a problem in families. It is important to tell parents that learning Arabic can benefit their child's academic and professional development. It is crucial to depoliticize the Arabic language to make it simpler and more open to all. Alas, it is difficult to give advice, but to get your language back and for your daughter, it is essential to understand that bilingualism is no longer an issue in families.

Nabil: It is important to remember that the Arabic language is not linked to Islam and that most Muslims in the world do not speak Arabic. Fighting against stereotypes and doing educational work to find concord is crucial. It is vital not to be afraid to speak Arabic and to pass it on to your family.

Fabrice: For a long time, teachers in the U.S. or in France encouraged families to speak only in English or French at home, not considering other languages important. Today, more and more people, including those in the national education system, are challenging this idea. By valuing each language's advantages, children can learn several languages, often better than adults. It is, therefore, a question of asking what place to give to each of the languages practiced and to what extent they are helpful in our lives.

I express myself differently in English, Spanish, and French and use different expressions and lexical fields in each language. In a family, especially in a blended family, where everyone speaks their native language, children can learn expressions, means, and tools in each language to deal with different situations in life.

Linguists say that there can be moments of difficulty for children who are confronted with several languages in the first years of their lives, but this quickly resolves itself, and the advantages far outweigh the disadvantages. This is why I repeat daily the importance of passing on one's mother tongue to one's children without fear of negative consequences.

Many French families in the United States claim the right to speak their native language and pass it on to their children, which is touching and shows how universal this need is. Bilingual education initiatives are multiplying in daycare centers, public schools, private institutions, or online.

Nabil: I think that France and the United States have different histories when it comes to language, with France having a history of unifying its territory and the French nation with the French language. At the same time, the United States has always been open to the linguistic richness brought by the different waves of immigration.

It is crucial to fight the idea that in France, one must speak only French because France has always been rich in languages, whether they are regional languages, languages of immigration, or overseas languages. Maintaining one's mother tongue is a real asset for children, allowing them to maintain links with their family and culture.

However, it is essential that children enjoy practicing their mother tongue and do not feel additional pressure from their parents or society. Children respond primarily to pleasure, so they should be encouraged and helped to feel happy to speak their mother tongue, not forced to learn a complex language.

Fabrice: Children must be happy with their mother tongue now and in the future. For example, teaching Arabic in France is a hot topic, as public schools do not consider the request of many parents to teach Arabic. As a result, many parents turn to religious education and mosques in France, where religious associations often provide education based on learning religious texts. This can lead children to perceive Arabic as a fixed language that is not very dynamic without deciding whether learning Arabic in a mosque is preferable to public school. So, there is a debate about that.

Nabil: I think that what is essential is to learn modern languages, especially languages that are part of our heritage and that we want to pass on. It is sometimes difficult to make them live and attractive in the country where we live. In my experience, when I was a child and teenager, Arabic did not attract me at all. It was a language that I did not want to learn, but my parents did not care why I did not want to learn it. So, it is important to ask ourselves how to make the languages we want to teach our children attractive and accessible.

Fabrice: You are not alone in this view. I think you got testimony from politicians, journalists, and researchers in your quest to write your book. Can you tell us about your background and your research process?

Nabil: Initially, my journey began with introspection, drawing upon personal experiences. However, I quickly realized this alone wouldn't suffice to craft a compelling narrative. To enrich the tapestry of my story, I sought out diverse perspectives, engaging with individuals whose stories could provide depth and contrast to my own. This led me to interact with a spectrum of influential figures, including the talented singer Camélia Jordana, esteemed former ministers Marylise Lebranchu and Najat Vallaud-Belkacem, prominent journalists from the French television landscape, and distinguished members of the Arab community who have achieved notable success both professionally and socially. Through these encounters, I aimed to weave a richer, more nuanced narrative that reflects a broad array of experiences and viewpoints.

Inquiring about their connection to the Arabic language, I was taken aback to find that many shared a narrative akin to mine. As a Lebanese from a Christian background, I anticipated my experience to be unique. Yet, I found common ground between individuals of North African descent and those of Egyptian or Sudanese heritage. The recurring theme was an introspection on whether their integration into French society necessitated sidelining their Arab identity. This concern extended to those with children, pondering over the transmission of their linguistic heritage.

The response to my book has been overwhelmingly positive, sparking significant interest. I have been moved by the influx of letters and heartfelt accounts from parents torn over imparting their native tongue to their offspring. These stories aren't limited to Arab descendants but span cultures from Breton to Portuguese. It appears language is a deeply personal matter, fraught with unresolved dilemmas about family dynamics, child-rearing, and interactions with extended family members. It's a sensitive topic that often stirs emotions, leading to tears or unspoken words among educators and parents alike. The universality of this issue is striking, and I am gratified to play a role in catalyzing this critical conversation.

Fabrice: The question that concerns me the most, and that often comes to mind, is how to find teachers, train them, and get them to teach what we want to teach.

Nabil: We have very little room in France to recruit Arabic teachers for the public teaching exams. This is problematic because it was evident that to teach, we need teachers and hours of teaching. So, we have to train teachers. The French tradition is that we seek to train experts and the best language practitioners. That's fine, but we could also follow the example of English and have language assistants who help teachers allocate class time. It is a question of political will and resources to put in place tricks that allow as many children as possible to be exposed to the language.

When discussing the two-block school, I mentioned the importance of educational continuity. In France, a big problem is that children who took Arabic in middle school may not find it in high school, or conversely, students who took Arabic in elementary school no longer have it in their local middle school. The true challenge lies in maintaining consistent educational progress for children over an extended period without compelling them to learn an unwanted language. Instead, we should equip them with the resources necessary to engage with the language voluntarily.

Fabrice: The continuum issue concerns us all here in New York's French community. Of course, some outstanding high schools offer a blended baccalaureate program, but there are very few options in the public system that allow this continuum. And therein lies the big concern: What will the kids do? What are they going to choose? Have their years of primary school been enough to reach a level of fluency and bilingualism to make them able to write in French and Arabic? This phenomenon, resonating between France and the United States, signifies a lot. It reflects a shared experience, perhaps even mirrored when viewed from the opposite perspective. The emergence of bilingual programs in elementary schools, particularly in New York, showcases a diverse linguistic offering, including Chinese, Spanish, Korean, Hebrew, Italian, Russian, German, and more, with up to fifteen languages available. These programs herald the advent of bilingual education, yet this momentum often halts at the middle school level, leaving a void in continued language education. This gap underscores the need for a paradigm shift to foster an understanding that multilingualism opens global doors for individuals and cultivates world-wise, skilled citizens.

Nabil: Indeed, recognizing the value of bilingualism is crucial, but the real challenge lies in igniting a passion for languages among children and teenagers and showcasing the cultural wealth it can unlock. My journey to learning English in high school was fueled by my love for English music and the desire to watch Star Wars in its original language - an enchanting experience. Similarly, my attraction to Spanish stemmed from its melodious nature and my aspiration to immerse myself in Spain's culture. In its broadest sense, this underscores the importance of a cultural approach to make languages appealing to the younger generation. It's about presenting language learning as an academic exercise and a gateway to exploring new worlds - through music, movies, friendships, and global connections. My proficiency in English and Spanish improved significantly when I started communicating with friends who spoke these languages. However, I missed out on this enriching experience with Arabic, as I didn't engage in such exchanges with my grandmother or cousins. Unfortunately, this aspect of language learning - the real-world application and cultural immersion - is often absent from textbooks.

Fabrice: Multilingualism is increasingly vital in today's global landscape, with Canada leading the way in North America. Language immersion programs, which allow children to spend part of their schooling in a foreign language, began to develop in the United States in the 1970s, and there are now nearly 180 for French in some 30 states and thousands for Spanish.

Nabil: In France, immersion programs are not yet well developed, but this seems to be a growing demand, including in rural areas. However, in France, we often think that monolingualism is the norm when it is an exception. In many countries, people practice several languages daily, such as in French-speaking Africa. It is, therefore, essential to consider this linguistic diversity and accept it as a richness, even within the same language.

This also raises the question of accent and norm. In France, there is a tendency to standardize how people speak, but this can lead to a denial of the country's linguistic and cultural diversity. In the United States, on the other hand, the size of the country and the regional differences lead to a greater openness to linguistic and accentual diversity. Thus, speaking English with a French accent is often well perceived, while speaking French with a North African or Ch'ti accent is frequently derided.

It is, therefore, important to promote multilingualism by showing children and teenagers that practicing a foreign language can be a means of discovering a new world, cultures, and people. To do this, it is necessary to make languages attractive and arouse the desire to learn them by showing their usefulness and richness.

With the confinement during the pandemic and the closure of schools, many French people have rediscovered learning foreign languages, turning to films, songs, or online courses. It is crucial to continue this momentum, valuing multilingualism and recognizing our country's linguistic and cultural diversity.

Fabrice: You recently spoke about your desire to reconnect with the Arabic language. Could you tell us a little more about this?

Nabil: Yes, indeed, I realized that it was essential to integrate the Arabic language into my life if I wanted to embrace my culture. Although I can write a few pages in Arabic, I don't practice it regularly, which is a shame. Right now, I'm in a phase of cultural reclamation. This is an important step for me, but I know it will take time.

Fabrice: What about pronunciation and understanding of the Arabic language?

Nabil: Well, some pronunciation specificities are very important to remember. In Arabic, there are letters and sounds that don't exist in French, like "rat", "la" and "règne" which are guttural sounds. As a former Arabic speaker, I have retained some of the sounds I learned as a child. However, comprehension, reading, and vocabulary diversity are more difficult for me. Standard Arabic is quite different from the Arabic spoken in other countries. For example, Lebanese, Moroccan, and Egyptian Arabic are everyday languages, while Standard Arabic is more elitist and, therefore, more difficult to access.

Fabrice: Regarding your daughter, what are your aspirations for her journey in learning Arabic?

Nabil: My daughter is French-Lebanese, so there is this dilemma of whether she should be French-American, French-Lebanese, or all three. We don't have a specific plan, but I'm open to suggestions.

Fabrice: In your book, you articulate a vision of optimism regarding the state of the Arabic language in France. Could you elaborate on this perspective?

Nabil: I believe that French and American histories are rich tapestries woven with narratives of immigration and cultural amalgamation. In France, individuals often form unions across borders, nurturing children within a mosaic of cultural backgrounds and bequeathing a legacy encompassing ancestral recipes, melodies, cinematic treasures, and familial lore. This melding of cultures constitutes the very essence of French historical identity. It presents a unique opportunity to cultivate a milieu ripe with social, cultural, and professional prospects for the younger generation. Embracing this diversity offers a chance to transcend the simplistic and reductive perceptions of a French identity encapsulated in a bygone era. Bilingualism, in this context, serves as a conduit for inclusivity and understanding, enabling a deeper insight into the varied ways of life, thoughts, and traditions of others, thereby fostering a more empathetic and open-minded citizenry.

Embracing linguistic diversity: Reflections on Arabic language education in France

In conclusion, the teaching of the Arabic language in France embodies a complex challenge that underscores broader issues surrounding language education, cultural identity, and integration within a multicultural society. Nabil Wakim's insightful exploration in "*L'arabe pour tous, pourquoi ma langue est taboue en France*" sheds light on the intricate landscape of Arabic language education and delves into the personal narratives that intersect with broader socio-political debates. Our dialogue above brings to the forefront the nuanced realities of bilingualism, the struggles of transmitting heritage languages, and the potential for linguistic diversity to enrich personal and collective identities. As France grapples with the practicalities of language education and the cultural implications of multilingualism, the experiences shared in Wakim's work offer a poignant reflection on language's power to connect and divide. The discussion emphasizes the importance of fostering an environment that values linguistic diversity as a cultural asset, encouraging a more inclusive approach to language education that respects and celebrates the multitude of linguistic heritages within the nation.

One pivotal area of inquiry revolves around the pedagogical approaches to language teaching in multicultural settings. How can educational systems adapt to accommodate and celebrate linguistic diversity, ensuring language education extends beyond mere academic pursuit to embrace cultural heritage and identity?

Another critical aspect is the role of language in shaping individual and collective identities, particularly in contexts where linguistic heritage intersects with migration and integration narratives. What does the choice of language—the pursuit of Arabic, Breton, German, or other languages—tell us about personal and communal identities in a globalized world?

Moreover, the challenges and opportunities presented by bilingualism or multilingualism, especially in transmitting heritage languages to younger generations, warrant a closer examination.

How do families navigate the complexities of bilingual upbringing, and what support mechanisms are essential to facilitate this process?

Finally, the societal perceptions and political dimensions associated with particular languages, as evidenced by the contentious status of Arabic in France, raise important questions about the intersection of language, power, and social inclusion. How do societal attitudes towards specific languages influence educational policies and practices, and what steps can be taken to foster a more inclusive and respectful linguistic landscape?

By exploring these questions, we can unravel the intricate tapestry of language education, cultural identity, and societal integration, shedding light on the multifaceted challenges and opportunities ahead.

17. The history and development of the teaching of the Arabic language to students of Arab origin in Florence and Tuscany

Haifa Alsakkaf

Good World Citizen

When I arrived in Italy in the mid-nineties, the scenery of immigration was starting to change. Immigrant workers started bringing their families and settling in Italy, and many of these immigrants came from North Africa and other Arab countries. The new Arab and Islamic communities started carrying out cultural and social activities, generally aimed at the children of their communities. Among these activities were classes on Arabic language and culture carried out by volunteer teachers. As a member of the Arab community of Florence, I participated in such initiatives. I followed the progress of the activities, at first in the local community's headquarters and then in public spaces, such as schools or libraries. In 2001, I was among the founders of the Arabic language school Alshuruk, which continues its activities to date.

Today, children of Arab origin are showing more interest in learning the language of their parents and family. However, there are many challenges in maintaining and promoting Arabic language teaching and providing a more significant offer to heritage learners and all students interested in learning the Arabic language.

Students of non-Italian origin in the Italian education system

The presence of students of non-Italian origin

There are over 860,000 international students in Italian schools, representing about 10% of the total school population, most of whom

(64%) are born in Italy to non-Italian parents. When examining the larger Italian geographical areas, we find that the majority of students with non-Italian citizenship are concentrated in the northern regions (65%), followed by the central regions (22%), and finally, the southern regions (13%). At a regional level, the Italian region with the highest percentage of international students is Emilia-Romagna (16.4%), followed by Lombardy (15.5%), and in third place comes Tuscany (14.1%). The national portrait is reflected at the local level, with the Metropolitan City of Florence being the fourth metropolitan city, after Milan, Rome, and Turin, for the number of legally residing non-E.U. citizens.

Taking into consideration the ranking of countries of origin of non-Italian students, we find that in the first 12 positions, there are 3 Arab countries, which are Morocco (12.2%), Egypt (3%), and Tunisia (2.3 %). In addition to these three countries, some students come from all the other Arab countries, bringing the total percentage of students of Arab origin to over 18% of the total students of non-Italian origin. This is a significant figure because most of these students are born in Italy and generally do not need to learn the Italian language. If, in the early 2000s, the students of non-Italian citizenship were inserted into the Italian education system having already started a school course in their country of origin, now more and more start their educational path without literacy in the Italian language. This involves a change in the methods of integration that the school must implement towards these students, which should move towards a cultural and not just a linguistic approach.

Regulations and norms of the Ministries of Education in Europe and Italy

Multiculturalism in Italian and European societies is a matter of fact. The transition from a monocultural pedagogy to one in which there is interaction and exchange between the various cultures of the students has become a necessity. In this process, the role of the school is essential. Due to the intensification of migratory flows in the past few decades, the European Ministries of Education and European Institutions have issued numerous recommendations and regulations regarding including students with foreign citizenship in schools.[227] Their integration is understood as a two-way process that provides rights and duties for immigrants and the society that welcomes them, considering the current concept of interculturalism. This process involves the various institutions operating at the micro level with families, teachers, educators, and the school context in general, as well as at the macro level at the political level with the various regulations.

At the European level, Member States take appropriate measures to promote the teaching of the mother tongue and culture of the country of origin, coordinating it with regular teaching. Since the 1980s, the inclusion of international students in compulsory education at the Italian level has been the subject of a ministerial *circulaire* for promoting and coordinating intercultural initiatives. Subsequently, the broader dimensions of migratory flows and the needs of non-E.U. students required careful consideration and a series of specific interventions. These actions are to be implemented by the administration and school offices to promote and develop common operational strategies and ensure the necessary connection between the different school grades. In school practice, efforts should be made to enhance the language and culture of origin by coordinating it with teaching the compulsory subjects included in the study plan. This makes it clear that Italian schools today face a critical turning point and must renew themselves to favor the insertion and integration of students of non-Italian origin. Adopting a global, transversal perspective capable of investing the entire socio-cultural educational system in an intercultural pedagogical direction is necessary.

---

[227] Council of Europe, 2008; European Commission, 2008.

Since 2000, single schools, even though part of the national school system, have had their own administrative, didactic, and organizational autonomy in compliance with the general State rules on education. In this autonomy of educational institutions, it is possible to apply didactic projects according to options that conform with their educational offer. Such choices can enhance diversity by adopting all the initiatives useful for achieving intercultural academic success. The Italian school system has a structurally inclusive character but needs to go beyond the mere reception or insertion to become intercultural. The Ministry of Education published 2006 "*Guidelines for the Reception and Integration of Foreign Students*" and 2007 "*The Italian Way for an Intercultural School and the Integration of Foreign Students*." These documents refer to the presence of students of non-Italian origin as an advantage and an opportunity for change for the entire school. Among the objectives of these documents is identifying a model that highlights the specificity of the Italian experience, its strengths, and the weaknesses that should be addressed with new practices and resources.

Despite these indications, Italian school programs do not offer adequate intercultural teaching or courses on the cultures and languages of non-Italian students' countries of origin. The theoretical and regulatory developments probably have not been accompanied by sufficient investments in resources to allow the school to make a systemic and far-reaching institutional change. Therefore, very often, the teaching of the languages and cultures of origin of non-Italian students is managed by single communities.

The teaching of the Arabic language and Arab culture in Florence and Tuscany

The initial experiences

Most immigrants from Arab countries are of Islamic religion, and in the new social and cultural context, they began to look for ways to maintain their specificity. In the 1980s, Islamic centers were initially established as student associations. In later years, this model changed to better organize the activities and needs of its members, including young adults and families. One of these organizations was that of the city of Florence: The Islamic Cultural Association of Florence and Tuscany (CIFT).

As the CIFT grew, the challenges it had to face also grew. While the first generations of immigrants arriving in Italy had a more or less structured linguistic, religious, and cultural formation, their children, especially those born in the new host country, face difficulties acquiring adequate knowledge of these aspects. These children, born and raised in Italy, learn the Italian language like their native peers, and with it, they also learn the local habits and customs. Often, however, they have no means of learning the language and culture of origin, which usually leads to an intergenerational communication crisis. The new generations of children of Arab origin face, in addition to changes related to the growth processes, those concerning their insertion into a social organization and a cultural tradition different from those of their families. For these reasons, my first experiences teaching the Arabic language and culture began within the cultural centers of the various Islamic communities in Tuscany in the form of courses for children held on weekends. Families also bring their children to socialize with others with whom they share the social and cultural context. Nonetheless, this system had difficulties, mainly concerning the complex organization and limited programs.

The Alshuruk Arabic language school

The situation of the Arab and Islamic communities became very complicated after September 11, 2001. In Italy, negative representations of immigrants of Arab origin and Muslims in the media were present even before this event, which further contributed to the growing intolerance. The prejudices about Islam propagated by the mass media spread a hostile attitude towards Arabs and Muslims among the Italian population. In this intricate scenario, a novel proposal was put forward to create a school dedicated to teaching the Arabic language and culture, welcoming all children.

The proposal was formulated during the visit of the then-president of the Tuscany Region, Claudio Martini, to the headquarters of CIFT. During this meeting, attended by Arab and Muslim families with their children, the importance of making one's culture and religion known appropriately was reaffirmed as the most effective way to counter prejudice. This endeavor could be done through teaching not only to the community's children but also to the entire society.

In November 2001, the Alshuruk school for Arabic language and Arab culture was established. The first lessons were held at the Giorgio La Pira International Student Centre on Saturday mornings. These lessons were aimed mainly at children whose mother tongue was Arabic, but among the students, there were also Italian children whose parents wanted them to learn Arabic. The first group of students was divided by age and level of knowledge of the Arabic language. The teachers, all holding suitable qualifications, offered their work and time on a volunteer basis. Another activity to highlight was the Italian language course for the mothers of these children, which was carried out at the same time as the Arabic lessons for children.

After a few years, Alshuruk School moved its location to a public school due to the increasing number of students. An agreement between the Municipality of Florence, the Office of Public Education, and the Islamic Community permitted the lessons to be held at a public school during extra-school hours. Thus, the Arabic school was formal, with various classes and a defined program, timetable, and calendar. In its first year as a public school, Alshuruk had about 70 students divided into six classes. The course included a first preparatory class for students aged 5 to 6, then subsequent classes based on age and level of knowledge of the Arabic language.

In addition to teaching the Arabic language, lessons were dedicated to Arab culture. There are many elements common to the various Arab countries, in particular those concerning history, religious traditions, and holidays. However, each country has specific characteristics linked to local customs. During the lessons, the students had the opportunity to learn about the plurality of the Arab countries and their customs, elements of history, and mentions of the local dialects. In all classes, teachers almost exclusively use modern standard Arabic (MSA) in a simplified variety. Especially in the first levels, teachers used simplified language and grammar with a limited vocabulary that they gradually enriched with every lesson. This is also to address the differences in dialect and levels between students and to dedicate more space to oral production and pronunciation, mainly some Arabic letters absent in the Latin alphabet. Following the example of the Alshuruk school, eight other schools were established throughout the province of Florence in the Tuscany Region. These schools had programs and an administration similar to that of Alshuruk. They were all self-managed by volunteer associations and held their activities in public schools. This has allowed students living in various areas to reach one of these schools more efficiently. Other initiatives by local communities were carried out and held in libraries, literary circles, etc.

Challenges facing the teaching of the Arabic language

In Italy, Arabic is the third most widespread language among residing foreign citizens and the second language for school students. Therefore, it is necessary to consider the richness of the cultural panorama of origin and the linguistic repertoire these students possess, which is often composed of more than one language (dialect, MSA, classical Arabic, the language of colonization, etc.). This complexity is frequently summarily sacrificed on the altar of the need for insertion and integration, a cultural impoverishment for these students and society.

The general linguistic profile of the student of Arabic origin depends on several relevant factors such as country of origin, family background, level of schooling, and linguistic competence in the mother tongue, with the distinction between MSA and dialect. In Italy, Arabic-speaking students find themselves divided between two very different languages in which there are no standard tools that can be useful for metalinguistic reflections. In the current situation, in most cases, we cannot speak of Italian as a second language since we are faced with bilingualism. The concept of bilingualism has also taken on a more open character in the case of children of immigrants of Arab origin. Those who use the mother tongue at home, be it a dialect or a regional language, and another language at school are considered bilingual. Adequately supporting the correct use of both languages to use bilingualism is not easy. Research has highlighted the difficulty in achieving authentic bilingualism, both because the apparent rapidity with which learning occurs in childhood is often misleading and because there are different and more specific methods and types of expression within it. Most of these students often speak their parents' language of origin at home, which is a dialect of Arabic. In this case, the question would possibly concern competence in Arabic rather than Italian, and the difficulties that could arise would affect the sphere of cultural identity and not only the linguistic aspect.

Young second-generation Arabs represent a fascinating case: like all bilinguals, they have mastered two codes, Italian and an Arabic dialect. However, the term Arabic language does not always coincide with the language they have perfect command of. Instead, it refers to the classical language, the custodian of the literary and religious heritage of the Arab world. A language that many of them learn like any other language. In the various Arabic language classes, we find students from different Arab countries familiar with a particular dialect. Teachers, therefore, must apply a more significant commitment to teaching Arabic than other languages due to this diglossia and variety of dialects.

For this reason, it is impossible to refer to a single country's paths or a specific dialect. In addition, some students of Arabic origin may have not learned their mother tongue and have not had the opportunity to familiarize themselves with it. In this case, their first approach to the Arabic language is precisely the school of Arabic. This problem does not exist in the countries of origin, as the language of schooling is the classic literary Arabic or MSA, while the local dialect is used orally. Another consideration is religion since classical

Arabic is the language of the Qur'an and liturgy. A third consideration is strictly linguistic due to the superiority of classical Arabic and MSA over the dialect's vocabulary, expressions, grammatical rules, and grammatical correctness. Consequently, teaching the classical language to learn and not lose this cultural heritage is necessary.

Some teaching models commonly used in other European countries (Amsterdam and Jerusalem) incorporate a particular dialect. In Italian reality, the two communities most present are the Moroccan and Egyptian, which have two very different dialectal languages. This presents the difficulty of an eventual choice of the dialect to use. Therefore, the best option is to adopt the traditional model based on teaching MSA in the initial training phase. The emphasis is mainly on competence in written production, gradually including oral production and reception skills. The student first learns the standard variety, which is considered more valuable because it is expected to the whole of the Arab world and because it is mainly prevalent in writing. Despite these considerations, dialects remain widely used in daily social communication, especially among the second generation, and their use is not expected to decrease.

For this reason, we cannot simply ignore this reality and its value in social contexts, and the issue of dialect differences is also addressed in the Arabic language schools in Florence and Tuscany. The teaching goal in these schools is that of any other language. That is to develop language skills and to achieve effective learning of the Arabic language, starting with basic skills: comprehension, reading, and written and oral production. To achieve these objectives, it is up to the teacher to create a path according to the reference models and directives, considering the surrounding context. Also, concerning assessment, there is not yet a comprehensive framework in Italy for assessing proficiency in Arabic. However, there have been several initiatives to build an assessment tool and establish the requirements for language certification, at least for the basic skills and levels.

Future opportunities

Italy has a long history of emigration and yet a concise immigration experience. It was only starting from the early 1980s that Italy began to attract substantial flows of immigrants from other countries. Until then, Italian society was linguistically and culturally homogeneous. This puts Italy in a particular situation for the rapidity with which its society is changing. The presence of immigrants from other cultures who are actively involved in public life and contact with local institutions represents a valuable resource and an element of change and improvement for society.

The topic of language in this process is of fundamental importance. Language transmits cultural aspects, attitudes, values, norms, etc., from the parents to their children. The language spoken in the family profoundly affects how the second generations identify and place themselves in relation to society. The intergenerational relationship between parents and children has delicate dynamics that, in this case, could be affected by linguistic and cultural barriers. Young people of Arab origin who were born and raised in Italy learn the Italian language at school and know the habits and customs of Italian society, while their parents may not. Thus, an additional barrier between parents and their children may be created. By learning the language and culture of origin, the children of immigrants can overcome other cultural barriers besides the language barrier, thus understanding their parents and getting closer to a substantial part of their identity.

The integration process occurs in many ways, both at and outside the school. The collaborations implemented between the Italian school and civil society actors, including the Arab communities and the associations that refer to them, have certainly produced positive results. These results also align with the principles set by the Ministry of Labor and Social Policies regarding the policies for the social integration of foreign immigrants, particularly minors. Teaching the mother tongue to students of non-Italian origin is considered a fundamental tool for cognitive and psychological growth at schools.

Unfortunately, the various initiatives for teaching the mother tongues of students of non-Italian origin are still minimal, sporadic, and fragmented. Moreover, the COVID-19 pandemic has devastated all the initiatives to teach the Arabic language in the past two years. Since the pandemic started in early 2020, all these activities have been suspended and have not resumed as they are considered extracurricular activities. The best solution to optimize the outcome of this teaching with a lower expenditure of effort is to have it included within the content of the school's educational program. It would further enhance the learning of the mother tongue as it is part of the school activity and would allow more students of Arab origin to learn it.

Furthermore, courses could be offered to all students interested in learning this language, one of the world's most widely used languages. Projects can be activated in single schools to make learning the language and culture of origin possible as supplementary courses throughout the school year. This proposal provides for the activation, among the educational initiatives, of lessons aimed at bilingual and monolingual students to promote interculturalism and peaceful coexistence.

In recent years in Italy, there has been a significant and increasing interest in including Arabic as a foreign language in schools, especially in high schools. The activation of the teaching of the language and culture of origin in this way presents numerous advantages. A significant advantage is making this teaching available to all students of Arab origin, who do not have to travel or find extra time to attend classes. Furthermore, all other students who would like to benefit from this teaching could also do so. A second advantage is creating further opportunities for intercultural exchange and relationships. Another advantage is for the school itself; this activity has to do with the pedagogical and didactic management of the changes in the school and society. Among these are the encounter processes, the challenges of social cohesion, the conditions of intercultural exchange, and the relationships between diversities. In this case, through teachers' awareness, the training process would respond to multilingualism with bottom-up actions to enhance linguistic diversity and increase skills that include all the actors operating on the educational scene as recipients.

18. Linguistic consciousness-raising: A reflection on critical thinking and mainstreaming gender vocabulary in the Arabic language

Munirah Eskander
American University of Iraq, Sulaimani (AUIS)

Developing critical thinking skills is often imperative for student success in universities worldwide, including the Middle East and North Africa (MENA).[228] This is demonstrated in the emphasis on critical thinking across university curricula and in the numerous initiatives undertaken to instill this skill in teachers and students alike in Arab countries.[229] Although such initiatives are not limited to the MENA region,[230] studies have suggested that critical thinking skills are not well developed among students in Arab universities.[231]

As a bilingual Arab woman who was taught such skills in a university in the United Arab Emirates and the Netherlands, I am particularly interested in how language and independent thinking intersect to influence how students acquire the ability to think critically, especially concerning gender. This chapter explores my personal and academic journey in navigating discussions of critical thinking and gender in the English and Arabic languages as a student and educator. In light of realizing the extent to which gender discussions are confined to intellectuals, I further reflect on the

---

[228] Yousef, 2021.
[229] Schwartz, 2012; Genkin, 2021; Eurasia Foundation, 2016.
[230] Sellars et al., 2018.
[231] Yousef, 2021; Allamnakhrah, 2013; Al-Mahrooqi and Denman, 2020.

discourse on gender and sexuality in Arabic and how it can become more accessible to laypeople and academics alike.

The first section of this chapter describes my linguistic and academic studies in school and university, followed by a discussion relating my experience teaching critical thinking and gender as an instructor. The final section offers suggestions on how the discourse on gender and sexuality can become more mainstream and inclusive in Arabic. Lastly, I would also like to note that as someone who is not a specialist in sociolinguistics, this chapter reflects my personal opinion and perspective on how the Arabic language can be used to stimulate critical thinking about gender, both in the classroom and in society.

Personal linguistic and academic journey

During my childhood and adolescence in Saudi Arabia and the U.A.E., I attended schools where secular and religious subjects were taught in Arabic, except for English class. However, I studied English grammar, composition, and reading at a basic level, which involved understanding anodyne texts at face value, otherwise known as "decoding."[232] Also known as the first level of comprehension in reading, decoding is followed by the inferential and evaluative levels, which are higher levels of reading comprehension. At the second level of inferential engagement, readers must "read between the lines, connect information from different parts of the text, and draw conclusions."[233]

Readers are only then equipped to engage in evaluative reading, which necessitates the "use of numerous higher order thinking skills and strategies, among which are analyzing, synthesizing, hypothesizing, and identifying bias."[234] Together, these three levels

---

[232] Alderson, 2000.
[233] Alderson, 2000, p. 3.
[234] Freimuth, 2014. P. 3.

enable readers to engage in critical thinking, which can be understood as involving all three abovementioned processes, as well as Paul's additional dimension of approaching matters "with an open mind and from multiple perspectives."[235]

Although I was not taught to read and comprehend Arabic texts as a critical thinker in school, the religious and secular texts I studied enabled me to engage inferentially with reading material. However, the approach of my instructors and the textbooks we were assigned to read continued to reinforce specific ideas, including nationalism, religiosity, and the superiority of Arabic as the language of the Qur'an.[236] As such, the educational system's intentional glorification of the Arabic language and Islamic heritage discouraged (or even prohibited) instructors from teaching students to evaluate reading material, which made it far more challenging to cultivate critical thinking skills in high school.

I enrolled in the American University of Sharjah after graduating from high school. At this liberal arts university, the predominant language of instruction was English, although I studied a few courses in Arabic.[237] The move from school to university was very challenging, manifesting not only in a shift in the language of instruction from Arabic to English but also in the transition from rote learning to independent thinking.

One of the first courses which stimulated me to think critically was "Introduction to Women's Studies." As a teenager, I was puzzled by how men and women were treated differently in society,

---

[235] Paul, 1984.
[236] Kermani, 2017.
[237] The Arabic courses I took included "Readings in Arabic Heritage I," "Readings in Arabic Heritage II," "Readings in Arabic Philosophy," "Introduction to Translation," "Maqamat," and "Islamic Texts in Translation."

especially concerning religion[238] and education. For example, while I was studying in Saudi Arabia in elementary school in the 1990s, boys and girls followed different curricula, with girls compelled to take courses that would teach them homemaking skills and embroidery classes instead of sports classes, which were reserved for boys.[239] My prior questioning related to gender encouraged me to take the course on women's studies, which equipped me with the linguistic and conceptual tools to address questions about gender inequality, including institutional sexism. My intellectual journey began at this point, and I started to identify as a feminist and critical thinker.

I believe that how a person is taught critical thinking is important. In my experience, I was encouraged by my professors to question everything that was considered an indisputable truth, even if it were religious scripture. Even more importantly, my instructors provided me with a safe, nonjudgmental space to acknowledge the cognitive dissonance I was experiencing personally and intellectually. This process of questioning made me appreciate the value of academic endeavors and pursue a career in the field to become an educator committed to shaping minds, especially in the MENA countries. As such, I completed my master's degree in Modern Middle Eastern Studies and recently began teaching at a higher education institution, which I discuss further below.

From student to educator: Gendered language and critical thinking

In the Spring Semester of 2022, I officially joined the American University of Iraq, Sulaimani (AUIS) as a Jan Warner Visiting

---

[238] The literature I engaged with, including magazines and novels, along with the religious content I encountered, such as televised *fatawas* or religious edicts, delineated distinct rights and obligations for men and women, framing these differences as equitable.
[239] Al Rawaf and Simmons, 1991.

Scholar at the Center for Gender and Development Studies (CGDS). Since then, I have continued to serve as an Adjunct Lecturer and taught different courses, including "History of the Middle East," "Social Justice in Theory and Practice," and "Critical Reading and Writing." Reflecting on my intellectual background and expertise, I designed the "Critical Reading and Writing" course to include reading material on topics about gender, sexuality, inequality, exploitation, religion, culture, and politics, amongst others.

As a facilitator of learning, my pedagogical approach involves gauging the academic and cultural environment I am teaching to establish a safe space where students can voice their opinions and ideas freely. This is particularly important in the MENA countries, where censorship is often imposed in both social and political domains upon various social groups, especially women.[240] Since I aim to measure students' preexisting knowledge and encourage them to think outside the box, I believe this can only be done by removing taboos, emphasizing mutual respect and active listening, and urging them to be inquisitive and analytical.

Although most of my students are Kurdish, some understand Arabic better than English, and I also have Arab students in my classroom. In a few one-to-one meetings with pupils with limited comprehension skills, I occasionally code-switch between Arabic and English to explain some ideas better. I consider this practice a necessity because of the different levels of fluency that my pupils and I have in the various codes we speak.

However, this is also a struggle due to the multi-layered code-switching between Arabic and English, as this process applies not only to switching between different languages but also to different varieties within a language.[241] Due to the academic setting in which my meetings take place, several of these meetings entail

---

[240] Skalli, 2006.
[241] Myers-Scotton, 1993.

codeswitching between Modern Standard Arabic (MSA) [the highly valued (H) variety of Arabic], colloquial Arabic [the low (L) variety of Arabic], and English.[242] The complexity of this process, in light of my academic studies in English, has been challenging to navigate. This is because I am not as familiar with intellectual terms in Arabic since English was the dominant language of instruction in both my alma maters.

While this could be easily overcome by researching certain (gender or other) terms online before specific meetings, I have encountered a second problem. In this case, my students are also not as familiar with intellectual terms in Arabic, which often originate in MSA, and are typically restricted to conversations amongst intellectuals or the well-educated.[243] This could be attributed to high illiteracy rates in some parts of the MENA region, where education is less accessible to the underprivileged.[244] In addition, the absence of a reading culture can perpetuate reliance on traditional media and social media for information instead of books.[245] Academic vocabulary acquisition in Arabic has proven difficult for many native speakers, partly due to the diglossic nature and linguistic characteristics of the Arabic language.[246] As such, even if I were to familiarize myself with gender-specific terms in Arabic, for example, I would only be able to converse with others with this vocabulary more efficiently, typically academics or practitioners in the development field.[247]

Aside from Arab societies' lack of widespread knowledge of gender-related terms, including those about the LGBTQ+ community, many Middle Easterners, including intellectuals,

---

[242] Bassiouney, 2009.
[243] Badawi, 1973.
[244] Hashemi and Intini, 2015.
[245] Martin et al., 2017.
[246] Makhoul et al., 2018.
[247] Kamal, 2018.

perceive such concepts to be a Western imposition that must be opposed in the name of religion or tradition.[248] There is also much resistance to the word "gender," in particular, and little consensus on using a single term in Arabic with the same connotation as the English equivalent.[249]

A personal experience as an educator showed me first-hand how removed the term "gender" can be from the lived experience of my Arabic- and Kurdish-speaking pupils. For example, one of the writing assignments I gave my students asked them to discuss how they perform gender roles within their society critically. However, the submissions demonstrated that the vast majority of them could not reflect on how they "do gender" and transgress gender norms in their personal lives. Although they could engage with the concept of gender in class while also reflecting on it as a feature of Western society, they could not comprehend that their manhood or womanhood could be socially constructed.

This inability to connect gender to their personal lives, in my opinion, is a reflection of their subconscious resistance to it as a concept that they continue to see as Western and not truly indigenous or Middle Eastern. For example, since gender performativity is more publicly visible in the West, such as in the form of cross-dressing or drag,[250] it is easier to see active resistance to gender roles therein. While the subversion of gender roles also exists in the MENA countries, the transgression of gender norms is not as overt or explicitly political in the contemporary age[251] despite having a long history in the region.[252] This is in part due to greater persecution of

---

[248] Al-Hasan, 2021; Dalacoura, 2014.
[249] Kamal, 2008.
[250] Lorber, 1995.
[251] Nigst and Garcia, 2010.
[252] Massad, 2007.

non-gender conforming individuals or (perceived) members of the LGBTQ+ community in the MENA region.[253]

However, in my perspective, the manifestation of "gender" as a concept—despite originating as a "field of knowledge from the North"—exists everywhere and in all societies, being "borrowed, followed, or adapted… and producing a localized politics" in various contexts.[254] All societies have their understanding and theorization about gender orders and ways of transgressing against gender norms, such as in the emergence of the phenomenon of *boyat*, or "girls who behave like men," in the Gulf states.[255] However, while the performance of drag in the West is dominated by drag queens who are performing femininity in contrast to drag kings performing masculinity, *boyats*' performance of masculinity reflects the privilege associated with it, whereby "all positivity is placed on the side of masculinity and…femininity is emptied of all value".[256] Hence, the behavior of *boyat* is perceived to be a revolt against gender norms that provide them with greater access to public spaces and challenge privileges bestowed upon men by patriarchy.[257] Nonetheless, while it is frowned upon for women to "behave like men," it is far more acceptable for them to do so than for men to behave like women due to the devaluation of women's bodies and femininity embedded in patriarchal systems.[258]

As such, in my perspective, the unintentional dismissal of gender and sexuality as Western concepts—as embodied in my students' writings—delegitimizes the need for specialized vocabulary on the topic to exist in languages native to the region, including Arabic and

---

[253] Youssef and Stack, 2017.
[254] Millan, 2016, 10.
[255] Nigst and Garcia, 2010.
[256] Nigst and Garcia, 2010, 12.
[257] Nigst and Garcia, 2010.
[258] Johnson, 2014.

Kurdish. I believe such vocabulary needs to exist and be widely circulated to have a more open and accessible discourse on gender in society. Simultaneously, existing terms that manifest in the form of slurs and heteronormative lexicon, which are far more well-known than neutral terms, must also be challenged in the Arabic language.

For example, the United States-based National Immigrant Justice Center's (2021) Arabic LGBTQ Terminology Guide lists twelve pejorative terms used to describe effeminate men, including "mukhannath," "khaniith," "khawwal," and "zanaana." The text further comments, "These terms appear grouped together because they are all generally used to emasculate people who are perceived as failing to perform their expected roles as men" (p. 11). The embodiment of linguistic sexism in these insults demonstrates how gender roles are reinforced in how the Arabic language is used. Moreover, although the Guide does not categorize the following terms as necessarily attributable to "effeminate men," other pejoratives could be attributed to them, including "man with a woman's appearance," "shemale," "shadhdh/a" (sexual deviant), and "luutiyy" (sodomite). Of the neutral terms for identity descriptors that exist, the Guide notes that the terms "mithliyy" (gay) and "mithliyya" (lesbian) are most likely to be recognized by speakers of Arabic.[259] However, the lack of recognition of other terms such as "aabir/a al-jindar" (transgender) and "thunaaíyy/a al-mayl al-jinsiyy" (bisexual) is still problematic because these terms are descriptive (neutral) as well, thereby not explicitly connoting support or rejection of any particular cause or sexual orientation. The following section discusses my reflections on how some of the abovementioned forms of linguistic sexism can be deconstructed.

---

[259] National Immigrant Justice Center, 2021.

Moving forward: Deconstructing linguistic sexism.

In my perspective, deconstructing linguistic sexism in Arabic is a two-fold process. Firstly, this involves tackling the root of resistance against the term "gender," its derivatives, and other concepts as Western impositions. I believe it is essential to continue to raise awareness about and highlight the existence of historical women's rights and feminist movements in the region, dating back to the 20th century[260]. This will help root existing discourses on gender and sexuality in indigenous women's experiences while shedding light on the historicity of non-heteronormative sexual practices therein.[261]

Secondly, it is essential to produce and circulate educational content on gender that is not exclusively confined to academic or intellectual circles and is more accessible to the general public. Such material can also be important in denouncing the casual and pervasive use of pejoratives and circulating neutral gender terms. For example, this is evident in the digital initiative "Khateera,"[262] a Facebook page and online magazine that critically discusses gender and women's issues in Arabic. Various educational and satirical posts and videos on the Facebook page that critique sexism and raise awareness about Arab women's struggles are regularly shared (Khateera, n.d.). By using accessible and inclusive language, Khateera is an example of how gender-related content can be widely shared and circulated online in a more captivating form, catering to a more diverse audience.

Another example of how educational content can be circulated in the Arabic language, thereby promoting the use of positive sexuality-related terms, is evident in the content posted on social

---

[260] Al-Ali, 2002.
[261] Massad, 2007.
[262] The term "khateera" literally means "dangerous" singular feminine in Arabic. However, in colloquial slang Arabic, "khateera" is often used to denote a fearless woman.

media by Dr. Sandrine Atallah, a consultant in sexual medicine and certified psycho-sexologist. While not strictly related to gender, Atallah posts material on sexual education and health. Since many misconceptions and myths stem from this taboo topic, Atallah challenges stereotypes about sexual reproduction and health and encourages sex positivity. One way in which she has been promoting pleasure is by changing the language used to describe sexual relations.

For example, by pointing out that many terms denoting sexual activity have negative connotations,[263] she pushes for the need to use positive terms meant to shed any shame associated with intimacy and enjoying sex, especially for women.[264] Moreover, she encourages people to come up with "#NewSexSlang" in Arabic through an initiative begun by the International Planned Parenthood Federation to circulate more favorable terms for sexual acts (International Planned Parenthood Federation, n.d). This encourages people to not only become recipients of knowledge but also to actively partake in constructing language by coining new and inclusive terms in Arabic. Such educational endeavors not only raise awareness in the public and bring more equality into intimate relationships but also aid in grounding the discourse on sexuality in the activities of the general public. Hence, this exclusively challenges such discourse's confinement to academics and intellectuals.

Through such content, both Atallah and the platform Khateera help disseminate more neutral or positive gender and sexuality-related terms in Arabic, thereby supporting such vocabulary. Such

---

[263] For example, the term "'adah sirriyyah," or "masturbation" in Arabic literally means "secret habit," and has a shameful connotation in the Arabic language. In the content posted on social media, Atallah debunks myths about masturbation while also raising awareness about its benefits, further encouraging the use of more positive names for the term in Arabic Atallah, 2021.

[264] Atallah, 2021.

linguistic consciousness-raising, in the case of pejoratives, and the circulation of neutral terms that reflect Arab history, culture, and heritage can play an important role in challenging sexist practices that violate the bodies and rights of women, men, and other sexual minorities. It is only by thinking critically about language that discussions on gender and sexuality in Arabic can become more neutral and inclusive. In other words, it is only by constructing a more accessible, critical discourse on gender that the Arabic language can become a more powerful tool to challenge patriarchy and promote greater gender equality.

Mosaic of languages: Shaping the future of education in the Arabic-speaking world

Carine Allaf, Fabrice Jaumont, Selma Talha-Jebril

The journey towards multilingualism for the Arabic-speaking world is rich in promise and fraught with complexities. It is a journey underscored by multiple advantages, including enhanced communication and connection within culturally diverse communities, economic benefits, and improved access to the global stage. The examples shared by our authors underscore the potential of effective multilingual education in creating global citizens proficient in multiple languages and, in so doing, unlocking expansive opportunities.

Simultaneously, multilingualism contributes to cognitive development and social cohesion. Studies consistently affirm the role of multilingualism in honing cognitive abilities, such as problem-solving, memory, and cognitive flexibility. Furthermore, being a polyglot is more than an intellectual asset—it encourages a broader cultural understanding, fosters mutual respect and empathy, and ultimately creates more inclusive, harmonious societies.

Case studies from Morocco and the United Arab Emirates present valuable insights into successfully implementing multilingual education, showcasing the benefits of language diversity and active governmental support. The journey towards multilingualism extends to the Arabic-speaking diaspora as well. In countries like France and the United States, where significant Arabic-speaking immigrant communities reside, multilingualism often opens doors to economic opportunities and better access to services. However, it is paramount to address the lack of institutional support for language learning and overcome perceptions that consider multilingualism a hindrance to societal integration.

Our book's exploration of multilingual learning underscores the imperative of embracing a multilingual revolution that recognizes Arabic as a global language of significant import. A revolution that empowers learners, educators, and societies to cherish the beauty of linguistic diversity and leverage it for cultural, cognitive, and economic advancements. A revolution that views Arabic not just as a language of heritage but as a vital means of communication in our globalized, interconnected world. This revolution is not a distant dream but a palpable reality, achievable through concerted efforts in language education policy, teacher training, curriculum development, and societal mindset change.

Our shared vision is an equitable and inclusive multilingual society that values the rich tapestry of languages and cultures. In this society, embracing multilingualism leads to greater understanding, tolerance, peace, and progress. It is a vision we can all partake in, learn from, and contribute to, and it is a vision that this book hopes to inspire. Together, we can traverse the path toward a multilingual future, unlocking limitless possibilities for the Arabic-speaking world and beyond.

It is crucial to address the existing challenges systematically to move toward this vision of a multilingual world. Firstly, increasing resources and support for learning languages like Arabic is imperative. This involves improving the availability and quality of language learning materials and investing in teacher training to ensure educators are well-equipped to teach a second or third language.

Secondly, it is essential to challenge and change societal attitudes that view multilingualism as threatening cultural identity. This can be achieved through public education campaigns that highlight the benefits of multilingualism and showcase successful examples of individuals and communities who have embraced multiple languages without losing their cultural identity.

Thirdly, it's crucial to reassess and revise language policies to promote multilingual education, especially for languages that are less widely represented. This includes revising school curriculums to include more language learning opportunities, implementing policies that promote the use of multiple languages in the public and private sectors, and creating incentives for individuals to learn and use various languages.

Fourthly, more research must be conducted to understand the challenges and opportunities for multilingual learning in Arabic. This research could inform policy decisions and help develop more effective language-learning strategies.

Fifthly, collaboration among stakeholders, including educators, policymakers, parents, and students, is crucial. These stakeholders can work together to promote multilingualism and create a more inclusive, diverse, and globally connected Arabic-speaking world through dialogue and cooperation.

The examples of Qatar and the United Arab Emirates demonstrate that a multilingual education strategy can lead to increased economic opportunities and improved access to global markets. The experience of these countries can serve as a model for other Arabic-speaking countries looking to promote multilingualism. However, it is also essential to recognize that each country is unique, and what works in one context may not be effective in another. Therefore, local conditions, cultural norms, and societal attitudes must be considered when designing and implementing multilingual education strategies.

In the Arabic-speaking diaspora, efforts should also be made to support multilingualism. In countries like France and the United States, this could include providing more resources and support for Arabic language learning in schools, encouraging the use of Arabic in public spaces, and promoting cultural events that celebrate the Arabic language and culture.

Within the dynamic mosaic of the Arabic-speaking world, individuals from diverse backgrounds blend a rich cultural tapestry, nurturing the next generation within a spectrum of traditions, and transmitting a legacy rich with cherished recipes, tunes, artistic works, and ancestral tales. This intricate interplay of cultures lies at the core of our linguistic heritage, creating a fertile landscape ripe with social, cultural, and professional possibilities for the younger demographic. Embracing the intricate diversity of this mosaic challenges outdated and simplistic notions of identity, showcasing this linguistic community's dynamic and multifaceted nature. Multilingualism emerges as a pivotal element in this setting, serving as a bridge to inclusivity and deeper insights, enabling a fuller recognition of the varied lifestyles, viewpoints, and customs that weave the elaborate fabric of our region, thereby nurturing a community more attuned to and accepting of the world's broad array of perspectives.

About the authors

Originally from Tunisia, **Rym Akhonzada** holds a BA in English Language and Linguistics. She started her career in research at Queen's University Belfast. She currently runs her language school "Interlingua" in Belfast, and she is the founder of a social enterprise called "Yallaa" which aims to promote Arab culture, arts, and heritage in the region. Rym is also a visiting lecturer at the School of Education at Ulster University.

Sarab Al Ani's research interests focus on the use of technology in language teaching, overcoming challenges that students of Arabic in the U.S. face, the means to achieve desired language skills with minimum difficulty, and optimal testing methods. She has taught Arabic at the Middlebury Language Summer Schools and Michigan State University and linguistics, morphology, and phonology at the University of Baghdad. She is currently the Arabic Language program director at Yale University and teaches all levels of Arabic.

Issam Albdairat is a Lecturer in the Arabic program at the Middle Eastern Languages & Cultures department at Indiana University Bloomington. Dr. Albdairat's research interests include teaching Arabic as a second language and being interested in Arabic phonology and sociolinguistics. Dr. Albdairat earned his Ph.D. in Near Eastern Languages and Cultures from Indiana University Bloomington.

Aisha Alfadhalah is a trilingual Speech-Language Pathologist at the Center for Autism and Related Disorders at Kennedy Krieger Institute. She focuses on the treatment and evaluation of multilingual students. Her research interest is multilingualism, specifically the importance of maintaining the home language to develop the cultural and linguistic identities of children with and without developmental disabilities.

Carine Allaf is the Senior Programs Advisor for QFI programs. Although she works across all programming, she focuses primarily on our international programs, elementary Arabic immersion schools, monitoring and evaluation, and research. Carine has worked in the education, development, and non-profit fields for over 15 years as a teacher, scholar, and practitioner in the United States and the Arab world. Carine holds a Ph.D. in Comparative and International Education from the University of California, Los Angeles.

Fatema M. Al-Malki is the Project Manager of Qatar Reads, passionate about reading for the cause of social progress. She received her MA in Creative and Cultural Industries from King's College London and focuses on impact-based program design for the Qatar National Library.

Haifa Alsakkaf holds a Ph.D. in Intercultural Pedagogy and is the visionary founder of the Good World Citizen organization. With a rich 18-year tenure teaching within the Italian educational landscape, she also played a pivotal role as a co-founder and decade-long director of the Alshuruk Arabic Language School. Dr. Alsakkaf's academic prowess extends to her contributions through articles and conference participation, addressing interculturalism, cultural heritage, the experiences of second-generation immigrants in Italy, and nuanced insights into intercultural pedagogy.

Hakim Benbadra is French-Algerian. He grew up in Paris with an Algerian background. He supports African family businesses in their development and growth. Hakim is also committed to ensuring equal opportunities for youth. He helped to expand International Day for Equal Opportunities' (IDEO) programming from 5 countries to 23 and led IDEO's effort to achieve UN recognition. Hakim is passionate about empowering underserved communities and supporting youth in France and Africa.

Marina Chamma is a Beirut-based political economist and author. After starting her studies at Sophia University in Tokyo, she graduated from the American University of Beirut with a B.A. in Political Science. She obtained a M.Sc. in International Political Economy from the London School of Economics. As a freelance writer and blogger, she established eyeontheeast.org in 2011. Her first book, *And So We Drive On: Short Stories*, was published in 2020. Her writing has also appeared in, among others, *Liban: Messages pour un pays* (Collective Work. Editions Noir Blanc, etc., 2019) and *Beyond Shattered Glass: Voices from the Aftermath of the Beirut Explosion* (Collective Work. Interlink Books, August 2023).

Logan Cochrane is an associate professor at Hamad bin Khalifa University and an associate dean for academic affairs in the College of Public Policy. He is an Associate Fellow of the Ethiopian Academy of Sciences and an Adjunct Professor at Hawassa University (Institute for Policy and Development Research).

Anna Dillon is an Associate Professor at Emirates College for Advanced Education. She has worked in the U.A.E. and Ireland as a mainstream class teacher, school principal, and head of faculty, and more recently, as a teacher educator and higher education administrator at Zayed University. Her research interests include bilingual education, language education, classroom-based research, and more recently, international education, Third Culture Kids, and accreditation in teacher education.

After obtaining her degree from Istanbul University's Department of Arabic Language and Literature in 2006, **Zeynep Ertürk** spent nearly a decade teaching Arabic at the Izmir Private Cemre Language Institute. Pursuing a Ph.D. in the field, she researched Arabic training sets within the European framework, underscoring the value of bilingual education. By 2022, she was teaching at Boaziçi University. With a rich background in bilingual instruction, Dr. Ertürk has specialized in teaching Arabic and English to Turkish speakers and vice versa and has extensively studied the interplay between native and target languages, even exploring bilingual education approaches in Jordan and Kuwait.

Munirah Eskander is an Adjunct Lecturer at the American University of Iraq, Sulaimani (AUIS). She holds a BA in International Studies and a BSc in Chemical Engineering from the American University of Sharjah in the United Arab Emirates and an MA in Modern Middle East Studies from Leiden University in the Netherlands.

Janaan Farhat is a Research Associate at the Sheikh Saud bin Saqr Al Qasimi Foundation for Policy Research. She holds a BA in International Studies from Leiden University in the Netherlands, specializing in the Middle East. Her research interests include language and identity, comparative education, cultural heritage, youth employment, and gender in the Middle East and North Africa.

Born in Demnate, Morocco, **Mohammed Foula** has been an Arabic language teacher at the preparatory secondary level since 2004. He is a Moroccan novelist with three notable works: *Qabil Againv*, 2019, *Remnants of Memory*, 2020, and *Never Be a Forensic Doctor*, 2021. He is also the author of the lexicon *Boundaries of Languages*, 2022. He has been acknowledged with the Sharjah Prize for the novel *Qabil Again* in the UAE, 2012, and the Maroun Abboud Award for the story *Extraordinary Ambassador* in France, 2022.

Fabrice Jaumont is a scholar-practitioner, award-winning author, non-profit leader, and education advisor based in New York. He is President of the Center for the Advancement of Languages, Education, and Communities, a nonprofit publishing organization based in New York and Paris. He has published nine books on bilingualism and education, philanthropy, and higher education, including *The Bilingual Revolution: The Future of Education is in Two Languages* and *Conversations on Bilingualism*.

Hanieh Khataee is the Director of the Strategy and Impact Department at Qatar Foundation. Hanieh brings over 20 years of international experience leading organizations to achieve national development priorities through community-centered solutions. She is passionate about impact-driven programs that can transform societies and has worked in the fields of health, sustainability, and education.

Mehdi Lazar is an international educator, author, and geographer. He is the Academic Director of the International School of Boston and a Research Associate at Panthéon-Sorbonne University. Mehdi, a certified teacher and school administrator, received his Ph.D. in Geography from Panthéon-Sorbonne University. An international workshop leader and former Education Inspector, Mehdi is the author of several books and articles on international education and the geography of the MENA region. His current research focuses on multilingual education, global citizenship education, and current affairs.

As the World Language & Dual Language Immersion Specialist for the Utah State Board of Education, **Gregg Roberts'** work led to groundbreaking changes in how second language education is viewed and funded within Utah's K-12 schools and nationwide. The "Utah Model" has impacted K-12 educators in school districts and states nationwide. Gregg was named "State Supervisor of the Year" in 2009 by the National Council of State Supervisors of Foreign Languages; in 2015, he received ACTFL's prestigious "Leo Bernardo Award for Innovation in K-12 Language Education." Gregg has also received the Palmes Académiques from the French Government.

Majd Sarah, Founder and CEO of Sin Fronteras Language Center LLC., is an accomplished language educator and visionary leader with over 15 years of experience in higher education. Dr. Sarah has a Master's degree in Applied Linguistics and a Ph.D. in Teaching, Learning, and Culture from the University of Texas at El Paso and currently serves as the School Age Administrator for over 40 YWCA After School programs across the county of El Paso. Specializing in literacy and biliteracy, Dr. Sarah is committed to empowering educators and promoting an inclusive learning environment by nurturing critical thinking and resilience in teachers and students, aiming to inspire them to reach their fullest potential.

For more than three decades, **Robert Slater** has been a national leader in creating innovative solutions to language issues nationwide. Formerly the Director of the National Security Education Program, Dr. Slater created and launched the Language Flagship effort, the National Language Service Corps, and numerous scholarship and fellowship programs that support the study of languages by U.S. students from kindergarten through post-secondary education.

Selma Talha Jebril is the Research, Policy, and Partnership Manager at Qatar Foundation. Before joining the Qatar Foundation, Selma was a Monitoring & Evaluation Specialist at IIE. Selma also worked with Chemonics International and Search for Common Ground on projects implemented in the Middle East and North Africa. Selma is originally from Morocco and holds a master's degree in sustainable development, international policy, and management from SIT Graduate Institute and a bachelor's degree in international relations and Trade from Université de Cergy-Pontoise (France).

References

Abid-Houcine, S. (2007). Enseignement et éducation en langues étrangères en Algérie : la compétition entre le français et l'anglais. Droit et cultures, 54, 143-156.

Abourehab, Y. and Azaz, M. (2020). Pedagogical translanguaging in community/heritage Arabic language learning. Journal of Multilingual and Multicultural Development, 1-14.

Abu Ali, D. and Habash, N. (2016). Botta: An Arabic dialect chatbot. In: Proceedings of COLING 2016, 26th International Conference on Computational Linguistics: System Demonstrations, 208–212.

Abushihab, I. M. (2015). Contrastive analysis of politeness in Jordanian Arabic and Turkish. Theory and Practice in Language Studies, 2017-2022.

Aksan, D. (2015). Her yönüyle dil ana çizgileriyle dilbilim. Ankara: Türk Dil Kurumu Yayınları.

Aktaş, O. (2019). kelime ve cümle yapıları bakımından arapça ve farsçanın karşılaştırılması, Ankara Yıldırım Beyazıt Üniversitesi, Ankara.

Alabd, A. (2016). Heritage language learners in L2 Arabic classes: Challenges and Instruction Strategies (master's thesis). The American University of Cairo.

Al-Ali, N. (2002). Women's movements in the Middle East: Case studies of Egypt and Turkey. United Nations Research Institute for Social Development.

Al-Batal, M. (2007). Arabic and national language educational policy. The Modern Language Journal, 91(2), 268-271.

Al-Batal, M. and Belnap, K. (2006). The teaching and learning of Arabic in the United States: Realities, needs, and future directions. In K. Wahba, Z. Taha, L. England, Handbook for Arabic language teaching professionals in the 21st century. 389–399. Mahwah, NJ: Erlbaum.

Albdairat, I. S. (2021). Sociolinguistic study of phonological variation in Jordanian Arabic in Al-Karak (Doctoral dissertation, Indiana University).

Albirini, A. (2014) The socio-pragmatics of dialectal code-switching by Al-'Keidaat Bedouin speakers. Intercultural Pragmatics. 11(1): 121–147.

Albirini, A. (2014). The role of colloquial varieties in the acquisition of the standard variety: The case of Arabic heritage speakers. Foreign Language Annals, 47(3), 447-463.

Al-Dajani, B.A.S. (2019). The function of Arabic literature in Arabic language teaching: A gateway to cultural literacy. In Dirasat: Human and Social Sciences, vol. 46, n. 1, pp. 281-293.

Alderson, C. (2000). Assessing reading. Cambridge University Press.

Al-Ghanim, K. and Watson J. (2021). Language and nature in Southern and Eastern Arabia. European Journal of Multi-disciplinary Studies, Volume 6 Issue 1.

Alhasan, A. (2022). An Islamic vision of gender: An application in Sudan. Islamic Dawa Landmarks Magazine, 15(1), 174-228.

Ali, S.A. (2013). Exploring motivational strategies for second language learners amongst first-year Japanese students. Institutional Repositories DataBase Takenoko Institutional Repository.

Alim, H. S. (2016). Introducing raciolinguistics. Raciolinguistics, 1–30.

Alkhlaifat, E., Yang, P., and Moustakim, M. (2020). Code-switching between Arabic and English in Jordanian GP consultations. Crossroads: A Journal of English Studies, 30(3), 4-22.

Allamnakhrah, A. (2013). Learning critical thinking in Saudi Arabia: Student perceptions of secondary pre-service teacher education programs. Journal of Education and Learning, 2(1), 197-210.

Al-Mahrooqi, R. and Denman, C. J. (2020). Assessing students' critical thinking skills in the humanities and sciences colleges of a Middle Eastern university. International Journal of Instruction, 13(1), 783-796.

Al-Rawaf, H. S. and Simmons, C. (1991). The education of women in Saudi Arabia. Comparative Education, 27(3), 287-295.

Alsahafi, M. (2017). Pluricentricity and heritage language maintenance of Arab immigrants in the English-speaking new world countries. International Journal of Research Studies in Language Learning, 7(2), 93–102.

Al-Saleemi, E. (1987). A contrastive study of the verb systems of English and Arabic. Durham University. Durham E-Theses.

Al-Tamimi, F. (2001). Phonetic and phonological variation in the speech of rural migrants in a Jordanian City. Unpublished doctoral dissertation, University of Leeds, UK.

Amara, A. (2010). Langues maternelles et langues étrangères en Algérie : conflit ou cohabitation ? Algérie Synergies, 11, 5-121.

Angouri, J. (2012). I'm a Greek kiwi: Constructing Greekness in discourse. Journal of Language, Identity Education, 11(2), 96-108.

Archer, L., Francis, B., and Mau, A. (2010). The culture project: Diasporic negotiations of ethnicity, identity, and culture among teachers, pupils, and parents in Chinese language schools. Oxford Review of Education, 36(4), 407–426.

August, D., Shanahan, T., and Escamilla, K. (2009). English language learners: Developing literacy in second-language learners—Report of the national literacy panel on language-minority children and youth. Journal of Literacy Research, 41(4), 432–452.

Ayouby, K. K. (2007). "Speak American!" or language, power, and education in Dearborn, Michigan: A case study of Arabic heritage learners and their community—doctoral dissertation.

Azlan, N. I. and Narasuman, S. (2013). The role of code-switching as a communicative tool in an ESL teacher education classroom. Procedia - Social and Behavioral Sciences, 90, 458-467.

Badawi, E. M. (1973). Mustawayat al-'Arabiyya al-mu'asira fi Misr. Dār al-ma'arif.

Baker, C., Wright, W. E. (2021). Foundations of bilingual education and bilingualism. Multilingual Matters.

Baker, C. (2014). A parents' and teachers' guide to bilingualism, 4th Edition, Bristol, UK: Multilingual Matters.

Bamoshmoosh, M. (2015). Vecchie e nuove barriere (linguistiche) metropolitane, in Quale città per un nuovo umanesimo, Rivista Associazione Incontri, Edizione Polistampa, vol. VII, n. 13, Firenze, 65-70.

Bassiouney, R. (2009). Arabic sociolinguistics. Edinburgh University Press.

Bassiouney, R. (2013). The social motivation of code-switching in mosque sermons in Egypt. International Journal of the Sociology of Language, 220.

Bauer, E. B. and Mkhize, D. (2012). Supporting the early development of biliteracy: The role of parents and caregivers. In Early Biliteracy Development, 23-42. Routledge.

Belfarhi, K. (2019). Languages' interaction in Algeria: Dialectical text and French graphic. Open Journal for Studies in Linguistics, volume 2, 51-58.

Belmihoub, K. (2018). English in a multilingual Algeria. World Englishes, 207–227.

Bessaid, A. (2020). The quest for Algerian linguistic independence. Translation Literary Studies, 4(2), 105-119.

Bhatia T. K. and Ritchie W. C. (2004). The handbook of bilingualism. Blackwell Pub.

Bialystok, E. (2001). Bilingualism in development: Language, literacy, and cognition. Cambridge University Press.

Blom, J. P. and Gumperz, J. (1972). Social meaning in linguistic structures: Code-switching in northern Norway. In J. Gumperz and D. Hymes: Directions in Sociolinguistics: The Ethnography of Communication, 407-434. NY: Holt, Rinehart, and Winston.

Bloomfield, L. (1935). Language. London: Allen Unwin.

Blumenfeld, H. K. and Marian, V. (2013). Parallel language activation and cognitive control during spoken word recognition in bilinguals. Journal of Cognitive Psychology, 25(5), 547–567.

British Council. (2013). Which languages the U.K. needs most and why? Languages for the future report.

Bronkhorst, J. (2001). Etymology and magic: Yaska's Nirukta, Plato's Cratylus, and the riddle of semantic etymologies. Numen-International Review for The History of Religions, 147-203.

Bucholtz, M. and Hall, K. (2004). Language and identity. In A. Duranti, A Companion to Linguistic Anthropology, 369-394. Blackwell.

Bullock B. E. and Toribio A. J. (2009). The Cambridge handbook of linguistic code-switching. Cambridge University Press.

Burgess, J. (2021). Translanguaging and wonder: a poetic inquiry into newcomer belonging. In Blaikie, F. Visual and Cultural Identity Constructs of Global Youth and Young Adults.

Burnett, C. (2013). Arapça mantık eserlerinin orta çağ ve rönesansta latinceye tercümesi. Sakarya İlahiyat Üniversitesi İlahiyat Fakültesi Dergisi, 263-273.

Canagarajah, S. and Silberstein, S. (2012). Diaspora identities and language. Journal of Language, Identity Education, 11(2): 81-84.

Carey, M. (2012). Qualitative research skills for social work: Theory and practice. Ashgate Publishing.

Carreira, M. (2004). Seeking explanatory adequacy: A dual approach to understanding the term 'Heritage Language Learner.' Heritage Language Journal 2, no. 1: 1–25.

Ceccatelli S. (2013). Pluralità linguistica: A scuola di arabo. In "Nel cuore di Firenze". December, 37-39

Chami, A. (2009). A historical background of the linguistic situation in Algeria. 395-387 (1)4 ,مجلة المواقف.

Cochrane, L., Ozturk, O., Alhababi, R., Khataee, H., Al-Malki, F., and Nourin, H. (Under Review). The impact of household traits and parental educational attainment on reading habits in Qatar.

Cochrane, L., Ozturk, O., Khataee, H., Alhababi, R., Al-Malki, F., & Nourin, H. (2022a). Fostering a reading culture in Qatar: Evidence from Qatar Reads. Development Studies Research 9: 82-94.

Cochrane, L., Ozturk, O., Khataee, H., Alhababi, R., Al-Malki, F., and Nourin, H. (2022b). تعزيز ثقافة القراءة: أدلة من 'قطر تقرأ. [Arabic translation] QScience Connect 2022(1):4.
Collier, V. P. and Thomas, W. P. (2017). Validating the power of bilingual schooling: Thirty-two years of large-scale, longitudinal research. Annual Review of Applied Linguistics, 37, 203–217.
Commissione Europea contro il razzismo e l'intolleranza. (2005). Terzo Rapporto sull'Italia, 16 dicembre.
Cook, V. (1980). Rules and representations. Oxford: Basil Blackwell.
Coppola D. and Moretti R. (2018). Valorizzare la diversità linguistica e culturale: Uno studio di caso, in La didattica delle lingue nel nuovo millennio. In C.M. Coonan, A. Bier, E. Ballarin, Studi e ricerche, Edizione CaFoscari, vol. 13, 15. 397-412.
Cordel, A.S. (2014). La diffusion de l'anglais dans le monde : le cas de l'Algérie. Thèse de linguistique, Université de Grenoble.
Council of Europe. (2008). The White Paper on Intercultural Dialogue.
Cummins, J. (1979). Linguistic interdependence and the educational development of bilingual children. Review of educational research, 49(2), 222-251.
Cummins, J. (2008). BICS and CALP: Empirical and theoretical status of the distinction. Encyclopedia of language and education, 2(2), 71-83.
Cummins, J. (2008). Teaching for transfer: Challenging the two solitudes assumption in bilingual education. Encyclopedia of language and education, 1528–1538.
Dakhli, L. (2020). L'esprit de la révolte. Paris : Éditions du Seuil.
Dalacoura, K. (2014). Homosexuality as cultural battleground in the Middle East: Culture and postcolonial international theory. Third World Quarterly, 35(7), 1290-1306.
De Bot, K. (2007). Language teaching in a changing world. The Modern Language Journal, 91(2), 274-276.
De Jong, E. and Howard, E. (2009). Integration in two-way immersion education: Equalising linguistic benefits for all

students. International Journal of Bilingual Education and Bilingualism, 12(1), 81–99.

Deaux, K. (2006). To be an immigrant. Russell Sage Foundation.

Della Puppa, F. (2018). Lingua araba a scuola: nuove prospettive glottodidattiche, in La didattica delle lingue nel nuovo millennio edited by C.M. Coonan, A. Bier, E. Ballarin, Edizione CaFoscari, in Studi e ricerche, vol. 13, 15. May. 429-440.

DeLoache, J. S., Chiong, C., Sherman, K., Islam, N., Vanderborght, M., Troseth, G. L., Strouse, G. A., and O'Doherty, K. (2010). Do babies learn from baby media? Psychological Science, 21(11), 1570–1574.

Demetrio D. and Favaro G. (1999). Immigrazione e pedagogia interculturale: Bambini, adulti, comunità nel percorso di integrazione, Edizione La Nuova Italia, Firenze.

Department of Education and Skills. (2019). Primary language curriculum (English medium schools). curriculumonline.ie

Desinan C. (1997). Orientamenti di educazione interculturale, Franco Angeli Editore, Milano.

Dhahir, O. (2015). Studying Arabic as an additional language together with Arab heritage language learners: The intercultural aspects of sociocultural-interactive strategies. Al-'Arabiyya, 43–59.

Dillon, A., Salazar, D., and Al Otaibi, R. (2015). Leading learning to support bilingual co-teaching at kindergarten level in the UAE. Middle Eastern & African Journal of Educational Research, 16, 21-33.

Consiglio dell'Unione europea. (1977). Direttiva del Consiglio dell'Unione Europea del 25 luglio 1977 relativa alla formazione scolastica dei figli dei lavoratori migranti (77/486/CEE).

Drissner, G. (2023). The new tool that can even transcribe Gaddafi's speeches in Arabic. Arabic for Nerds. March 3.

Drozdik L. (2008). Simplified Arabic or bilingualism? Academic discourse confronted with literary evidence. Asian and African Studies, vol. 17, n. 2, 224-249.

Dunlevy, D.A. (2020): Learning Irish amid controversy: how the Irish Language Act debate has impacted learners of Irish in Belfast, Journal of Multilingual and Multicultural Development.

Edwards, J. (2009). Language and identity: An introduction. Cambridge University Press.

El-Fevzân, A. I. (2014). al-'Arabiyye beyne yedeyk. Riyad: al-'Arabiyye li'l-cem'i.

El Salman, M. (2003). Phonological and morphological variation in the speech of Fallahis in Karak (Jordan). PhD dissertation. Durham University.

Ertük, Z. (2021). Avrupa dil portfolyosu ve dilbilgisi kuramları çerçevesinde arapça dil eğitim setlerinin dilbilgisi içerik incelemesi (Unpublished Master Thesis). İstanbul Üniversitesi, İstanbul.

Et-Tonsi, A. (2013). al-Kitâb fî Ta'allumi'l-'Arabiyye. America: Georgetown University Press.

European Commission. (2008). Green paper on Migration and Mobility: Challenges and Opportunities for E.U. Education Systems.

Evans, M. and Phillips, J. (2007). Algeria: Anger of the dispossessed. New Haven, CT London: Yale University Press.

Faas D., Hajisoteriou C., and Angelidies P. (2014). Intercultural education in Europe: policies, practices, and trends, in British Educational Research Journal, vol. 40, n. 2, April. 300-318.

Farghaly, A. and Shaalan, K. (2009). Arabic natural language processing. ACM Transactions on Asian Language Information Processing, 8(4), 1–22.

Fasold, R. (1997). The sociolinguistics of society. Oxford: Blackwell Publishers.

Filiu, J-P. (2019). Algérie, la nouvelle indépendance. Paris : Éditions du Seuil.

Fishman, J.A. (2000). 300-plus years of Heritage Language Education in the United States. Heritage Languages in America: Preserving a National Resource. Ed. J. K. Peyton, D. A. Ranard, and S. McGinnis. New York: ACTFL, 81-98.

Flores, N. and Rosa, J. (2015). Undoing appropriateness: Raciolinguistic ideologies and language diversity in Education. Harvard Educational Review, 85(2), 149–171.

Freimuth, H. (2014). Challenges to building a 'knowledge society': The role of literacy in promoting critical thinking in the UAE. Sheikh Saud Bin Saqr Al Qasimi Foundation for Policy Research, 10, 1-12.

Friend, M. (2015). Welcome to co-teaching 2.0. Educational Leadership, 73(4), 16-22.

Friend, M., Cook, L. (1992). Interactions: Collaboration skills for school professionals. White Plains, NY: Longman Publishing.

Furman, N., Goldberg, D., and Lusin, N. (2010). Enrollments in languages other than English in United States institutions of higher education, Fall 2006. New York: MLA.

Gallagher, K. (2019). Introduction: Education in the UAE—context and themes. In K. Gallagher. Education in the United Arab Emirates: Innovation and Transformation, 1-18. Springer: Singapore.

García, O. and Lin, A. M. (2017). Translanguaging in bilingual education. Bilingual and multilingual education, 117-130.

García, O., Lin, A. M. Y. (2016). Translanguaging in bilingual education. Bilingual and Multilingual Education, 1–14.

Gardner, R. C. and MacIntyre, P. D. (1991). An instrumental motivation in language study. Studies in Second Language Acquisition, 13, 57-72.

Gardner, R. C. and Lambert, W. (1972). Attitudes and motivation in second language learning. Rowley, MA: Newbury House.

Gardner-Chloros, P. (2009). Code-switching. Cambridge University Press.

Genkin, S. (2021). Helping students build critical thinking skills in Oman through the Fulbright Specialist Program. World Learning. April 13.

Godwill, E. A. (2015). Fundamentals of research methodology: A holistic guide for research completion, management, validation, and ethics. Nova Science Publishers.

Goodman, B. and Tastanbek, S. (2021). Making the shift from a codeswitching to a translanguaging lens in English language teacher education. TESOL Quarterly, 55(1), 29-53.

Gort, M. and Bauer, E. B. (2012). Holistic approaches to bilingual / biliteracy development, instruction, and research. Early biliteracy development: Exploring young learners use of their linguistic resources, 1-7.

Grandguillaume, G. (1998). Langues et représentations identitaires en Algérie. In coll., 2000 ans d'Algérie. Carnets Séguier, Atlantica Editions, Biarritz.

Greer, M. and Johnson, D. (2009). National survey of schools teaching Arabic as a core course. Paper presented at the ACTFL 2009, Washington, DC.

Gregory, L., Thomure, H. T., Kazem, A., Boni, A., Elsayed, M. A. A., and Taibah, N. (2021). Advancing Arabic language teaching and learning: A path to reducing learning poverty in the Middle East and North Africa. World Bank.

Grine, N. (2009). Les représentations linguistiques et leur incidence sur la réussite ou l'échec d'une politique linguistique. Thèse Doctorat. Université de Mostaganem.

Grosjean, F. (1982). Life with two languages. An introduction to bilingualism. Cambridge, MA: Harvard University Press

Gumperz, J. (1976). Conversational code-switching. In Gumperz, J. Discourse Strategies. Cambridge: Cambridge University Press.

Günay, V. D. (2004). Dil ve İletişim. İstanbul: Multilingual Yayınları.

Haeri, N. (2009). The elephant in the room: Language and literacy in the Arab world. In D. Olson & N. Torrance, The Cambridge Handbook of Literacy, 418-430. Cambridge University Press.

Hajjej, A., Almawi, W.Y., Arnaiz-Villena, A., Hattab, L., and Hmida, S. (2018). The genetic heterogeneity of Arab populations as inferred from HLA genes. PLoS One, 13(3), 1-24.

Hamman, L. (2018). Translanguaging and positioning in two-way dual language classrooms: A case for criticality. Language and Education, 32(1), 21-42.

Harbi, M. (1998). Naissance d'une nationalité. In coll., 2000 ans d'Algérie. Carnets Séguier, Atlantica Editions, Biarritz.

Hathorn, C. and Dillon, A. M. (2018). Action research as professional development: Its role in education reform in the United Arab Emirates. Issues in Educational Research, 28(1), 99-119.

Hillman, S. (2019). "I'm a Heritage Speaker of the Damascene dialect of Arabic": Negotiating the identity label of Arabic Heritage Language Learner. Heritage Language Journal, 16(3), 296-317.

Hoff, E. and Core, C. (2013). Input and language development in bilingually developing children. Seminars in Speech and Language, 34(4), 215–226.

Holes, C. (1995). Community, dialect, and urbanization in the Arabic-speaking Middle East. Bulletin of the School of Oriental and African Studies 58(2). 270–287.

Hornberger, N. H. and Wang, S.C. (2008). Who are our heritage language learners? Identity and biliteracy in Heritage Language education in the United States. In D. Brinton, O. Kagan, and S. Bauckus, Heritage Language Education: A New Field Emerging, 3–35. New York: Routledge.

Hughes, C. E., Shaunessy, E. S., Brice, A. R., Ratliff, M. A. and McHatton, P. A. (2006). Code-switching among bilingual and limited English proficient students: Possible indicators of giftedness. Journal for the Education of the Gifted, 30(1), 7–28.

Husen, A. A. (2011). A new understanding of heritage: A case study of non-Arab Muslims in the Arabic classroom. Doctoral dissertation.

Husseinali, G. (2012). Arabic Heritage Language Learners: Motivation, expectations, competence, and engagement in learning Arabic. Journal of the National Council of Less Commonly Taught Languages, 11, 97-110.

Husseinali, G. (2006). Who is studying Arabic and why? A survey of Arabic students' orientations at a major university. Foreign Language Annals, 39(3), 395-412

İşler, E. (2002). Karşıtsal çözümleme ve arapça öğretimi. Nüsha. 123-134.

Istrate, A. M. (2019). The impact of the Virtual Assistant (VA) on language classes. Conference paper published by "Carol I" National Defence University.

James, C. (1980). Contrastive analysis. Essex: Longman.

Johnson, A. G. (2014). The gender knot: Unraveling our patriarchal legacy. Temple University Press.

Jones, S. (2020). Finding our true north: On languages, understanding and curriculum in Northern Ireland.' Curriculum Journal.

Kahrs, E. (1984). Yaska's Nirukta: The quest for a new interpretation. Indologica Taurinensia.

Kamal, H. (2008). Translating women and gender: The experience of translating the Encyclopedia of Women and Islamic Cultures into Arabic. Women's Studies Quarterly, 36(3-4), 254-268.

Kamal, H. (2018). Travelling concepts in translation: Feminism and gender in the Egyptian context. Literary and Translation Studies, 14(1), 131-145.

Kenner, C. (2004). Living in simultaneous worlds: Difference and integration in bilingual script-learning. International Journal of Bilingual Education and Bilingualism, 7(1), 43-61.

Kerimoğlu, C. (2017). Genel dilbilime giriş-kuram ve uygulamalarla dilbilim, göstergebilim ve türkoloji. Ankara: Pegem Akademi.

Kerin, M. and Murphy, C. (2018). Equal temperament: Co-teaching as a mechanism for musician–teacher collaboration. In Musician–Teacher Collaborations: Altering the Chord, 217-230. Routledge.

Kermani, N. (2017). Poetry and language. In A. Rippin J. Mojaddedi, The Wiley Blackwell Companion to the Qur'ān, 117–129. John Wiley Sons.

Khamis-Dakwar, R. and Makhoul, B. (2022). The relationship between children's explicit knowledge and awareness of diglossia and success in learning Arabic: A preliminary investigation. Journal of Multilingual and Multicultural Development.

Kıran, Z. (1984). Dilbilim ve temel ilkeleri. Hacattepe Üniversitesi Edebiyat Fakültesi Dergisi, 87-96.
Knut S.V. (2012). The Maghreb since 1800: A short history. London: Hurst & Company.
Kourouma, A. (1997). Le processus d'Africanisation des langues européennes. Littératures africaines : dans quelle(s) langue(s)? SILEX / Nouvelles du Sud, 135-140.
Labed, Z. (2015). Multilingualism in Algeria: The case of appellation of Algerian TV channels. Revue Traduction et Langues, 14(1), 117-131.
Lado, R. (1957). Linguistics across cultures. Ann Arbor: University of Michigan Press.
Lancioni G. (2018). Insegnamento dell'arabo e certificazione: una panoramica, in Didattica dell'arabo e certificazione linguistica: riflessioni e iniziative, edited by G. Lancioni, C. Solimando, Roma Tre-Press, 11-30.
Lazar, M. and Nehad, S. (2014). L'Algérie aujourd'hui. Paris : Michalon.
Le Sueur, J. (2010). Algeria since 1989: Between democracy and terror. London: Zed Books.
Leikin M., Ibrahim R., and Eghabria H. (2014). The influence of diglossia in Arabic on narrative ability: Evidence from analysis of the linguistic narrative structure of discourse among pre-school children. Reading and Writing, Springer, n. 27, 733-747.
Lewis, G., Jones, B., and Baker, C. (2012). Translanguaging: Origins and development from school to street and beyond. Educational Research and Evaluation, 18(7), 641-654.
Lorber, J. (1995). Paradoxes of gender. Yale University Press.
Mackenzie, N. and Veresov, N. (2013). How drawing can support writing acquisition: Text construction in early writing from a Vygotskian perspective. Australasian Journal of Early Childhood, 38(4), 22-29.
Madrid, D. and Hughes, S. (2011). Studies in bilingual education. Bern: Peter Lang.

Makhoul, B., Olshtain, E., Sabah, K., and Copti-Mshael, T. (2018). The development of academic vocabulary among Arabic native-speaking middle school pupils: How much do they really know? Psychology, 9, 323-339.

Mancini, T. (2008). Adolescenza, identità e immigrazione: continuità e discontinuità culturali nelle seconde generazioni d'immigrati, in Ricerca Psicoanalitica, year XIX, n. 2, 137-160.

Martin, J., Martins, R. J. and Naqvi, J. (2017). Do Arabs really read less? 'Cultural tools' and 'more knowledgeable others' as determinants of book reliance in six Arab countries. International Journal of Communication, 11, 3374-3393.

Massad, J. (2007). Desiring Arabs. University of Chicago Press.

Massaro, D. W. (2017). Reading aloud to children: Benefits and implications for acquiring literacy before schooling begins. The American Journal of Psychology, vol. 130, no. 1, 63–72,

McDougall, J. (2017). A history of Algeria. Oxford: Cambridge University Press.

McKendry, E. and McKendry, M. (2019). Multilingualism and diversity in Northern Ireland schools and teacher education. In Teaching Content and Language in the Multilingual Classroom. Mercator European Research Centre on Multilingualism and Language Learning, 2019.

McMullen, J., Harris, J., Jones, S., McConnellogue, S., and Winter, F. (2021). School-based Support for Syrian Refugee Pupils in Northern Ireland, Belfast: Centre for Research in Educational Underachievement, Stranmillis University College

Menken, K. and Kleyn, T. (2010). The long-term impact of subtractive schooling in the educational experiences of secondary English language learners. International Journal of Bilingual Education and Bilingualism, 13(4), 399–417.

Milan G. and Cestaro M. (2016). We can change! Seconde generazioni, Mediazione interculturale, Città, Sfida pedagogica, Pensa Multimedia Editore, Lecce.

Milan, G. (2009). Multiculturalità, cittadinanza e educazione interculturale. Uno sguardo alle indicazioni presenti in recenti documenti in materia, in Studium Educationis, vol. 3.

Millán, M. (2016). The traveling of 'gender' and its accompanying baggage: Thoughts on the translation of feminism(s), the globalization of discourses, and representational divides. European Journal of Women's Studies, 23(1), 6-27.

Ministero dell'Istruzione. (1990). La scuola dell'obbligo e gli alunni stranieri. L'educazione interculturale. Circolare Ministeriale. 26 luglio 1990, n. 205.

Ministero dell'Istruzione. (1989). Inserimento degli stranieri nella scuola dell'obbligo: promozione e coordinamento delle iniziative per l'esercizio del diritto allo studioCircolare Ministeriale. 8 settembre 1989, n. 301.

Ministero del Lavoro e delle Politiche Sociali. (2018). La presenza dei migranti nella città metropolitana di Firenze.

Montrul, S. (2008). Incomplete acquisition in bilingualism: Reexamining the age factor. Amsterdam, the Netherlands: John Benjamins.

Montrul, S. (2010). Current issues in heritage language acquisition. Annual Review of Applied Linguistics, 30, 3–23.

Mor–Sommerfeld, A. (2002). Language mosaic. Developing literacy in a second–new language: a new perspective. Reading, 36(3), 99-105.

Motha, S. (2006). Decolonizing ESOL: Negotiating linguistic power in U.S. public school classrooms. Critical Inquiry in Language Studies, 3(2–3), 75–100.

Moussaoui, M. (2020). Le hirak, la langue en mouvement. Insaniyat, 87, 105-117.

Murat Özgen, Ö. K. (2020). Dünya dillerinden örneklerle dilbilimsel tipoloji. Ankara: Pegem Akademi.

Muysken, P. (2000). Bilingual speech: A typology of code-mixing. Cambridge University Press.

Myers-Scotton, C. (1993). Dueling languages: Grammatical structure in code-switching. Oxford: Oxford University Press (Clarendon Press).

Myers-Scotton, C. (1993). Social motivations for code-switching: Evidence from Africa. Oxford University Press.

Myhill, J. (2014). The effect of diglossia on literacy in Arabic and other languages. In Saiegh-Haddad, E., Joshi, R. Handbook of Arabic Literacy. Literacy Studies, vol 9. Springer, Dordrecht.

Naji, N. (2021). The motivation and attitude of Arab heritage children and their parents' perspectives toward learning Arabic.

National Immigrant Justice Center. (2021). Arabic LGBTQ terminology: A guide for NIJC interpreters and staff. Heartland Alliance.

National Standards in Foreign Language Education Project. (2006). Standards for foreign language learning in the 21st century. National Standards in Foreign Language Education Project.

Nawafleh, A. M. (2008). Code-switching in the Jordanian society. (Unpublished thesis), Al Hussein Bin Talal University. Amman: Jordan.

Newman, J. (2014). To Siri, with love. New York Times. Oct. 17.

Nguyen, A., Shin, F., and Krashen, S. (2001). Development of the first language is not a barrier to second-language acquisition: Evidence from Vietnamese immigrants to the USA. International Journal of Bilingual Education and Bilingualism, 4(3), 159–164.

Nickel, G. K. (1968). Contrastive linguistics and language teaching. International Review of Applied Linguistics in Language Teaching, 233-256.

Nigst, L. and García, J. S. (2010). Boyāt in the Gulf: Identity, contestation, and social control. Middle East Critique, 19(1), 5-34.

Nilep, C. (2006). Code-switching in sociocultural linguistics. Colorado Research in Linguistics, 19.

Northern Ireland Office. (2020). New Decade, New Approach. Agreement. 9 January.

Northern Ireland Statistics and Research Agency. (2014). Census - key statistics for district electoral areas in Northern Ireland (2011, 2014).

Norwegian Agency for Development Cooperation. (2017). EduApp4Syria. NORAD.

Osservatorio nazionale per l'integrazione degli alunni stranieri e per l'educazione interculturale. (2007). La via italiana per la scuola interculturale e l'integrazione degli alunni stranieri, MIUR.

Özen, U. (2015). Chomsky'nin bilişselci dil yaklaşımının yabancı dil eğitiminde uygulanabilirliğine ilişkin bir soruşturma, Uludağ Üniversitesi, Bursa.

Pancsofar, N. and Petroff, J. G. (2016). Teachers' experiences with co-teaching as a model for inclusive education. International Journal of Inclusive Education, 20(10), 1043-1053.

Paresh, D. (2023). ChatGPT is cutting non-English languages out of the AI revolution. Wired.

Parks, J. (2008). Who chooses dual language education for their children and why. International Journal of Bilingual Education and Bilingualism, 11:6, 635-660.

Parlak, M. (2015). Başlangıçtan günümüze türkçe dilbilgisi çalışmalarına bakış, Akdeniz Üniversitesi, Antalya.

Paul, R. (1984). Critical thinking: Fundamental for education in a free society. Educational Leadership, 42, 4 -14.

Pehlivan, A. A. (2020). Dilbilgisi öğretimi. Ankara: Pegem Akademi.

Pokorn, N. K. (2005). Challenging the Traditional Axioms: Translation into a non-mother tongue. Amsterdam Philadelphia: John Benjamins.

Poza, L. (2017). Translanguaging: Definitions, implications, and further needs in burgeoning inquiry. Berkeley Review of Education, 6(2), 101-128.

Prashad, V. (2008). The darker nations: A people's history of the third world. The New Press.

Qualey, M. L. (2020). For kids: A summer of Arabic podcasts, readings, and online activities. Al-Fanar.

Rabin, C. (2020). Co-teaching: Collaborative and caring teacher preparation. Journal of Teacher Education, 71(1), 135-147.

Ramadan, T. (2002). Essere Musulmano Europeo, Città Aperta Edizione, Enna.

Redattore Sociale. (2002). Rapporto sulla situazione dei musulmani in Italia rispetto alla fruizione di beni e servizi. Agenzia Quotidiana di Informazione.

Redazione. (2008). Da oggi Firenze parla arabo. Il Reporter, 11 marzo 2008.

Rhazzali, K. and Equizi, M. (2019). I musulmani e i loro luoghi di culto, in Le religioni nell'Italia che cambia: Mappe e bussole, edited by di E. Pace, Carocci Editore, Roma.

Rhodes, N. and Pufahl, I. (2010). Foreign language teaching in U.S. schools: Results of a national survey. Washington, DC: Center for Applied Linguistics.

Romaine, S. (2007). Preserving endangered languages. Language and Linguistics Compass. 1/1-2: 115-132.

Ruedy, J. (2005). Modern Algeria: The origins and development of a nation. Bloomington/Indianapolis: Indiana University Press.

Saad, Z. (1992). Language planning and policy attitudes: A case study of Arabization in Algeria. Unpublished doctoral dissertation, Columbia University, U.S.A.

Saîd el-Ebraş, M. Â. V.-S.-'. (2013). Silsilet'ul-Lisân. el-Lisânu'l-Umm.

Saiegh-Haddad, E. and Spolsky, B. (2014). Acquiring literacy in a diglossic context: Problems and prospects. In Saiegh-Haddad, E., Joshi, R. Handbook of Arabic Literacy. Literacy Studies, vol 9. Springer, Dordrecht.

Sakarna, A. (1999). phonological aspects of 9abady Arabic, a Bedouin Jordanian dialect. Ph.D. Dissertation. University of Wisconsin, Madison.

Salim, J. A. (2013). A contrastive study of English-Arabic noun morphology. International Journal of English Linguistics, 122-132.

Scalera, D. (2004). The Invisible learner: Unlocking the heritage language treasure. Language Association Journal, 55.2.

Scanu R. (2009). Testi di scrittori di origine araba per una riflessione interculturale, in Lingua Nostra e Oltre, online journal of Università di Padova, vol. 2, n.1, 36-55.

Schor, L. (2023). How can you use ChatGPT to learn Arabic? Arabic for Nerds. February 4.

Schwartz, A. (2012). Bringing critical thinking to education in the Arab world. Fast Company. October 16.

Sellars, M., Fakirmohammad, R., Bui, L., Fishetti, J., Niyozov, S., Reynolds, R., Thapliyal, N., Liu-Smith, Y. L., and Ali, N. (2018). Conversations on critical thinking: Can critical thinking find its way forward as the skill set and mindset of the century? Education Sciences, 8(4), 1-29.

Shay, O. (2015). To switch or not to switch: Code-switching in a multilingual country. Procedia—Social and Behavioral Sciences, 209, 462-469.

Shendy, R. (2022). Learning to read in an "estranged" language: Arabic diglossia, child literacy, and the case for mother tongue-based education. Creative Education, 13, 1247-1301.

Sibel Dokuyucu, S. A. (2022). Arapçada mefulun fih ve türkçedeki zarfların karşıtsal çözümlemesi. Journal of Strategic Research in Social Science (JoSReSS), 1-12.

Siebetcheu, R. (2018). La scuola del nuovo millennio: tra italiano, dialetti e altre lingue, in La didattica delle lingue nel nuovo millennio, edited by C.M. Coonan, A. Bier, E. Ballarin, Edizione CaFoscari, in "Studi e ricerche", vol. 13, 15, 117-134.

Skalli, L. H. (2006). Communicating gender in the public sphere: Women and information technologies in the MENA. Journal of Middle East Women's Studies, 2(2), 35-59.

Skutnabb-Kangas, T. and Mohanty, A. K. (1995). Bilingualism in a multilingual society: Psycho-social and pedagogical implications. TESOL Quarterly, 29(4), 775.

Sonnenschein, S. and Munsterman, K. (2002). The influence of home-based reading interactions on 5-year-olds' reading motivations and early literacy development. Early Childhood Research Quarterly, vol. 17, no. 3, 318–37.

Soslau, E., Gallo-Fox, J., and Scantlebury, K. (2019). The promises and realities of implementing a coteaching model of student teaching. Journal of Teacher Education, 70(3), 265-279.

Steele, J. L., Slater, R. O., Zamarro, G., Miller, T., Li, J., Burkhauser, S., and Bacon, M. (2017). Effects of Dual-Language Immersion Programs on Student Achievement: Evidence From Lottery Data. American Educational Research Journal, 54, 282S–306S

Steward, B. (2019). IPA Regional Seminar, Amman (day 1): Digital disruption to humanitarian action. International Publishers Association.

Stora, B. (2001). Algeria, 1830–2000: A short history. Ithaca: Cornell University Press.

Stora, B. (2001, 2004). Histoire de l'Algérie depuis l'indépendance. Paris: Editions La Découverte.

Suleiman, Y. (2003). The Arabic language and national identity: A study in ideology. Edinburgh University Press Ltd.

Suleiman, Y. (2011). Arabic, self and identity: A study in conflict and displacement. Oxford University Press.

Tadesse, S. (2014). Parent involvement: Perceived encouragement and barriers to African refugee parent and teacher relationships. Childhood Education, 90(4), 298–305.

Temples, A. L. (2010). Heritage motivation, identity, and the desire to learn Arabic in U.S. early adolescents. Journal of the National Council of Less Commonly Taught Languages, 9, 103- 132.

Tessa, A. (2015). L'impossible éradication. L'enseignement du français en Algérie. Préface Amin Zaoui, Alger: Édit. Barzakh.

The Languages Company. (2009). Towards an integrated curriculum CLIL National Statement and Guidelines.

Ufficio Patrimonio Informativo e Statistica. (2019). Gli alunni stranieri in Italia: I dati del Ministero, sito ufficiale-area prove nazionali. INVALSI.

Ufficio Patrimonio Informativo e Statistica. (2020). Gli alunni con cittadinanza non Italiana - a.s. 2018/2019.

Ufficio per l'integrazione degli alunni stranieri. (2006). Linee guida per l'accoglienza e l'integrazione degli alunni stranieri. Circolare ministeriali n. 24, MIUR, Dipartimento per l'Istruzione.

Ufficio Scolastico Regionale per la Toscana. (2017). Focus: Sedi, alunni, classi e dotazioni organiche del personale docente della scuola statale a.s. 2017/2018 per la Toscana—avvio anno scolastico, MIUR.

Ünal, E. (2009). fransızcanın ikinci yabancı dil olarak öğrenilmesinde birinci yabancı dil ingilizcenin ve karşılaştırmalı dilbilgisinin rolü, Çukurova Üniversitesi, Adana.

U.S. Department of State. (2022). 2021 Report on international religious freedom: Jordan. June 2.

Valdés, G. (2001). Heritage language students: profiles and possibilities. In J. Peyton, D. Ranard, S. McGinnis, Heritage languages in America: preserving a national resource, 37–77. Washington, DC: Center for Applied Linguistics.

Valdés, G. (2005). Bilingualism, heritage language learners, and SLA research: opportunities lost or seized? Modern Language Journal, 89(3), 410-426,

Valenzuela, A. (1999). The subtractive elements of caring and cultural assimilation. In Subtractive schooling: U.S.-Mexican youth and the politics of caring, 10–20. SUNY Press.

Van den Bosch, L. J., Segers, E., and Verhoeven, L. (2020). First and second-language vocabulary affect early second-language reading comprehension development. Journal of Research in Reading, 43(3), 290-308.

Van Deusen-Scholl, N. (2003). Toward a definition of heritage language: Sociopolitical and pedagogical considerations. Journal of language, identity, and education, 2(3), 211-230.

Velasco, P. and García, O. (2014). Translanguaging and the writing of bilingual learners. Bilingual Research Journal, 37(1), 6-23.

Vikør, Knut, S. (2012). The Maghreb since 1800: A short history. London: Hurst Company.

Wahba, K., Taha, Z. A., and England, L. (2014). Handbook for Arabic language teaching professionals in the 21st century. Routledge.

Wamda. (2021). Edtech startup Adam Wa Mishmish raises $475,000 Seed funding. June 10.

Webb, J. B. (2003). Interview. I Speak Arabic. Diana Scalera. ispeakarabic.org. Video.

Wei, L. (2014). Negotiating funds of knowledge and symbolic competence in the complementary school classrooms. Language and Education, 28(2), 161-180.

Welles, E. (2004). Foreign language enrollments in United States institutions of higher education, Fall 2002. ADFL Bulletin, 35(2–3), 7–26.

White, L. (1986). Implications of parametric variation for adult second language acquisition: An investigation of the 'pro-drop' Parameter. V. Cook içinde, Experimental Approaches to Second Language Acquisition. Oxford: Pergamon Press.

Wilder, S. (2014). Effects of parental involvement on academic achievement: A meta-synthesis. Educational Review, 66(3), 377–397.

Williams, C. (2000). Llythrennedd deuol: Trawsieithu–pecyn datblygiad staff. Dual literacy: translanguaging–staff development pack. Cardiff, UK: BBC.

XXIX Rapporto Immigrazione. (2020). Conoscere per comprendere, Caritas e Migrantes, Tau Editrice, Perugia, 92.

Yaseen, M. M.S., Sa'di, R. A. and Sharadgah, T. A. (2021). Functions of code-switching from Arabic to English among Jordanian pilots in their daily informal conversations: A case study. Arab World English Journal, 12 (2) 109-124.

Younes, M. and Chami Y. (2014). Arabiyyât al-Naaas. New York: Routledge.

Yousef, W. (2021). An assessment of critical thinking in the Middle East: Evaluating the effectiveness of special courses interventions. PLoS ONE, 16(12).

Youssef, N. and Stack, L. (2017). Egypt expands crackdown on gay and transgender people. NY Times. October 3.

Zabarah, H. (2015). College-level Arabic heritage learners: Do they belong in separate classrooms? Journal of National Council of Less Commonly Taught Languages, 18, 93-120.

Zacharias, A. (2020). How do you say "Hey Siri" in spoken Arabic? NYUAD lab is working on Gulf dialects to find the answer. The National. June 2.

About TBR Books

a program of CALEC

TBR Books is a program of the Center for the Advancement of Languages, Education, and Communities. We publish researchers and practitioners seeking to engage diverse communities on education, languages, cultural history, and social initiatives. We translate our books into various languages to further expand our impact.

BOOKS IN ENGLISH

Bilingual Children: Families, Education, Development by Ellen Bialystok
The Heart of an Artichoke by Linda Ashour and Claire Lerognon
French All Around Us by Kathleen Stein-Smith and Fabrice Jaumont
Navigating Dual Immersion: by Valerie Sun
Conversations on Bilingualism by Fabrice Jaumont
One Good Question by Rhonda Broussard
Can We Agree to Disagree? by Sabine Landolt and Agathe Laurent
Salsa Dancing in Gym Shoes by T. Oberg de la Garza and A. Lavigne
Beyond Gibraltar; The Other Shore; Mamma in her Village by M. Lorch
The Clarks of Willsborough Point by Darcey Hale
The English Patchwork by Pedro Tozzi and Giovanna de Lima
Peshtigo 1871 by Charles Mercier
The Word of the Month by Ben Lévy, Jim Sheppard, Andrew Arnon
Two Centuries of French Education in New York by Jane Flatau Ross
The Bilingual Revolution by Fabrice Jaumont

كتب بالعربية (Books in Arabic)

فابريس جومون - حوارات حول الثنائية اللغوية
كيم, ماري تشي وي - أعوام كورية سعيدة مع الجدة
تيبوهو موجا - الأمر الجيد والسيء والرائع: فيروس كورونا - ما أحببته وخسرته واكتسبته
مارك هانسن - الرياضيات للجميع
تيبوهو موجا - الفستان الأزرق
ديانا سوبل ليدرمان - درس الخياطة
إديانا سوبل ليدرمان - كمامات
كريستين هيلوت - ماريمبا
ستيوارت ماكميل, دونيا - متعة جهاز المناعة
ستيوارت ماكميل, دونيا - متعة عملية التنفس
ستيوارت ماكميل, دونيا - متعة عملية الهضم
ديانا سوبل ليدرمان - نوح هنري رواية قوس قزح
جايل فوستر - هل تساعدني في اختيار حيوان أليف؟
فابريس جومون - الثورة ثنائية اللغة: مستقبل التعليم يكتب بلغتين

BOOKS FOR CHILDREN (available in several languages)

Lapin is Hungry

Franglais Soup e by Adrienne Mei

Rainbows, Masks, and Ice Cream by Deana Sobel Lederman

Korean Super New Years with Grandma by Mary Kim, Eunjoo Feaster

Math for All by Mark Hansen

Rose Alone by Sheila Decosse

Uncle Steve's Country Home; The Blue Dress; The Good, the Ugly, and the Great by Teboho Moja

Immunity Fun!; Respiratory Fun!; Digestive Fun! By D. Stewart-McMeel

Marimba by Christine Hélot, Patricia Velasco, Antun Kojton

Our books, such as paperback and e-book, are available on our website and in all major online bookstores. Some of our books have been translated into over twenty languages. For a listing of all books published by TBR Books, information on our series, or our submission guidelines for authors, visit our website at:

www.tbr-books.org

About CALEC

The Center for the Advancement of Languages, Education, and Communities (CALEC) is a nonprofit organization that promotes multilingualism, empowers multilingual families, and fosters cross-cultural understanding. The Center's mission aligns with the United Nations' Sustainable Development Goals. Our mission is to establish language as a critical life skill by developing and implementing bilingual education programs, promoting diversity, reducing inequality, and helping to provide quality education. Our programs seek to protect world cultural heritage and support teachers, authors, and families by providing the knowledge and resources to create vibrant multilingual communities.

The specific objectives and purpose of our organization are:

- To develop and implement education programs that promote multilingualism and cross-cultural understanding and establish an inclusive and equitable quality education, including internship and leadership training. [SDG # 4, Quality Education]

- To publish and distribute resources, including research papers, books, and case studies that seek to empower and promote the social, economic, and political inclusion of all, focusing on language education and cultural diversity, equity, and inclusion. [SDG # 10, Reduced Inequalities]

- To help build sustainable cities and communities and support teachers, authors, researchers, and families in advancing multilingualism and cross-cultural understanding through collaborative tools for linguistic communities. [SDG # 11, Sustainable Cities and Communities]

- To foster solid global partnerships and cooperation, mobilize resources across borders, participate in events and activities that promote language education through knowledge sharing and coaching, empower parents and teachers, and build multilingual societies. [SDG # 17, Partnerships for the Goals]

SOME GOOD REASONS TO SUPPORT US

Your donation helps:

- Develop our publishing and translation activities so that more languages are represented.
- Provide access to our online book platform to daycare centers, schools, and cultural centers in underserved areas.
- Support local and sustainable action in favor of education and multilingualism.
- Implement projects that advance dual-language education.
- Organize workshops for parents, conferences with large audiences, meet-the-author chats, and talks with experts in multilingualism.

DONATE ONLINE

For all your questions, contact our team by email at contact@calec.org or donate online on our website:

www.calec.org

معلومات حول كالِيْك (CALEC)

مركز النهوض باللغات والتربية والمجتمعات **كالِيْك** (CALEC) اختصار بالفرنسية لعبارة [The Center for the Advancement of Languages, Education, and Communities]، هو منظمة غير ربحية تعمل على تعزيز التعددية اللغوية ودعم الأسر متعددة اللغات وتعزيز التفاهم بين الثقافات. تتماشى مهمة المركز مع أهداف التنمية المستدامة للأمم المتحدة. نريد أن نجعل إتقان اللغات مهارة أساسية ومفيدة من خلال إنشاء وتطوير برامج التعليم الثنائي اللغة، وتعزيز التنوع، والحدّ من عدم المساواة وتوسيع نطاق الوصول إلى جودة التعليم. تهدف برامجنا إلى الدفاع عن التراث الثقافي العالمي مع دعم المعلمين والمؤلفين والعائلات من خلال تزويدهم بالمعرفة والموارد لتشكيل مجتمعات متعددة اللغات نابضة بالحياة.

الأهداف والغايات المحددة لمنظمتنا هي :

- تطوير وتنفيذ البرامج التعليمية التي تعزز التعددية اللغوية وكذلك التفاهم بين الثقافات ، وإنشاء تعليم جيد ومنصف وشامل، لا سيما من خلال التدريب الداخلي والتدريب (هدف التنمية المستدامة رقم 4 - جودة التعليم)

- نشر الموارد، مثل المقالات البحثية والكتب ودراسات الحالة، التي تهدف إلى دعم وتعزيز الإدماج الاجتماعي والاقتصادي والسياسي للجميع، مع التركيز بشكل خاص على التنوع الثقافي، والمساواة والشمول (هدف التنمية المستدامة 10 - الحد من عدم المساواة)

- المساعدة في بناء مدن ومجتمعات مستدامة ودعم المعلمين والمؤلفين والباحثين والأسر في تعزيز التعددية اللغوية والتفاهم بين الثقافات باستخدام الأدوات التعاونية (هدف التنمية المستدامة رقم 11 - المدن والمجتمعات المستدامة)

- تعزيز الشراكات العالمية من خلال تعبئة الموارد عبر الحدود، والمشاركة في الأحداث والأنشطة التي تعزز تعليم اللغة من خلال نشر المعرفة، والتدريب، وتمكين الآباء والمعلمين، وبناء مجتمعات متعددة اللغات (الهدف 17 من أهداف التنمية المستدامة - الشراكات لتحقيق الأهداف).

بعض الأسباب الجيدة لدعمنا

تبرعك يسمح لنا بالقيام بما يلي:

- تطوير أنشطة النشر والترجمة لدينا بحيث يتم تمثيل المزيد من اللغات
- امنح حق الوصول إلى منصتنا للكتاب عبر الإنترنت لدور الحضانة والمدارس والمراكز الثقافية في المناطق المحرومة
- دعم الإجراءات المحلية والمستدامة لصالح التعليم والتعددية اللغوية
- تنظيم اجتماعات مع المؤلفين والخبراء في التعددية اللغوية، وورش عمل للآباء ومؤتمرات مع جماهير كبيرة

لتقديم تبرع عبر الإنترنت

إذا كانت لديك أية أسئلة، اتصلوا بفريقنا عبر البريد الإلكتروني على contact@calec.org للتبرع عبر الإنترنت، قوموا بزيارة موقعنا على الإنترنت:

www.calec.org/?lang=ar

www.ingramcontent.com/pod-product-compliance
Lightning Source LLC
Chambersburg PA
CBHW021144160426
43194CB00007B/686